Georgia Land

A Collection of Georgia Recipes,
Historic Landmarks & Scenic Attractions

Published by
The Auxiliary to the Medical Association of Georgia
Atlanta, Georgia

Georgia Land

First Edition 1992   7,500 Copies

Second Edition 1993   10,000 Copies

Cover Illustration by Cheryl Dennis

ISBN 0-9632174-1-0

Library of Congress Catalog Card Number: 92-70647

Additional copies of **Georgia Land** may be obtained by using the order form provided in the back of this book.

Printed in the USA by

WIMMER BROTHERS

A Wimmer Company

Memphis • Dallas

TABLE OF CONTENTS

FOREWORD

Welcome to **Georgia Land**! The Auxiliary to the Medical Association of Georgia Cookbook Committee proudly presents this collection of Georgia recipes, historic landmarks and scenic attractions.

Travel with us across **Georgia Land**, share with us our "Sunday best" recipes, and treat yourselves to glimpses of scenic attractions and landmarks from Mountain Majesty to Scenic Lowlands. Journey across Georgia's Historic Heartland and Bountiful Plains, the Classic South and our very diverse Capital City. Discover ten sections of our state, each representing a food category and each illustrated by a talented Georgia artist.

Throughout **Georgia Land** many recipes reflect local cuisine and Georgia products. Others reflect our varied interests and backgrounds. Most are family favorites and all are offered for your enjoyment by members of the thirty-two county medical auxiliaries in Georgia. Recipes were tested in Auxiliary kitchens and evaluated by the very finest of critics — our families. We applaud the culinary skills and exceptional spirit of teamwork of all who participated in this project.

All profits from the sale of **Georgia Land** will provide community health projects and health education programs presented by county auxilians throughout the State. The Auxiliary to the Medical Association of Georgia gratefully acknowledges your support of our efforts through the purchase of this cookbook. We thank you for the opportunity of sharing **Georgia Land** with you.

Mary Ann Marks
Chairman
Cookbook Committee

ABOUT THE ORGANIZATION

The Auxiliary to the Medical Association of Georgia is composed of spouses of physicians from all parts of the state. We are committed to health related, charitable endeavors as a means to extend our goal to improve the health and quality of life for all people.

Some of the health issues addressed by the Auxiliary include the following:

1. Teen Sexuality
2. AIDS Education
3. Safety
4. Drug and Alcohol Abuse Prevention
5. Suicide Prevention
6. Comprehensive School Health Education
7. Healthy Lifestyles i.e., non-use of tobacco
8. The Elderly
9. Mammography Awareness
10. Family Violence
11. Environmental Concerns
12. Homeless Issues

The proceeds from this book will be used to promote health related projects for communities in Georgia. We are excited about the potential benefit from the sale of this outstanding cookbook *Georgia Land*.

Ingrid H. Brunt
President
The Auxiliary to the
Medical Association of Georgia
1991-92

COOKBOOK COMMITTEE

Mary Ann Marks, **Chairman**

Recipe Chairman	Carol Ann Hardcastle
Recipe Collection Coordinator	Grace Walden
Recipe Testing Coordinator	Jeanne Smiley
Word Processor	Allyce North
Design/Format Chairman	Cheryl Dennis
Editorial Chairman	Jan Collins
Marketing Committee	Maureen Vandiver
	Connie Menendez
	Jana Hill
Finance Chairman	Nancy Wolff
Advisor	Sally Darden

Credits

Georgia on My Mind — The Official State Travel Guide, published by Georgia Travel Publications.

Georgia at Its Best — Jeanne Perkins Harman and Harry E. Harman, III, 1989, Rutledge Hill Press

The Georgia Almanac and Book of Facts - 1989-1990 — James A. Crutchfield, Rutledge Hill Press

Georgia - The WPA Guide to Its Towns and Countryside — Compiled by Workers of the Writers' Program of the Works Progress Administration in the State of Georgia, University of South Carolina Press

ACKNOWLEDGEMENTS

We extend our thanks:

To all members of the following county auxiliaries who sent us their recipes and who also gave freely of their time, energy and ingredients in testing the recipes. We sincerely regret that, because of space limitations, all recipes submitted could not be included.

Baldwin
Barrow
Bibb
Carroll-Haralson
Clayton-Fayette
Cobb
Colquitt
Crawford W. Long
DeKalb
Dougherty
Flint
Floyd-Polk-Chattooga
Georgia Medical
Glynn
Gwinnett-Forsyth
Hall

Jackson-Banks
Laurens
Medical Association of Atlanta
Muscogee
Newton-Rockdale
Ogeechee River
Peachbelt
Randolph-Stewart-Terrell
Richmond
South Georgia
Sumter
Thomas Area
Tift
Walker-Catoosa-Dade
Ware
Whitfield-Murray

To our families who encouraged us with their patience, love and enthusiasm throughout this project.

To Jean Thwaite, former Food Editor of *The Atlanta Constitution*, who offered many helpful suggestions and spent many hours editing recipes.

To Talitha Russell, our executive director, and Medical Association of Georgia staff personnel who assisted us in countless ways.

To Ingrid Brunt, 1991-92 President of the Auxiliary to the Medical Association of Georgia. Her leadership and her commitment to improved health and quality of life inspired us to publish **Georgia Land.**

MEET THE ARTISTS

Cheryl Dennis of Atlanta produced the graphic design and the cover of *Georgia Land*. Cheri, a past president of the Auxiliary to the Medical Association of Atlanta, earned a BFA from Wesleyan in Macon. In addition to her free-lance graphic design business, she has worked with McDonald Little in Atlanta and W. B. Doner in Baltimore. Recent years have found Cheri sharing her artistic talents with Pace Academy and the community in a volunteer capacity.

Margaret Bartholomew of Atlanta created the art for the title pages of each section of *Georgia Land*. She, too, is a past president of the Auxiliary to the Medical Association of Atlanta. Margaret majored in art at Auburn University and has studied at the High Museum of Art and with private instructors. "I have always been interested and involved in the visual and performing arts," says Margaret. She has been a docent at the Woodruff Arts Center and is a charter member and past president of Callanwolde Guild.

Ann Bryant Cowart — *"The Classical South"* — Ann lives on the family farm in Jenkins County near Millen, Georgia. For many years Ann, along with her husband Jimmie, operated a restaurant in Statesboro. Since retiring in 1983, she has pursued her art full-time. Ann studied watercolor with Ruth Hibbs for several years and has attended watercolor workshops by other noted artists but is mainly self-taught. She has had several one-woman and group shows. Ann's paintings hang in banks, offices, and private collections throughout the region.

Yvonne Worley Randall — *"The Confederate Trace"* — Yvonne, a Marietta native, knows this area well as her family has lived in this section of Georgia for seven generations. Her keen interest in the Civil War is stimulated by living with her physician husband in the shadow of Kennesaw Mountain. Yvonne has studied at Sweet Briar College, Atlanta College of Art, Georgia State University, The Center for Creative Studies in Detroit, and Cortona, Italy. The body of her work is primarily figurative in drawing, painting and sculpture. Yvonne has been the recipient of many awards for her art including Governor's Artist of Excellence and Cobb Arts Council Professional Achievement Award.

Ashley Ivey — *"Pineland Plantations"* — Ashley, a young artist from Thomasville, is a graduate of the University of Georgia with a Bachelor of Fine Arts degree in drawing and painting and certification in art education. She has also studied art in Cortona, Italy. Ashley has participated in and won awards in numerous local, regional, and national juried exhibitions. Her works can be found in private collections in Georgia, Florida, South Carolina, Illinois, and New Mexico, as well as in the offices of the U. S. House of Representatives in Washington, D. C.

Terri Frolich — *"The Historic Heartland"* — Terri, a resident of Macon, earned her first degree in medical technology and is married to a physician. Recently, she earned a second degree from Wesleyan College, a Bachelor of Fine Arts. Terri is a partner in the J. H. Webb Gallery, located in the historic district of Macon at Vineville and Oakhaven. Her gallery specializes in three dimensional original art by predominantly Georgia artists and in custom framing.

Mary George Poss — *"Mountain Majesty"* — Mary George lives in Rabun County, and her love of the Georgia mountains is expressed in her many limited edition scenes of the area. She studied at The University of Georgia under Lamar Dodd and Howard Thomas. The artist has exhibited at such places as the Georgia Museum of Art, Augusta Museum of Art and the Atlanta Piedmont Art Show. She has been featured in numerous one-woman art shows. Mary George, a native of Athens, started Athens' first art gallery in 1962. Her present art gallery in Clayton opened in 1983.

Dee Jackson — *"Bountiful Plains"* — Dee, a native of Savannah, now lives among the tall pines in Statesboro. She is an accomplished artist in a variety of media, including watercolor, oil, graphics, and calligraphy, with a special interest in combining watercolor and calligraphy. Dee has studied in numerous locations in the U. S., as well as such diverse locations as Okinawa and Australia while traveling with her Air Force husband. She teaches watercolor and calligraphy through Georgia Southern University and maintains a private studio in her home.

Blanche Nettles — *"Golden Isles"* — Blanche, who grew up on the Golden Isles of Georgia, earned a Bachelor of Fine Arts from the Savannah College of Art and Design and a Master of Education in the field of art from Georgia Southern University. She is currently working at Savannah Country Day School as an art educator. Blanche, a physician's daughter, enthusiastically supports **Georgia Land's** purpose to support community health projects throughout Georgia.

Bebe Davidson — *"The Capital City"* — Bebe has been painting the Atlanta scene for fifteen years. These pen and ink drawings are typical of the studies she does for her large watercolor paintings. Her originals and limited edition lithographs hang in many collections, including those of the mayor of Atlanta, Marriot Hotels and the faculty club of Emory University. She is a signature member of the Georgia Watercolor Society and a past president of the Auxiliary to the Medical Association of Atlanta. Bebe's art training includes early study with her artist grandmother in Columbus, Wesleyan Conservatory, Stratford College, and the Royal Conservatory in Toronto.

Gloria Sampson — *"The Chattahoochee Valley"* — Gloria has been drawing seriously since a child growing up in Montana. After graduation from the California College of

Arts and Crafts in Oakland, she worked for many years as a professional interior designer, with week-ends devoted to drawing and painting the Victorian architecture in the Bay Area. This whetted her interest in historic preservation and now she and her husband live in Columbus and are currently restoring four houses on The National Register. In 1987, Mercer University Press published a book of 120 of Gloria's original watercolor paintings entitled *Historic Churches and Temples of Georgia*. These have been exhibited in four of Georgia's major museums.

Tina Highsmith Rowell — *"The Scenic Lowlands"* — Tina is a native of Waycross, mother of 3 daughters, and married to William A. Rowell, a DME Respiratory Repair Technician. Tina has worked at Brantley Printing Company as a graphic artist and at Belk Hudson's as Advertising Manager, Special Events Coordinator, and Visual Display Merchandiser. She currently manages Obediah's Okefenok, Waycross' newest Tourist attraction. Her most recent work includes a coloring book, informals, post cards, etc. for Obediah's. Tina also serves on the Waycross/Ware County Tourism Committee and the 1996 Olympic Committee for the Chamber of Commerce.

Classical South: BEVERAGES & APPETIZERS

The Classical South

"The Classical South" lies to the east midway between the mountains and the sea. This is a land steeped in Southern tradition with columned mansions and town squares, game-filled woods, and well-stocked lakes.

In the spring, the eyes of the world focus on this area to view the greatest spectacle in golf, The Masters Tournament, played at the Augusta National. This golf course, designed by Georgia's own Bobby Jones and opened in 1932, is not only one of the game's most challenging, but also one of its most beautiful.

The Old Medical College building, typical of the Greek Revival architecture popular in 19th century Georgia, is also in Augusta, once the state capital. Erected in 1835 for the Medical Academy of Georgia, the first school of medicine in the state, the Old Medical College has been beautifully restored to serve again the Medical College and the community.

Artists:
Margaret Bartholomew — Title Page
Ann Bryant Cowart — "The Clasical South"

Champagne Punch

1 bottle champagne
1 cup cognac

2½ liters ginger ale
1 6-ounce can frozen lemonade
(optional)

Have all ingredients cold. Stir ingredients to mix. Serve in punch cups or champagne glasses. Optional: Make small ice ring with lemonade, some cognac, and enough ginger ale to fill small ring.

Serves 25 to 30   *Nancy Steinichen*

Slushy Punch

Serve with mint sprig

1 ounce citric acid (from pharmacy)
3 cups sugar
3 quarts water
16 ounces frozen orange juice
   concentrate, thawed

16 ounces frozen lemonade
   concentrate, thawed
46 ounces canned pineapple juice

Combine all ingredients in large plastic container, one that can go in the freezer. Stir well with a large wooden spoon. Place in freezer overnight and stir in the morning before serving.

Serves 50   *Pam Woodard*

Christmas Hot Punch

Wonderful holiday scent

½ gallon apple cider
1 46-ounce can pineapple juice
1 6-ounce can frozen orange juice
   concentrate
1 6-ounce can frozen lemonade juice
   concentrate

5 6-ounce juice cans water
1 12-ounce can apricot nectar
1 cup sugar
24 whole cloves
2 sticks crushed cinnamon

Combine all ingredients in large pot. Bring to boil and let simmer 1 hour. Gets better when reheated.

Serves 30   *Sundra Purser*

Christmas Cider

Smells wonderful

½ cup brown sugar
1 teaspoon whole allspice
1 teaspoon whole cloves
¼ teaspoon salt

Dash of nutmeg
1 3-inch stick cinnamon
2 quarts cider

Boil all ingredients. Simmer for 20 minutes. Strain to remove spices. Can be simmered in crockpot on low for 2 hours.

Serves 12   *Dorraine Smith*

Cranberry-Apple Cider

2 64-ounce jars apple cider
1 32-ounce jar cranberry juice
4-5 cinnamon sticks

20 plus whole cloves
1 cup brown sugar

Pour juices in 30 cup percolator. Put cinnamon, cloves, and sugar in basket of percolator. Perk.

Jane Mullins

Ultimate Piña Colada

With or without spirits

1 can frozen Piña Colada mix
3 scoops vanilla ice cream
Rum, optional

Ice cubes
Fresh pineapple spears
Maraschino cherries

Make Piña Colada mix according to directions with desired amount of rum and ice. Put all ingredients except ice cream in blender as instructed on container. When ice is crushed and blended into mix add ice cream. Garnish with fresh pineapple spear and cherry on toothpick or straw.

Paula Rymuza

Sangria

Olé

Base:

4 oranges

2 lemons

1 lime

3 pounds (6¾ cups) sugar

3 cups water

Sangria:

1 cup base

1 fifth dry red wine

1 small bottle soda water

To make base: Slice all fruit very thinly. Combine ingredients in a heavy metal pot and bring to a boil. Simmer for 30 minutes. Place in container and refrigerate until ready to serve.

To serve Sangria: Mix Sangria ingredients and serve over ice. Garnish with fruit slices.

Makes about 1 quart base mix

Jeanne Smiley

Homemade Sweet Wine

An old recipe from Coweta County

You will need:

1 quart measure

1 gallon measure

1 cup measure

Churn with loose-fitting lid

Clean cloth

Muscadine or Scuppernong grapes

Sugar

Yeast

Water

Scrub out churn and set aside. Mash enough grapes to fill quart measure, leaving skins and pits in mash. Put into gallon measure. In cup of lukewarm water, dissolve 1 envelope yeast. Put in gallon measure with mashed grapes. Add 6 cups white sugar and enough water to make one gallon. Put mixture in churn. Repeat until churn is full. Cover churn with clean cloth and put lid on loosely. Put churn in cool quiet place and leave it alone. In a few days you will hear it begin to "work" and it will make a bubbling sound. In 21-28 days strain and put into clean bottles.

Mary Martin Bowen

Birdsville Plantation, 1780's, Jenkins County

Ice Cream Grasshoppers

2 ounces Crème de Menthe
2 ounces Crème de Cacao

1 quart softened vanilla ice cream

Add ingredients to blender, mix until smooth. Serve in crystal wine glasses.

Carolyn Hoose

Jaclyn's Yogurt Drink

*Jaclyn created this for National Dairy Week
for 4-H club and received kudos for it!*

8 ounces vanilla yogurt
1 cup frozen fruit (strawberries,
    blueberries, peaches, etc)

1 cup skim milk

Put all ingredients in blender and blend until smooth.

Serves 4

Jaclyn Rymuza

Annie's Russian Tea

A favorite fall and winter drink

¾ cups sugar
1½ cups water
Tea ball filled with whole allspice and
    cloves
3 sticks cinnamon

46-ounce can unsweetened orange
    juice
46-ounce can pineapple juice
16-ounce can apricot nectar
1 cup weak tea

Bring first four items to a boil. Cover and simmer for 15 minutes. Add this to a large pot with rest of ingredients. Simmer for 1 to 2 hours.

Makes one gallon

*Cathy Dohrmann
Becky Smalley*

Hot Crabmeat Appetizer

Adds seafood to your buffet without great expense

1 8-ounce package cream cheese
1 tablespoon milk
6½ ounce can crabmeat
2 tablespoons finely chopped onion

½ to 1 teaspoon horseradish
Dash of salt and pepper
Dash of Worcestershire
½ cup sharp cheddar cheese

Soften cream cheese with milk. Add all other ingredients except the cheese. Grate cheese over top and bake at 375 degrees for approximately 15 minutes.

Jan Collins

Crab Mountain

Easy to prepare and serve - always a big hit

8 ounces cream cheese
1 tablespoon mayonnaise
1 teaspoon lemon juice
1 tablespoon Worcestershire
Garlic and salt to taste

¼ cup minced onion, optional
1 cup fresh crabmeat or 1 7-ounce
   can drained crabmeat
1 12-ounce bottle chili sauce
Round buttery crackers

Mix cream cheese with next 5 ingredients. Shape into ball. Refrigerate. When ready to serve place cheese ball on plate. Pour chili sauce over, then sprinkle crabmeat on top. Serve with crackers.

Serves 6-8   *Dr. and Mrs. Wayne Rentz*

Shrimp Spread

8 ounces cream cheese, softened
1 cup mayonnaise
1 small onion grated

2 teaspoons Worcestershire
½ teaspoon salt
1 pound shrimp, cooked, peeled,
   deveined, and chopped fine

Combine cream cheese, mayonnaise, onion, Worcestershire, and salt. Add shrimp. Serve with party crackers.
Note: Substitute 1 tablespoon horseradish and ½ cup catsup for Worcestershire.

Talitha Russell
Becky Smalley

Oyster-Artichoke Appetizer

A "Big Easy" favorite

½ cup butter or margarine
8 tablespoons flour
1 bunch green onions, chopped
½ green pepper, chopped
3 stalks celery, chopped
1½ large white onion, chopped

1 pint raw oysters, halved (reserve liquid)
Salt and pepper to taste
2 large fresh artichokes
2 tablespoons lemon juice

Make a roux with butter and flour by melting butter in a heavy pot and adding flour. Stir constantly until a very dark brown color is achieved - do not let burn. Add chopped vegetables. Roux will become very thick. Cook about 5 or 6 minutes, stirring occasionally. Add reserved oyster liquid. Stir. Cook on low approximately one hour, stirring occasionally until a very thick consistency is achieved. Boil artichokes in salted water with a little lemon juice until fork tender. Cool artichokes and remove leaves, saving larger leaves to use as dippers. Remove hearts of artichoke and chop. Add this to the roux. Mix. Add oysters. Mixture will thin considerably. Cook until desired consistency is achieved. Serve in chafing dish with artichoke leaves.
Variation: This may be served without artichokes in small patty shells.

Serves 12 to 16   *Carol Ann Hardcastle*

Shrimp Pâté

¾ pound shrimp, steamed, peeled, and deveined
3 tablespoons Bermuda onion chopped
¼ teaspoon hot pepper sauce
3 ounces cream cheese
1 tablespoon lemon juice

½ cup mayonnaise
1 tablespoon white horseradish
1 teaspoon Dijon mustard
1 teaspoon dill
½ teaspoon sugar
½ teaspoon salt

Chop shrimp in food processor. Add onion. Set aside. Into processor, add cream cheese and mayonnaise. Blend. Add shrimp and remaining ingredients. Blend briefly. Refrigerate several hours to 2 days in prepared mold. Serve with crackers

Serves 10-12   *Arlene Axelrod*

Marinated Shrimp

2 to 3 pounds shrimp, cooked, peeled, and deveined
1 large mild onion, sliced thin
1 lemon, thinly sliced
1 jar capers
½ cup wine vinegar
1 cup water

2 teaspoons salt
1½ tablespoons sugar
1 teaspoon dry mustard
1 bay leaf
Dash hot pepper sauce
½ cup oil
2 to 3 cloves garlic, minced

Layer first four ingredients in large bowl. Simmer next 7 ingredients and let cool. Add the oil and garlic and pour over the layered mixture. Allow to marinate overnight in refrigerator. Serve with toothpicks.

Note: Tester suggests the addition of quartered artichoke hearts.

Janet Darden

Pickled Shrimp

Serve as an appetizer or toss with spinach noodles for pasta salad

2 cups light oil
1 cup vinegar
2 tablespoon mixed pickling spice
2 pounds cooked deveined shrimp
    (can be frozen)

1 large green pepper, sliced in rings
1 large onion, sliced in rings
Salt and pepper to taste

Mix oil, vinegar, and pickling spices. Layer shrimp, peppers, and onions in deep casserole or bowl. Pour mixture over each layer. Store in refrigerator overnight. Serve with toothpicks.

Note: Tester suggests placing spices in cheesecloth, especially if serving as a salad.

Jana Hill

Souffléed Crackers

From Helen Corbitt's Cooking School

24 saltine or common crackers, singles

Ice cold water
¼ cup melted butter or margarine

Preheat oven to 450 degrees. Dip each cracker into ice cold water. Drain. Place on cookie sheet. Drizzle each cracker with melted butter. Bake at 450 degrees until puffed! When nearly brown reduce heat to 350 degrees and bake until dry inside.

Serves 12

Jeanne Smiley

Buried Treasure

1 6-ounce can pitted ripe olives
1 6-ounce can water chestnuts
2 cups mayonnaise
½ cup well-drained horseradish
2 teaspoons dry mustard
2 teaspoons lemon juice
½ teaspoon salt

1 basket cherry tomatoes (about 2 cups)
1 pound medium shrimp, cooked, peeled, and deveined
1 8-ounce can whole mushrooms
½ head cauliflower or broccoli, broken into florets

Drain olives and water chestnuts. Make sauce of mayonnaise and seasonings. Mix in other ingredients except cauliflower or broccoli, which is added just before serving. Serve in shallow glass bowl with toothpicks. Best made day before.

Mary Williams

Mrs. Ross' Cheese Straws

Versatile addition to morning coffees, luncheons, or cocktail parties

1 pound New York sharp cheddar cheese, grated
2 cups butter or margarine

4½ cups flour
½ teaspoon cayenne
¼ teaspoon salt

Cream cheese and margarine together. Sift flour, pepper, and salt and gradually add to cheese mixture, blending well after each addition. This will make a stiff dough. Press through a cookie press onto ungreased cookie sheet. Bake at 350 degrees for 10-15 minutes. Cool before removing from pan.

Makes 6 dozen   *Mary Ann Marks*

Jalapeño Cheese Spread

Great with crackers or spread on toasted bread and English muffins

2 pounds processed cheese
1 quart mayonnaise

6 green onions, chopped with tops
6 pickled jalapeños, chopped with seeds

Melt cheese. Blend with mayonnaise. Add onions and peppers. Mix well. Place in crocks or glass containers. Chill.

Makes 1 quart   *Jeanne Smiley*

Barbara's Party Cheese Ball

16 ounces cream cheese, softened
1⅓ cup flaked coconut
2 tablespoons stuffed olives, chopped
2 slices bacon, fried crisp and
    crumbled

½ teaspoon Worcestershire
2 tablespoons grated onion
⅛ teaspoon curry powder
Celery salt to taste
Pepper to taste

Combine all ingredients, saving 1 cup coconut. Blend thoroughly. Shape into ball. Roll in coconut. Chill. Serve with crackers. Can be frozen.

Serves 12   *Jeanne Smiley*

Pretzel Dip

2 8-ounce packages cream cheese
2 cups shredded cheddar cheese
1 package dry ranch dressing mix

½ cup beer
Dash garlic salt
Dash seasoned salt

Mix all ingredients. Chill one hour before serving. Serve with pretzels.

Carolyn Moon

Beef-Tomato-Cheese Dip

Microwave easy and tasty and spicy

1 2-pound package processed cheese
    spread, diced
2 10-ounce cans diced tomatoes with
    chilis

1 10-ounce can mushroom soup,
    undiluted
1 pound ground beef

Brown beef. Drain. Mix all ingredients in 3 quart microwave dish. Microwave on medium until cheese melts. Stir intermittently to keep from sticking. Serve with taco or corn chips.

Ross Vandiver

Almond Pine Cones

1¼ cups whole almonds, plain or roasted and salted
8 ounces cream cheese, softened
½ cup mayonnaise

5 bacon slices, cooked crisp and crumbled
1 tablespoon chopped green onion
½ teaspoon dill weed
⅛ teaspoon black pepper

Spread almonds in single layer in shallow pan. Bake at 300 degrees for 15 minutes, stirring often until almonds just begin to turn color. (If almonds are already roasted skip this step.) Combine cream cheese and mayonnaise. Mix well. Add bacon, onion, dill, and pepper. Mix well. Cover and chill overnight. Form mixture into shapes of 2 pinecones on serving platter. Beginning at narrow end, press almonds at slight angle into cheese mixture in rows. Continue overlapping rows until all cheese is covered. Garnish with artificial pine sprigs. Serve with crackers.

Mary Williams

River Walk, Augusta, Georgia

Garlic-Herb and Cheddar Cheese Spread

Especially nice if you grow fresh herbs

Garlic-Herb Spread:

½ cup fresh parsley leaves

1 tablespoon fresh thyme leaves

1 tablespoon chopped fresh basil
  leaves

1 tablespoon fresh tarragon leaves

1 clove garlic, coarsely chopped

16 ounces cream cheese cut into
  chunks

½ cup butter, softened

1 teaspoon Worcestershire

½ teaspoon red wine vinegar

Cheddar Spread:

12 ounces sharp cheddar cheese,
  shredded

⅓ cup sour cream

¼ cup milk

¼ cup butter, softened

3 tablespoons chopped fresh sage
  leaves

1 tablespoon chopped fresh chives

1 teaspoon Dijon-style prepared
  mustard

Prepare Garlic-Herb Spread: In food processor with chopping blade, process parsley, thyme, basil, tarragon, and garlic until finely chopped. Add cream cheese, butter, Worcestershire, and vinegar. Process until well mixed and creamy. Line a 1¼ quart bowl with plastic wrap. Spread herb cheese into bowl. Refrigerate while preparing Cheddar Spread.

Cheddar Spread: In food processor, combine cheddar cheese, sour cream, milk, and butter. Process until smooth and creamy. Add sage, chives, and mustard. Process just until well mixed. Spoon Cheddar Spread over Garlic-Herb Spread. Cover and refrigerate at least 3 hours or overnight. To serve, uncover bowl and invert cheese onto serving plate. Remove bowl and plastic wrap. With small spatula, smooth surface of cheese. Garnish top and sides of cheese with fresh herbs and herb flowers, if desired. Let cheese stand 15 minutes at room temperature until soft and spreadable. Serve with crackers.

Makes about 5 cups

Susie Jarrett

Ginger Chicken Wings

1 pound chicken wings (cut the whole
    wing in half at joint and discard
    the end part)
¼ cup soy sauce

3 tablespoons minced fresh ginger
    root
½ cup flour or corn starch
4 cups oil

Marinate the chicken wings in soy sauce and ginger mixture for several hours or
overnight. Roll in flour or cornstarch. Deep fry in oil until slightly brown.
Note: Tester suggests as a variation, omit coating and bake in oven.

Serves 4
                                                                  Choon Turner

Cove on Lake Oconee

Polynesian Wings

A party hit

5 pounds chicken wing drumettes
½ cup butter or margarine
1 cup brown sugar

1 cup soy sauce
1 cup water
1 teaspoon dry mustard

Place drumettes in 9x13 inch flat baking dish. Melt butter and brown sugar over medium heat. Add soy sauce, water, and mustard. Heat. Do not boil. Cool completely. Pour over drumettes. Marinate several hours, turning several times. About 2 hours before serving time, bake in same pan at 350 degrees for 1¼ to 1½ hours. Drain on paper towel and arrange on serving tray.

Mary Ann Marks

Spicy Sweet and Sour Meatballs

1 pound hot pork sausage
¾ cup catsup
¾ cup brown sugar

¾ cup red wine vinegar
2 tablespoons soy sauce
1 teaspoon ground ginger

Shape sausage into one-inch balls. Fry in large skillet until browned and cooked. Drain. Combine remaining ingredients in a saucepan. Simmer five minutes. Add meatballs. Simmer for 15 minutes. Serve warm in a chafing dish.

Serves 10-12   *Susie Jarrett*

Mini Cheeseburgers

3 packages party rolls
1 cup margarine, softened
1½ teaspoons poppy seeds
1½ teaspoons dry mustard
1½ teaspoons onion salt

½ teaspoon garlic salt
¾ pound lean ground beef, mixed
   with 1 beaten egg
1 pound pasteurized process cheese
   spread

Slice through middle of entire package of rolls, forming a top and bottom. Cream margarine and seasonings. Spread mixture on top and bottom of rolls. Place small amount of ground beef mixture on bottom layer of roll so there is a small amount on each individual roll. Top with cheese. Place tops over all and keep in aluminum tray. Cover with aluminum foil. Bake at 350 degrees for 30 to 40 minutes. These can be made ahead and frozen.

Serves 12   *Carol Ann Hardcastle*

Sacred Heart Church, Augusta, Georgia. Sacred Heart, originally built as a cathedral in 1898, now serves as Augusta's cultural center.

Ham Delights

1 cup butter
3 tablespoons poppy seeds
1 teaspoon Worcestershire
3 tablespoons mustard

1 small onion, minced
3 packages small dinner rolls
1 pound thinly sliced boiled ham
¾ pound sliced Swiss cheese

Slice through middle of entire tray of rolls, forming a top and bottom. Cream butter, poppy seeds, Worcestershire, mustard, and onions and spread this mixture inside tops and bottoms of rolls. Place ham and cheese over bottom layer of rolls. Put roll top over all other ingredients, making a sandwich. Cut into individual servings and put back in roll pan. Bake at 400 degrees for 10-15 minutes or until hot. Can be used for breakfast or as an appetizer or with soup and salad

Makes 24-36

Betty Hatcher

Virginia's Ham and Curry Cheese Spread

Delicious and a bit different

1 pound cooked ham, cubed
1 small onion, quartered
½ pound sharp cheddar cheese, cubed
½ cup dried apricots
½ cup golden raisins
¾ cup mayonnaise

½ teaspoon curry powder
¼ teaspoon paprika
8 ounces cream cheese, softened
2 tablespoons milk
Extra paprika

Using blender, mix first four ingredients. Pour into 4 quart mixing bowl. Add raisins, mayonnaise, and curry. Mix thoroughly. Shape into one or two mounds using rubber spatula. Refrigerate until firm. Mix cream cheese and milk until smooth. Frost mound and sprinkle with paprika. Serve with crackers or cocktail bread.

Serves 24

Jeanne Smiley

Denise's Sausage and Cheese Goodies

Good appetizer or brunch dish

1½ cups biscuit baking mix
⅓ cup water
12 ounces sausage

2 cups frozen hash-brown potatoes
1 cup shredded cheddar cheese
1 cup Monterey Jack cheese

Mix biscuit baking mix and water. Spread in bottom of 9x13 inch greased pan. Pat down smooth. Brown sausage and potatoes. Place over biscuit mixture. Top with cheeses. Bake at 450 degrees for 15 minutes. Cut into squares.

Makes 24 squares   *Shirley Baskin*

Stromboli

1 pound frozen bread dough
½ pound salami, thinly sliced
½ pound mozzarella cheese, shredded

1 egg, beaten well
Parmesan cheese

Allow loaf of bread to thaw. On lightly floured board divide loaf in half. Roll each half into 9-inch square. Cover squares with layers of salami and cheese. Roll each square tightly in jelly roll fashion. Pinch ends and long edge of dough to seal. Place rolls on lightly greased baking sheet. Brush lightly with egg. Sprinkle with Parmesan cheese. Bake immediately at 350 degrees for 25-30 minutes. Slice thinly for appetizers.
Note: Tester suggests the addition of lightly sautéed onion and green pepper for variation.

Beverly Sabatino

Julie's Marinated Mushrooms

⅔ cup olive oil
½ cup water
Juice of 2 lemons
1 bay leaf
2 cloves garlic, minced

1 teaspoon dill weed
6 whole peppercorns
½ teaspoon salt
1 pound small whole fresh
   mushrooms

Combine olive oil, water, lemon juice, bay leaf, garlic, dill, peppercorns, and salt. Bring mixture to boil, simmer 15 minutes. Add mushrooms and simmer for 15 minutes, stirring occasionally. Cool. Chill for several hours, drain to serve. May keep for 2 days.

Serves 10-12   *Julie Davies*

Stuffed Mushrooms Rockefeller

Excellent hor d'oeuvres for elegant dinner

1 pound large mushrooms
½ cup butter or margarine, halved
1 12-ounce package frozen spinach soufflé
1 small green pepper, finely chopped
2 stalks celery, finely chopped
4 or 5 small green onions, finely chopped
3 tablespoons chopped parsley

3 tablespoons Worcestershire
2 or 3 drops hot pepper sauce
1½ ounces Anisette (liqueur), optional
Paprika
Salt to taste
¼ cup grated Parmesan cheese
Fine bread crumbs

Clean mushrooms with damp paper towels. Remove stems, reserving them to be eaten separately or minced and added to mixture. Sauté caps in half the margarine until they begin to discolor. Drain on paper towels. Cook the spinach soufflé according to the package directions. Remove spinach from tin slightly undercooked. Sauté vegetables in remainder of margarine. Stir vegetables into the spinach soufflé. Add Worcestershire, hot pepper sauce, Anisette, paprika, and salt. If mixture is too dry, add margarine and stir. Fill mushrooms; dust lightly with bread crumbs and cheese. Bake at 425 degrees for 5 minutes or until brown. Serve hot.

Makes 8-10 servings   *Juanita Sims*

Piggy Back Crackers

An old favorite

1 pound bacon   48 saltine crackers

Cut bacon slices in half. Wrap one half piece around each saltine cracker. Place on broiler pan. Cook in 200 degree oven for 2 to 2½ hours.

Makes 4 dozen   *Maureen Vandiver*

Vegetable Pizza

2 packages refrigerated crescent rolls
1 cup mayonnaise
8 ounces cream cheese
1 package ranch dressing mix
3-5 tablespoons milk
Broccoli florets

Cauliflower florets
Onions, chopped fine
Tomatoes, chopped fine
Green peppers, chopped fine
Cheddar cheese, grated

Spread rolls in pizza pan to form "crust". Bake at 375 degrees until golden brown. Cool. Combine mayonnaise, cream cheese, and dressing mix. Thin mixture with milk to spreading consistency. Spread on rolled crust. Put layer of mixed vegetables and top with cheese. Slice as you would a pizza and serve. Variation: top with alfalfa sprouts.

Serves 10

Jacqueline Clark
Sara Hogue

The Old Market in Louisville, believed to have been built when the town was the State Capital, 1796.

Mexican Dip

Chalupa grande crowd-pleaser

2 cans bean dip
2½ cups grated cheddar cheese
2-3 avocados
1 teaspoon salt
1 teaspoon lemon juice
1 cup mayonnaise
1 cup sour cream

1 package taco seasoning mix
1 6-ounce can ripe olives, sliced
1 cup green olives, sliced
2 fresh tomatoes, chopped
2-3 bunches green onions, chopped
Taco chips

Mix bean dip and cheese, saving enough cheese for topping. Spread in bottom of pie plate. Mix avocado with salt and lemon juice. Spread over bean dip. Mix together mayonnaise, sour cream, and taco seasoning mix. Spread mixture over avocado layer. Top all with shredded cheese and garnish with ripe olives, green olives, tomatoes, and onions. Serve with chips.

Note: As a variation, add 1 pound ground beef, cooked and drained, with the bean dip.

Serves 12

Raye Coplin
B. J. Worsley

Broccoli-Cheese Squares

3 tablespoons butter, melted
3 eggs
1 cup flour
1 cup milk
1 teaspoon salt
1 teaspoon baking powder

2 10-ounce packages chopped frozen
    broccoli, cooked and drained
1 8-ounce package shredded mild
    cheddar cheese
2 tablespoons chopped onion
Seasoned salt, sprinkle to taste

Pour butter into 9x13 inch baking dish. In large mixing bowl, beat eggs well. Add flour, milk, salt, and baking powder. Mix well. Stir in cooked broccoli, cheese, and onion. Spoon into prepared dish. Spread evenly. Sprinkle with seasoned salt. Bake at 350 degrees until set, about 30-35 minutes. Let stand 5 minutes before cutting into bite-sized pieces.

Makes approximately 30-36 bite size squares

Kimberly Jennings

Spinach Tarts

Your guests will want this recipe

1 10-ounce package frozen chopped
   spinach, thawed and drained
1 egg, beaten
¼ teaspoon salt
⅛ teaspoon pepper
2 tablespoons chopped onion

1 cup crumbled feta cheese
¼ cup butter or margarine, melted
Cream cheese pastry shells
2 tablespoons grated Romano cheese
Diced pimento, optional

Cream Cheese Pastry Shells:
3 ounces cream cheese, softened
½ cup butter or margarine, softened

1½ cups flour

Squeeze water from spinach. Combine spinach and next 6 ingredients. Mix well. Fill each pastry shell with 1 heaping teaspoonful of spinach mixture. Sprinkle with cheese. Bake at 350 degrees for 30-35 minutes. Garnish with pimento.

Cream Cheese Pastry Shell: Combine cream cheese and butter. Cream until smooth. Add flour and mix well. Shape dough into 30 1-inch balls. Place in ungreased 1¾ inch muffin pans and shape each ball into a shell.

Makes 30 tarts

Susie Jarrett

Jalapeño Squares

4 cups shredded cheddar cheese
4 eggs, beaten
1 12-ounce jar pimento, drained

3 canned Jalapeño peppers, chopped
   and seeded
1 teaspoon minced onion

Combine all ingredients in a medium bowl. Stir well. Spread mixture on a lightly greased 8-inch square baking pan. Bake at 350 degrees for 30-40 minutes. Cut into squares and serve immediately.

Makes 3 dozen squares

Moira Brigman

Maureen's Mock Pâté

Easy to make; beautiful and delicious

2 10¾-ounce cans beef consommé
   with gelatin
2 envelopes plain gelatin
Ripe olives
1 pound liverwurst at room
   temperature

8 ounces cream cheese, softened
1 tablespoon grated onion
½ teaspoon Worcestershire
2-3 dashes garlic powder

Heat consommé over medium heat. Add gelatin. Stir until dissolved. Set aside. Oil 1 quart mold or 2 metal ice trays. Thinly slice ripe olives and arrange on bottom of molds. Pour thin layer of consommé over olives. Set remaining consommé aside. Place molds in freezer until hard. With electric mixer beat together liverwurst and cream cheese until smooth. Add remaining consommé, onion, Worcestershire, and garlic powder. Blend until smooth. Pour into molds over olives. Chill for several hours. Unmold and serve with thinly sliced French bread or bland crackers. Keeps up to 3 weeks in refrigerator.

Makes a 1 quart mold

Mary Ann Marks

"I Don't Believe It's Spam!" Spread

1 large can Spam
2 teaspoons minced fresh green
   onions, including tops
2 tablespoons mayonnaise

6 ounces cream cheese, softened
1 3-ounce can ripe olives, drained and
   sliced

Process Spam to a thoroughly minced stage. Remove to bowl. Add green onions. Add mayonnaise. Stir. Line small bowl with plastic wrap. Add Spam mixture. Cover. Refrigerate several hours or overnight. Before serving turn onto plate. Frost with cream cheese. Cover top with olives arranged in concentric circles.

Ginny Plummer

Puerto Rican Antipasto

Very unusual and delicious

3 carrots, thinly sliced
3 large onions, chopped
3 green peppers, chopped
1 cup olive oil
1 8-ounce can tomato sauce
1 teaspoon vinegar
20 ounces tomato catsup

2 teaspoons Worcestershire
4 sweet pickles, chopped
2 4-ounce cans mushrooms
3 6-ounce cans white tuna, cut into
   bite size pieces
4 bay leaves
8-12 peppercorns

Boil carrots in water until tender. Drain and set aside. Sauté onions and peppers in olive oil in 5 quart pot. Add tomato sauce, vinegar, catsup, and Worcestershire. Cook 5 minutes. Add pickles and mushrooms. Cook for 3 minutes. Add tuna, carrots, bay leaves, and peppercorns. Cook all for 15 minutes. Store in a glass container in refrigerator. Serve with crackers. Will keep 4-5 months in refrigerator.

Makes a lot!   *Peggy Tuten*

"Liberty Hall," Pre 1845, Crawfordville, Georgia, home of Alexander Stephens, Vice President of the Confederacy and Governor of Georgia, 1882-1883.

Cheese Mousse

2 teaspoons unflavored gelatin
¼ cup cold water
2 cups sour cream (light may be used)
2 teaspoons Italian salad dressing mix

¼ cup Roquefort cheese
1 cup small curd, cream style cottage cheese
Parsley

Soften gelatin in cold water, then place over boiling water until gelatin dissolves. Stir gelatin into sour cream. Add dressing mix, Roquefort cheese, and cottage cheese. Beat with mixer until well blended. Pour into 3½ cup ring mold or small loaf pan. Chill until firm. Unmold, garnish with parsley and serve with carrot sticks or apple wedges.

Serves 8-10

Jeanne Smiley

Chili Dip

Popular with teenagers and the sporting crowd

1 pound hot sausage, cooked and drained
2 15-ounce cans chili without beans

1 package onion soup mix
1 pound pasteurized process cheese spread

Mix all ingredients and heat on medium heat until cheese is melted. Stir well.

Serves 8-10

Connie Weldon

Confederate
Trace: SALADS

The Confederate Trace

The cannons are silent now, but this section of Northwest Georgia once reverberated with the sounds of war. Sherman's march through Georgia during the Civil War started here.

The Chickamauga and Chattanooga National Military Park *is the country's oldest, largest, and most visited military park, encompassing 8,000 acres in Georgia and Tennessee. The Kennesaw Mountain National Battlefield Park was the scene of two Civil War battles leading to the siege of Atlanta so vividly portrayed in "Gone with the Wind."*

This area was also the site of the Cherokee nation, the largest and most important Indian tribe in the Southeast. Here the great Sequoya created the Cherokee alphabet, and the Cherokees practiced a republican form of government at their capital New Echota until 1838.

Artists:
Margaret Bartholomew — Title Page
Yvonne Worley Randall — "The Confederate Trace"

Chicken Cantaloupe Salad

Salad:

2 chicken breasts, cooked and diced
2 cups diced celery
2 cups mandarin oranges

½ cantaloupe, diced
1 cup slivered almonds
¼ cup chopped scallions

Dressing:

½ cup sour cream
3 teaspoons ginger

½ cup mayonnaise
2 tablespoons lemon juice

Combine salad ingredients in large bowl. Mix dressing ingredients and fold into salad mixture. Cover and chill overnight.

Serves 8   *Jane Schwartz*

Curried Chicken and Artichoke Salad

Richer flavor if made day before

1 8-ounce box chicken flavored rice
1½ cups mayonnaise
2 6-ounce jars marinated artichoke
    hearts (reserve ½ marinade from
    one jar)

½ teaspoon curry powder
2 cups cooked, cubed chicken
3 green onions, thinly sliced
15 green olives with pimentos, sliced

Prepare rice according to package directions, omitting butter. Cool. Mix mayonnaise with reserved marinade and curry. Combine all remaining ingredients. Toss until mixed well. Chill thoroughly.

Serves 6-10   *Moira Brigman*

Hot Chicken Salad

Nice for luncheon

3½ pounds cooked chicken, cubed
1 cup chopped celery
1 cup sliced water chestnuts
2 tablespoons chopped onions
1 can cream of chicken soup
1 cup mayonnaise

2 tablespoons lemon juice
1 4-ounce can sliced mushrooms
¾ teaspoon salt
¾ teaspoon pepper
Potato chips

Combine all ingredients except potato chips. Pour into greased 2 quart casserole dish. Top with crumbled potato chips. Heat at 350 degrees 30 minutes.

Serves 6   *Sally Woods*

Tahitian Chicken Salad

Good luncheon dish

2 cups chopped cooked chicken
1 bunch green onions (whites only) chopped
½ cup chopped celery
2 cups pineapple chunks

1 8-ounce can sliced water chestnuts
1 teaspoon curry powder
1 cup mayonnaise
2½ to 3 tablespoons chutney
1 3-ounce can Chinese noodles

In large mixing bowl combine first eight ingredients. Mix well. Refrigerate until ready to use. Just before serving fold in Chinese noodles. Serve on a bed of lettuce.

Serves 6-8   *Martha Hancock*

Etowah Indian Mounds, Cartersville, Georgia. The Etowah Indians occupied this area between AD 1000 and AD 1500.

Mock Taco Chicken Salad

A very low-fat luncheon dish - no oil!

¼ cup lemon juice
¼ cup yellow mustard
1 teaspoon ground cumin
1 teaspoon chili powder
4 skinless, boneless chicken breasts, grilled, baked, or microwaved, then cubed

1 unpeeled apple, cored and cubed
¼ cup chopped green onion
½ cup diced celery
1 teaspoon coarsely ground black pepper
8-12 romaine lettuce leaves

Mix lemon juice, mustard, cumin, and chili powder in medium bowl. Toss chicken and apple cubes in dressing; add onion, celery, and black pepper. Serve on 2 or 3 whole romaine leaves for each serving. Garnish with cherry tomatoes or strawberries if desired. You can pick up the lettuce leaf and eat it like a taco if you like.

Serves 4   *Sarah Schilling*

Cuban Chicken Salad

1 5-6 pound baking chicken, marinated in garlic, onion, salt, and lemon juice in refrigerator several hours before baking
1 15-ounce can green peas
1 15-ounce can asparagus
1 pound potatoes, boiled and chopped
2 apples, chopped

4 hard boiled eggs, chopped
¼ cup chopped celery
½ teaspoon pepper
2 tablespoons vinegar
4 tablespoons olive oil
Salt to taste
½ cup mayonnaise
Olives and pimentos for garnish

Bake chicken for 1 hour. Remove meat from bones and chop. Combine all ingredients with mayonnaise in glass bowl. Decorate with pimentos and olives. Refrigerate several hours before serving.

Serves 10   *Lidia Delgado*

Oriental Shrimp Salad

1 10-ounce package frozen green peas, thawed
2 cups cooked rice, white or brown
1 pound shrimp, cooked

1½ cups chopped celery
4 green onions, thinly sliced
1 5-ounce can chow mein noodles

Dressing:
½ cup canola oil
1 tablespoon soy sauce
1 teaspoon celery seed

2 tablespoons white wine vinegar
2 teaspoons curry powder

Combine all ingredients except noodles. Combine dressing ingredients. Toss with rice mixture. Cover and chill. Just before serving add noodles.
Note: May substitute chicken or ham for shrimp.

Serves 4-6

Barbara Meehan

Shrimp Salad for a Crowd

A luncheon favorite. Cheese straws add the perfect touch

7 pounds medium shrimp, cooked, peeled, and deveined
2 dozen hard boiled eggs, peeled and coarsely chopped
2 bunches celery, chopped fine
1 bunch parsley, chopped fine

2 bunches green onions chopped by hand (not food processor)
Salt and pepper to taste
Enough mayonnaise to moisten
6 small avocados, cut in bite size pieces
Lemon juice

Cut shrimp in bite size pieces and place in large bowl. Add eggs, celery, parsley, and green onions. Add enough mayonnaise to moisten and mix gently. Add salt and pepper. Chill several hours or overnight. Just before serving cut up avocados and toss with a little lemon juice. Add avocados to salad and toss gently.

Serves 24

Carol Ann Hardcastle

Jane's Shrimp Salad

1 7-ounce box vermicelli, cooked and drained

2 pounds shrimp, cooked, peeled, and deveined

1 16-ounce bottle slaw dressing

1 tablespoon mayonnaise

3 stalks celery, finely chopped

1 chopped green pepper

Juice of 1 lemon

4-6 tablespoons chopped parsley

Cayenne pepper to taste

Combine all ingredients, cover, and refrigerate overnight. Garnish with parsley. Serve on bed of lettuce or stuffed in a fresh tomato.

Serves 6   *Cathy Dohrmann*

Historic District, Marietta, Georgia. Park Square.

Korean Salad

Quite different

Salad:

2 10-ounce bunches fresh spinach, large stalks removed

1 7-ounce can sliced water chestnuts, drained

3 boiled eggs, chopped

1 8-ounce can bean sprouts, drained

1 medium red onion, chopped

½ pound bacon, cooked and crumbled

Dressing:

1 cup light corn oil

¼ cup cider vinegar

⅓ cup tomato catsup

⅓ cup sugar

2 teaspoons salt (or to taste)

1 tablespoon Worcestershire

Soak spinach in vinegar and water to clean. Drain. Mix all salad ingredients with spinach. Shake dressing ingredients in medium jar. Pour over salad and toss.

Serves 8

Sandra Brown

Broccoli Salad I

2 heads broccoli, cut into florets

2 medium onions, diced

1 cup shredded extra sharp cheddar cheese

1 pound bacon, fried crisp

Dressing:

1 cup mayonnaise

½ cup sugar

6 tablespoons wine vinegar

1 tablespoon bacon drippings

Combine broccoli, onions, cheese, and bacon in large bowl. Combine dressing ingredients. Pour over broccoli mixture. Mix well. Chill until ready to serve.

Serves 8

Brenda Dohn

Broccoli Salad II

Refreshing and beautiful for a summer buffet

1 bunch broccoli florets
½ pound fresh mushrooms, sliced
1 7-ounce can water chestnuts, sliced

1 pound fresh bean sprouts, optional
1 medium avocado, cut up
1 lemon, juiced

Dressing:
1 package original ranch dressing mix
1 cup buttermilk

1 cup mayonnaise

Place broccoli in bowl. Add mushrooms, water chestnuts, and avocado. Pour lemon juice over all. Refrigerate. Mix dressing ingredients. Refrigerate. Toss salad just before serving. Add bean sprouts just prior to serving if desired.

Serves 12   *Kathy Cundey*

Clock Tower, Rome, Georgia.

California Corn Salad

Great for picnics

2 12-ounce cans corn niblets
4 stalks celery, chopped
½ medium onion, finely chopped
1 teaspoon lemon pepper
1 teaspoon salt
1 tablespoon fresh lemon juice

2 heaping tablespoons sour cream
2 tablespoons mayonnaise
½ cup chopped walnuts
1 tablespoon chopped parsley
1 teaspoon paprika

Mix first seven ingredients well and refrigerate several hours or overnight. Drain when ready to serve. Combine sour cream and mayonnaise and add to mixture. Mix well. Garnish with nuts, parsley, and paprika.

Serves 6-8   *Julie Davies*

Mexican Corn Salad

Good substitute for potato salad at a picnic or cold meal

2 15-ounce cans shoepeg corn,
   drained
1 green pepper, chopped
1 large tomato, chopped

Purple onion
Mayonnaise
Salt
Pepper

Combine corn, pepper, and tomato with enough mayonnaise to bind. It doesn't take much. Add chopped onion, salt, and pepper to taste.

Serves 8   *Nancy Carr*

Deena's Green Pepper and Olive Salad

An unusual addition to any salad buffet

3 green peppers, sliced
1 cup chopped celery
1 large onion

Marinade:
⅓ cup vinegar
⅔ cup olive oil
1 teaspoon salt

1 large tomato or cherry tomatoes
1 cup sliced green olives or ½ cup ripe
   olives and ½ cup green

1 teaspoon pepper
1 tablespoon dried oregano

Mix marinade ingredients. Pour over chopped vegetables. Marinate at least overnight.

Serves 8-10   *Julie Davies*

Marinated Salad

Crunchy and unusual

1 head cauliflower
1 bunch broccoli
½ cup raisins soaked 10 minutes in
    warm water

1 cup unsalted peanuts
½ cup chopped celery
1 7-ounce can sliced water chestnuts
6 slices bacon, cooked and crumbled

Dressing:
1 cup mayonnaise
½ teaspoon curry powder

½ tablespoon vinegar
⅓ cup sugar

Steam and drain cauliflower and broccoli florets leaving them crunchy. Rinse with cold water. Drain well. Drain raisins and add to all the ingredients. Mix dressing and add just before serving.

Serves 8-10   *Raye Coplin*

Apple Tree Marinated Vegetable Salad

Marvelous for buffet. Good color. Looks pretty in
glass bowl for summer picnic or winter salad

Marinade:
1 cup oil
½ cup white vinegar
¼ cup wine vinegar
¼ cup lemon juice (fresh only)
1½ tablespoons salt

1 teaspoon oregano
1 teaspoon dry mustard
1 teaspoon dehydrated garlic
½ teaspoon anise seed, optional

Vegetables:
4 cups sliced zucchini
2 cups sliced yellow squash
2 cups broccoli florets
1½ cups cauliflower florets

1 cup sliced carrots
1 cup thinly sliced purple onion
1 cup halved cherry tomatoes

Mix marinade. Pour over prepared vegetables. Marinate several hours or overnight. Toss gently when ready to serve.

Serves 12   *Mary Beth Becton*

Italian Cabbage

Salad:

1 medium green cabbage, chilled and sliced about ¼ inch thick

3 tablespoons sugar

2 medium onions, sliced into rings

Dressing:

1 cup sugar

1 cup vinegar

1 cup safflower oil

1 teaspoon celery seed

1 teaspoon salt

1 teaspoon black pepper

Toss cabbage with sugar and onions. Bring dressing ingredients to a boil. Pour hot dressing over cold cabbage mixture. Cover immediately and chill. Toss every 30 minutes for 2 hours. Best made a day or two before serving. Keeps in refrigerator several days.

Note: Tester suggests using red and green cabbage for added color.

Serves 12   *June Snellin*

Layered Cabbage Salad

A nice variation of the layered salad

Salad:

1 medium head cabbage chopped

2 heads broccoli, florets only

1 onion sliced

1 pound bacon, cooked and crumbled

½ cup frozen green peas

1½ cups shredded Swiss cheese

Dressing:

1½ cups mayonnaise

½ cup plain yogurt

½ cup sugar

½ cup Parmesan cheese

½ teaspoon salt

½ teaspoon pepper

Layer salad ingredients in large, deep salad bowl in order given. Combine dressing ingredients, mixing well. Spread dressing over salad ingredients. Be sure to spread to edges of bowl to form a seal. Cover with saran wrap and refrigerate until chilled thoroughly. Toss before serving.

Serves 10   *Sally Woods*

Layered Potato Salad

1½ cups mayonnaise
1 cup sour cream
1½ teaspoons horseradish
1 teaspoon celery seed
Salt and pepper to taste

8-10 medium potatoes, boiled in
    skins, then sliced
2 medium onions, minced
1 cup fresh chopped parsley, tightly
    packed down

Mix mayonnaise, sour cream, horseradish, celery seed, salt, and pepper. Layer potatoes, onions, mayonnaise mixture, and parsley twice in 9x12 inch dish. Refrigerate several hours.

Serves 10-12   *Sally Swann*

Mother Essick's Hot or Cold Potato Salad

Great favorite with men

6 medium potatoes, peeled, cooked,
    and cubed
6 hard boiled eggs, sliced
1 medium onion, chopped
1½ tablespoons celery seed
Salt to taste

1¼ cups mayonnaise
4 slices bacon, cooked and crumbled
    (save drippings)
¼ cup red wine vinegar
¼ cup hot water
¼ cup sugar

Combine and toss potatoes, eggs, onion, celery seed, salt, and mayonnaise. Add vinegar, water, and sugar to drippings. Return to heat and simmer gently until sugar dissolves. Add potato mixture and heat through. Serve hot or cold.

Serves 6-8   *Deborah Johnson*

Peas and Smoked Almond Salad

1½ tablespoons curry powder
½ cup mayonnaise
1 pound frozen green peas, thawed

3 green onions, sliced thin
1 6-ounce can whole smoked almonds

Mix curry and mayonnaise. Toss with remaining ingredients. Chill. Better made the day before.

Serves 6-8   *Joan Turcotte*

Brazilian Black Bean Salad

1 8-ounce package dried black beans
2 teaspoons salt
2 tablespoons corn, peanut, or
   vegetable oil
3 cloves garlic
1 large carrot, scraped and chopped
1 large purple onion, chopped
2 stalks celery, chopped
1 small green pepper, chopped

1 teaspoon ground coriander
½ teaspoon ground cumin
Juice of 1 large navel orange
1 tablespoon sherry wine vinegar
1 teaspoon fresh lemon juice
Salt and coarse ground pepper to
   taste
1 small head lettuce (Boston or Bibb)
8 ounces sour cream or yogurt

Rinse beans in cold water and place in large bowl. Cover with water and let stand several hours. Drain beans and place in large sauce pan. Cover with 2 inches of water and bring to full boil. Lower heat, partially cover pot, and let beans simmer about 1 hour. Add 2 teaspoons salt and continue to simmer until beans are tender. Drain. Set aside in large bowl. Cook garlic in oil over low heat until tender. Remove and discard garlic. Add carrot and stir for 1 minute. Add onion, celery, and green pepper. Stir in coriander and cumin. Add mixture to beans. Add orange juice, vinegar, lemon juice, pepper, and salt and pepper to taste. Toss to mix. Refrigerate until 30 minutes before serving. Serve on lettuce with sour cream on side.

Serves 6-8   *Julie Davies*

Confederate Soldier, (Homage to Alfred Ward, Civil War artist), Resaca, Georgia.

Egyptian Tabouli

A famous middle eastern salad modified for American friends. AZ

1 cup bulghur wheat
1 cup boiling water
2 ripe medium tomatoes
1 green or yellow pepper
½-1 bunch green onions
2 cups chopped fresh parsley

1 teaspoon dried mint
Juice of one lemon
4 tablespoons olive oil
Pinch garlic powder
Salt and pepper to taste

Pour boiling water over bulghur in medium bowl. Let stand for 15-20 minutes. Stir to hasten cooling. Cut all vegetables into bite size pieces. Toss all other ingredients together with cooled bulghur wheat. Let stand for ½ hour or more to blend flavors.

Serves 6   *Afaf Zaki, M.D.*

Shrimp Mold

2 envelopes unflavored gelatin
8 ounces softened cream cheese
1 cup mayonnaise
1 10¾-ounce can condensed tomato
    soup

2-3 cups shrimp, cooked, peeled,
    deveined, and coarsely chopped
1 cup celery, finely chopped
⅓ cup onion, finely chopped
Salt and fresh lemon juice to taste

Dissolve gelatin in ½ cup cold water. Blend cream cheese and mayonnaise well. Heat undiluted soup on low and add gelatin and cream cheese mixture. Stir well or use mixer. Add shrimp, celery, and onion. Season to taste with salt and lemon juice. Makes 2 quart mold. Refrigerate until set.

Serves 8-10   *Jeanne Smiley*

Lime Vegetable Mold

Great side dish with barbecue

1 3-ounce package lime gelatin
1 cup boiling water
4 teaspoons vinegar
½ cup mayonnaise
1 cup shredded carrot

1 cup shredded cabbage
½ cup diced cucumber
1 tablespoon finely chopped onion
Salt and pepper

Dissolve gelatin in boiling water. Refrigerate until congealed. Turn gelatin into bowl and whip until fluffy. Fold in remaining ingredients. Place in large mold or 16 small molds. Chill until firm.

Serves 12-16   *Jeanne Smiley*

Gazpacho Salad Mold

Updated aspic. Great addition to any salad plate

3 envelopes unflavored gelatin
3 cups tomato juice
½ cup red wine vinegar
2 teaspoons salt
Hot pepper sauce
½ medium green pepper, diced

2 medium tomatoes, peeled and diced
½ cup chopped celery
½ cucumber, peeled and diced
1 tablespoon chopped chives
½ cup finely chopped red onion
1 cup stuffed olives

In large saucepan sprinkle gelatin over ¾ cup tomato juice. Over low heat stir constantly until gelatin dissolves. Remove from heat. Stir in remaining tomato juice, vinegar, salt, and pepper sauce to taste. Set pan in bowl of ice, stirring occasionally until mixture thickens to consistency of beaten egg whites, about 15 minutes. Fold in vegetables. Pour into 2 quart mold that has been rinsed in cold water. Refrigerate for at least 6 hours.

Serves 8-10   *Barbara Fortson*

*"The General," locomotive, of the Andrews Raid (or "Great Locomotive Chase")
of March 27, 1863. Housed in museum in Kennesaw, Georgia.*

Holiday Cranberry Salad

1 pound fresh cranberries
5 medium or 4 large crisp apples
  (Winesap or Red Rome)
1 cup sugar
1 envelope unflavored gelatin
2 3-ounce packages raspberry gelatin

¾ cup boiling water
2 oranges, juiced and seeded, using
  pulp
2 tablespoons grated orange peel
  (about 1 orange)

Clean, core, and grind cranberries and apples medium fine. Add sugar and stir. Soften unflavored gelatin in small amount of cold water. In large bowl, dissolve raspberry gelatin in boiling water. Stir until dissolved. Add softened gelatin. Stir. Add orange juice, ground fruit, peel, and sugar mixture. Mix well. Let stand several minutes. Mix again. Pour into serving dish or mold. Refrigerate until firm.

Serves 12-15   *Anne Staley*

Unbelievable Cranberry Salad

Special holiday salad

1 pound fresh cranberries, chopped
  fine
½ cup sugar
1 10-ounce can drained crushed
  pineapple

1 pound mini-marshmallows
½ pint whipping cream
1 cup chopped pecans

Place cranberries in large mixing bowl. Add sugar and pineapple. Stir well. Add marshmallows. Mix thoroughly. Cover. Refrigerate overnight. Before serving whip cream and fold into cranberry mix along with pecan pieces.

Serves 15   *Judith Joyner*

Holiday Apple Salad

1 cup whipping cream
⅓ cup flour
¾ cup sugar
1 20-ounce can crushed pineapple,
    drained
4 tablespoons margarine

3-4 large apples, peeled, cored, and
    diced
½ cup chopped maraschino cherries,
    optional
1 cup chopped nuts

Whisk cream into a mixture of flour and sugar. Add pineapple. Cook in double boiler until it begins to thicken. Add margarine. Cool. Add apples and nuts. Add cherries if desired. Refrigerate. Garnish with nuts if desired.

Serves 6-8   *Mary Williams*

Ellijay, Georgia. Apple Capital of Georgia.

Pineland Plantations: SOUPS & SANDWICHES

Pineland Plantations

Long favored by sportsmen from around the globe, the "Pineland Plantation" area was called the "best of the winter resorts of three continents," by Harper's Magazine back in 1887. The mild climate, plus the abundance of quail, turkey, dove, and deer make this a hunter's paradise.

In addition to its hunting preserves, other incentives to visit this section of Georgia are its abundant fishing lakes, well-groomed golf courses, charming communities, historic sites, and stately mansions.

Pebble Hill Plantation of Thomasville is a beautiful historic site that stands as a testimony to the sporting life. Now open to the public, it offers a glimpse of the extravagant lifestyle of wealthy Northern industrialists who "wintered" in South Georgia in the early 20th Century.

Artists:
Margaret Bartholomew — Title Page
Ashley Ivey — "Pineland Plantations"

Cucumber Soup

Easy and adds zip to any occasion

2 medium cucumbers, peeled
Salt and pepper to taste
⅛ cup margarine
2 scallions, chopped (optional)
1 tablespoon red wine vinegar

4 cups chicken broth
1 teaspoon dill weed
8 ounces sour cream
Chives for garnish

Cut cucumbers lengthwise and scoop out seeds. Cut into small chunks. Salt and pepper to taste. Melt margarine, add cucumbers, cover and cook on medium heat 10-15 minutes or until tender. Process in food processor or blender. Add scallions. Blend. Pour into mixing bowl. Add vinegar, broth, dill weed, and sour cream. Mix well. Chill before serving. Garnish with sprinkle of chives.
Note: May add sour cream to blender to aid in mixing.

Serves 6-8   *Betty Treadwell*

Yogurt Soup

Wonderful low-cal soup

2 quarts plain yogurt (non-fat)
4 medium cucumbers, peeled, seeded,
    shredded, and drained
2-4 cloves garlic, crushed
Salt and pepper to taste

1½ tablespoons fresh mint, chopped
    or 1½ teaspoons crushed dried
    mint
½ cup toasted pine nuts, optional
Garlic pita chips

Place yogurt in large bowl. Whisk until thinned and smooth. Add cucumbers, garlic, salt, pepper, and mint. Add pine nuts, if desired. Blend thoroughly. Taste to correct seasonings. Chill. Serve with pita chips.

Serves 10-12   *Claire Davison*

Iced Lebanese Soup

2-3 medium cucumbers, peeled and diced
Salt to taste
1 5-ounce can tomato juice or V-8 juice
2 large garlic buds
1 10½-ounce can chicken stock (or fresh)

2½ cups plain yogurt
1 hard cooked egg, grated
3 ounces small shrimp, cooked, peeled, and deveined or use rinsed canned shrimp
Parsley for garnish

Sprinkle cucumbers with salt. Rinse with cold water after 30 minutes. Crush garlic buds with enough salt to make paste. Mix all ingredients, except cucumbers and shrimp. Chill. Add cucumbers and shrimp before serving. Garnish with parsley. Serve chilled.

Serves 8-10   *Jeanne Smiley*

The Big Oak, listed on the National Register of Historic Places, dates from 1685 and is almost 70 feet high, 23 feet around, and 155 feet limb spread. Thomasville, Georgia.

Gazpacho

Worth the trouble

3 medium tomatoes, peeled and sliced
1 large cucumber, peeled and halved
1 large onion, halved
1 green pepper, quartered
1 2-ounce can pimento, drained
24 ounces tomato juice

⅓ cup olive oil
⅓ cup red wine vinegar
¼ teaspoon hot pepper sauce
1½ teaspoons salt
⅛ teaspoon coarsely ground pepper

Combine 2 tomatoes, ½ cucumber, ½ onion, ½ pepper, pimento, and ½ cup tomato juice. Purée mixture. In large bowl whisk pureed vegetables, oil, hot pepper sauce, vinegar, salt, and pepper. Chill at least 6 hours. Coarsely chop remaining vegetables and add to soup.

Serves 6   *Fran Kirsh*

Gazpacho II

Tasty low-calorie soup. Good in summertime

1½ cups tomato or V-8 juice
1 beef bouillon cube
2 tablespoons wine vinegar
1 tablespoon oil
½ teaspoon Worcestershire

3 drops hot pepper sauce
2 tablespoons chopped green pepper
2 tablespoons chopped onion
¼ cup cucumber, peeled and chopped
1 tomato chopped

Heat juice to a boil. Add bouillon cube. Stir until dissolved. Stir in vinegar, oil, Worcestershire, and pepper sauce. Refrigerate. Add all vegetables except tomato. Add tomato when ready to serve.
Note: May serve with chopped parsley and dollop of sour cream or yogurt for garnish.
Serves 4

Joan Mason

Leftover Salad Gazpacho

Soup:
5 cups salad with lettuce, radish, cucumber, and tomato

1-2 cups V-8 juice
¼ -½ cup half and half

Garnish:
1 ripe tomato chopped coarsely
4 teaspoons sour cream

2-3 tablespoons finely chopped green onion

Blend soup ingredients to thick consistency. Serve chilled with garnishes.

Serves 4   *Joan Turcotte*

Pat's Borscht

Delicious summer soup

1 jar pickled beets
½ cucumber, peeled, seeded, and chopped
2 cups buttermilk

2 hard cooked eggs
Sour cream, dill, green onion tops for garnish

Blend first four ingredients in blender. Chill very well. Serve topped with small amount of mixture of sour cream, dill, and chopped onion tops.

Serves 6   *Jeanne Smiley*

French Onion Soup

8-10 onions thinly sliced
½ cup olive oil
3 tablespoons butter or margarine, melted
6 10-ounce cans beef broth
¼ cup sweet vermouth

¼ cup sauterne
French bread, sliced
Parmesan cheese
8 ounces Gruyère cheese
8 ounces Swiss cheese

Sauté onions until clear in oil and butter over medium heat in 6 quart pot. Add broth. Bring slowly to boil. Add wines. Lower heat to allow flavors to blend. Stir and test for seasonings. Cover and simmer several hours. Before serving, sprinkle bread with Parmesan cheese and toast. To serve, ladle soup into crocks. Float cheese toast. Layer cheeses, first Gruyère, then Swiss. Place under broiler until cheese melts and is crusty.

Serves 6   *Susan Braun*

Potage Chou-Fleur Au Gratin

Cauliflower Soup with Cheese

3 chicken bouillon cubes
2 cups hot water
1 medium head cauliflower
1 cup French Colombard wine
4 tablespoons low-fat margarine
5 tablespoons flour

Salt and pepper to taste
2 percent milk, as needed
6 strips bacon, crisply fried and
   crumbled
4 ounces cheddar cheese, grated

Prepare chicken stock by dissolving bouillon in hot water in large pot. Remove leaves and stem from cauliflower and cook in chicken stock until tender, about 15-20 minutes. Remove cauliflower and chop into small pieces. Blend cauliflower and liquid with wine in blender until smooth and creamy. In large soup pot melt margarine, add flour and cook 3-4 minutes, stirring constantly. Add cauliflower mixture, season to taste and thin with milk to desired consistency. Heat or chill as desired. Garnish with bacon and cheese.

Serves 6   *Vincent Masters, M.D.*

Leek and Potato Soup

Wonderful Soup

2 leeks, white part only
1½ tablespoons unsalted butter
1 large baking potato, peeled and cut
   in chunks
¼ cup chopped onion

1 quart chicken stock
Freshly ground white pepper to taste
Vegetable seasoning to taste
2 tablespoons chopped fresh chives
   for garnish

Wash leeks carefully and chop coarsely. Melt butter in 2 quart pot. Cook leek over medium heat until softened. Add potato, onion, and stock. Bring to boil over high heat. Simmer, uncovered 30 minutes. Purée soup in several batches in blender or food processor. Season with pepper and vegetable seasoning. Pour into 4 heated soup bowls. Sprinkle with chives and serve.

Serves 4   *Arlene Axelrod*

Potage Courgettes Aux Dix Herbes

Ten herb zucchini soup

½ cup butter, melted
3 medium onions, cubed
3-5 potatoes, cubed
6-8 zucchini, sliced
2½ cups chicken stock
¼ teaspoon sage
¼ teaspoon marjoram
¼ teaspoon thyme
¼ teaspoon tarragon
¼ teaspoon oregano

¼ teaspoon rosemary
¼ teaspoon dill
¼ teaspoon basil
¼ teaspoon ground celery or celery
    salt
¼ teaspoon summer savory
Salt and pepper to taste
Dash hot pepper sauce
½ to 1 cup water
Cream or sour cream, optional

Sauté onions, potatoes, and zucchini in butter for 10 minutes, stirring. Add stock. Simmer 30 minutes. Add herbs and seasonings. Purée. Rinse blender or food processor with ½ to 1 cup water and add to soup. Reheat and serve or freeze for later use. For thicker, richer soup add cream, half and half, or sour cream as desired. May be served hot or cold. Garnish with chopped chives.

Makes 1 quart   *Elizabeth Smiley*

Sportsmen from around the world flock to South Georgia to hunt quail.

Potato Celery Soup

Excellent diet soup

1-2 ounces instant chicken bouillon
1 cup chopped celery
4 potatoes, peeled and grated
1 onion chopped
¼ cup butter or margarine
1 tablespoon chopped chives

1 tablespoon chopped parsley
½ teaspoon dill weed
¼ teaspoon pepper
½ pint milk or half and half or skim
    milk

In large pot boil 2 quarts water with bouillon. Add celery, potatoes, and onions. Cook 10-15 minutes until potatoes are soft. Add butter, spices, and milk. Cool 10 minutes. Process in blender. Reheat. Serve hot. Garnish with heavy cream, flaky crab, baby shrimp, or grated cheese.

Serves 10   *Cecilia Baute*

Nan's Herbed Potato Soup

8 medium potatoes, peeled
2 medium onions chopped (or 2
    tablespoons minced onion)
¼ cup butter
2 tablespoons chopped parsley
½ teaspoon crushed basil leaves

¼ cup flour
2 teaspoons salt
½ teaspoon pepper
2 cups cold milk
4 cups scalded milk
2 cups hot potato water

Cook potatoes and onion until tender with enough water to cover. Drain and save potato water. Put potatoes through ricer or coarse strainer. Add parsley and basil. To melted butter in 6 quart pot blend in flour, salt, and pepper. Gradually stir in cold milk. Add scalded milk and potato water. Cook over medium heat until mixture thickens slightly. Stir constantly. Stir in potato onion mixture. Heat and serve. Garnish with parsley or paprika. For smooth soup blend in blender.

Serves 4-6   *Judy Domescik*

Egyptian Lentil Soup

Nourishing and welcome on a cold winter night

1 cup yellow lentils
1 large onion coarsely chopped
2 medium carrots, coarsely chopped
2 garlic cloves

1 teaspoon ground cumin
2 tablespoons butter
2 beef or chicken bouillon cubes
Salt and pepper to taste

Rinse lentils with cold water several times. Soak for 15-20 minutes. Cover with water. Add remaining ingredients. Bring to boil in large pot. Reduce heat. Cook covered over medium heat until lentils are tender, about 30 minutes. When cool blend in blender. Serve with squeeze of lemon and sprig of parsley.

Serves 6-8

Afaf Zaki, M.D.

Black Bean Soup

Very good with crisp green salad and bread

1 pound black beans
2 quarts water
1 teaspoon salt for beans
2 cloves garlic
1 teaspoon salt for soup
1 teaspoon ground cumin
1 teaspoon oregano

¼ teaspoon dry mustard
2 tablespoons olive oil
2 onions, chopped
1 or 2 green peppers, chopped
1 teaspoon freshly squeezed lemon
   juice
2 cups cooked rice

Soak beans in water in dutch oven overnight. Next day, using same water, add one teaspoon salt. Bring to boil. Cook covered until beans are almost tender. Crush together garlic, salt, cumin, oregano, and mustard. In large skillet, heat oil. Sauté onions 5 minutes. Add green pepper and continue cooking until onions are tender. Stir in seasoning mixture, lemon juice, and ½ cup hot bean liquid. Cover and simmer 10 minutes. Add to beans and continue cooking 1 hour. Serve in bowls with mound of rice in center. Garnish with dollop of sour cream and finely diced green onion tops.

Serves 6-8

Evelyn Utke

Joe's Baked Garlic Soup

Serve with crusty bread. A one-dish summer meal that's easy and delicious

2 cups fresh tomatoes, peeled and diced
1 15-ounce can garbanzo beans, undrained
4 or 5 summer squash, sliced
2 large onions, sliced
½ green pepper, diced
1½ cups dry white wine

4 or 5 large garlic cloves, minced
1 bay leaf
2 teaspoons salt
1 teaspoon basil
½ teaspoon paprika
1¼ cups grated Monterey Jack cheese
1 cup grated Romano cheese
1¼ cups heavy cream

Generously butter inside of 3 quart baking dish. Combine all ingredients except cheeses and cream in dish. Cover and bake for 1 hour at 375 degrees. Stir in cheeses and cream. Lower heat to 325 degrees and bake 10-15 minutes longer. Serve warm.

Serves 4-6   *Jeanne Smiley*

Virginia Cream of Peanut Soup

Enjoy! And give a toast to Virginia

1 large onion, chopped
2 stalks celery, chopped
¼ cup butter or margarine
3 tablespoons flour
1 can cream of celery soup, undiluted

1 can cream of chicken soup, undiluted
1 cup white wine
2 cups smooth peanut butter
1½ cups milk

Sauté onions and celery in butter in large soup pot. Do not brown. Blend in flour. Add celery and chicken soups. Place mixture in food blender and blend. Return to pot. Add wine, bring just to boiling, stirring constantly. Do not boil. Add peanut butter and milk. Cook over low heat, stirring constantly, about 15 minutes. Thin as desired with milk or wine. Serve hot. Garnish with chopped peanuts.

Serves 6   *Judy Jay Masters*

Spinach Soup

An interesting variation

½ pound ground beef
Salt and pepper to taste
6 cups chicken stock

2 10-ounce packages frozen spinach
½ cup instant or regular rice, cooked

Season meat with salt and pepper. Form in 1 inch balls. Cook in enough water to cover for 5 minutes. Set aside. Heat stock to boiling. Add spinach. When stock returns to boil lower heat and simmer 4 minutes. Add rice. Let stand 5 minutes. Drain meat balls. Add to soup. Cover. Let stand 1 hour. Serve hot.

Serves 8   *Beverly Sabatino*

Potage d'Epinards

Spinach Soup

2 pounds fresh spinach, picked and
    washed
Or 2 10-ounce packages frozen leaf
    spinach, thawed
1 medium onion, sliced
1 bay leaf
1½ teaspoon salt

⅛ teaspoon freshly ground black
    pepper
4 cups chicken broth
1 tablespoon flour
1 cup milk
1 egg yolk, beaten
Nutmeg

Combine spinach, onion, bay leaf, salt, pepper and broth in large pot. Bring to boil. Cook over low heat 20 minutes. Discard bay leaf. Force the spinach mixture through a sieve or purée in blender. Return to pot. Mix flour and small amount of milk to make a smooth paste. Stir in remaining milk and add to spinach. Bring to boil, then cook over low heat 10 minutes. Add egg yolk slowly to hot soup, stirring constantly to prevent curdling. Do not boil. Serve hot with dash of nutmeg. Soup may be reheated, but do not boil again.
Note: Substitute 2 boxes squash for spinach and you'll have squash soup.

Serves 6   *Anne Jordan*

Ginny's Broccoli Soup

2 10-ounce boxes frozen chopped
  broccoli
2 10-ounce cans chicken consommé
2 10-ounce cans cream of chicken
  soup
2 cups whipping cream

1 cup milk
1 teaspoon curry
½ teaspoon ground nutmeg
½ teaspoon ground oregano
2 tablespoons lemon juice

Cook broccoli in consommé 5-6 minutes. Drain and save liquid. In food processor or blender blend broccoli and cream of chicken soup. Pour into large pot. Add whipping cream and milk. Heat but do not boil. Add broccoli liquid to desired consistency. Add spices. Heat, do not boil. May refrigerate and serve cold.

Serves 6　　　　　　　　　　　　　　　　　　　　　　　　　*Ginny Plummer*

Tortellini Soup

Quick, easy, and delicious

1 package tortellini, cheese filled
2 quarts chicken stock
2 cups chicken, cooked and diced

2 large escarole lettuce leaves, cut in
  thin julienne strips
Parmesan cheese

Cook tortellini until done. Drain and add to heated stock with chicken and escarole. Cook 5 minutes or until lettuce leaves are tender. Serve topped with Parmesan cheese.

Serves 6-8　　　　　　　　　　　　　　　　　　　　　　　　　*Paula Rymuza*

Corn-Sausage Chowder

Rich hearty soup. Good for cold weather

1 pound sausage
1 large onion thinly sliced
1 tablespoon bacon drippings
8 medium potatoes, peeled

2 15-ounce cans creamed corn
2 12-ounce cans evaporated milk
Salt and pepper to taste

Brown, crumble, and drain sausage. Set aside. Sauté onion in bacon drippings. Set aside. Cut potatoes in bite sized pieces and boil until tender. Add sausage, onion, corn, and milk to potatoes. Simmer but do not boil. Add salt and pepper to taste.

Serves 6　　　　　　　　　　　　　　　　　　　　　　　　　*Jamee Trotter*

Bishop's Corn Chowder

Easy Sunday night supper

¼ cup chopped green pepper
¼ cup chopped green onion
2 tablespoons butter or margarine
1 10½-ounce can cream of potato
  soup

1 16-ounce can creamed corn
1 cup milk
1 cup half and half
Salt and pepper

In large heavy pot, sauté pepper and onion in butter. Add soup and corn. Mix well. Add milk and half and half. Stir until thoroughly mixed. Salt and pepper to taste. Keep hot but do not allow to boil. Serve immediately or refrigerate. Reheat before serving.

Note: For heartier soup, add 8 ounces crabmeat.

Serves 6   *Mary Ann Marks*

The Lapham-Patterson House, Thomasville, 1884,
is a perfect example of Victorian Whimsey.

Crab Bisque

1 10-ounce can cream of asparagus soup
1 10-ounce can cream of mushroom soup
1½ soup cans whole milk
1 cup whipping cream
1 6½-ounce can crab meat, save juice

10-12 fresh mushrooms, sliced
3 tablespoons margarine
Dash each salt, pepper, onion salt, garlic salt, paprika
¼ cup cooking sherry
Parsley sprigs

Combine soups, milk, whipping cream, and crab meat including juice in saucepan. Simmer but do not boil. Sauté mushrooms in margarine and add to soup mixture. Add seasonings, then sherry. Garnish with sprig of parsley.

Serves 6-8   *Nancy Wolff*

Rita's Crab Bisque with Puff Pastry

Spectacular first course for a dinner party

3 tablespoons butter, melted
3 tablespoons flour
½ teaspoon salt
¼ teaspoon fresh ground pepper
3 cups half and half

1 10½-ounce can tomato soup
½ cup clam juice
1 pound lump crabmeat
Puff pastry (may be purchased)
1 tablespoon dry sherry

Combine butter, flour, salt, and pepper in sauce pan. Stir until mixture thickens. Add half and half, tomato soup, clam juice and gently fold in one pound of crabmeat. Divide in oven-proof bowls. Add sherry to top of soup but do not stir. Cut puff pastry circle one inch larger than diameter of bowl. Place circle of pastry on each bowl but do not crimp down tightly or pastry will not rise. Press gently around sides of bowl. Place bowls on cookie sheet and refrigerate until pastry is firm. Remove from refrigerator 30 minutes before baking. Uncover and bake in lower third of 400 degree oven for 20 minutes or until pastry is puffed and brown. You may omit puff pastry and serve without it.

Serves 6   *Julie Davies*

Oyster Stew

1 dozen oysters
¼ cup dried parsley
1 pint oyster water

1 pint milk
2 tablespoons butter
Salt and pepper to taste

Sauté oysters and parsley in oyster water until oysters are cooked and edges curl. Scald milk, but do not boil. Add butter to milk. Pour buttered milk into cooked oyster mixture. Add salt and pepper to taste. Serve hot. Add more butter if desired.

Serves 4   *Maureen Roshto*

Thomasville Farmers' Market.

Seafood Bisque

Blue Ribbon winner. Unexpected flavor

24 ounces cream cheese, softened
2 8½-ounce cans mushroom pieces
2 10¾-ounce cans cream of
    mushroom soup
1 8-ounce can water chestnuts

2 pounds shrimp, cooked, peeled, and
    deveined
1 pound crabmeat
2 tablespoons soy sauce
¼ teaspoon lemon juice
½ cup half and half

Combine all ingredients except half and half. Cook over very low heat until creamy and warm. Add half and half until soup-like consistency is reached

Serves 8-10
    Ruth Ann Price

Minestrone Soup

2 tablespoons olive or salad oil
1 large carrot, thinly sliced
1 large onion, thinly sliced
1 large celery stalk, thinly sliced
1 medium onion, chopped
1 garlic clove, cut in half
¼ pound fresh green beans, cut into
    1-inch pieces
6-8 cups water
1-2 teaspoons salt
½ teaspoon oregano
3 cups shredded cabbage

1 medium zucchini, diced
1 16-ounce can whole tomatoes
2 beef bouillon cubes
¼ cup ditalini macaroni
8 ounces fresh spinach, coarsely
    chopped
1 16-ounce can white kidney beans,
    drained
1 16-ounce can red kidney beans,
    drained
Grated Romano cheese, optional

In a large pan over medium heat, in hot oil, cook carrot, celery, onion, garlic, and green beans until lightly browned, about 15 minutes, stirring occasionally. Discard garlic. Add water, salt, oregano, cabbage, zucchini, tomatoes with liquid, and bouillon and heat to boiling, stirring to break up tomatoes. Reduce heat, cover, and simmer until vegetables are tender, about 45 minutes. Stir in macaroni, spinach, and beans. Cook until macaroni is very tender and soup is slightly thickened, about 10 minutes. Serve hot with grated cheese, if desired.

Makes about 12 cups or 10 first course servings
    Beverly Sabatino

Carolina Vegetable Soup

¾ pound leanest ground beef
2 large onions, chopped
2 10½ ounce cans beef broth
   undiluted
1 soup bone
2 28-ounce cans tomatoes
1 pound fresh green beans or 1 box
   frozen

2 carrots diced
1-2 small yellow squash, diced
1 tablespoon rice
2 16-ounce cans creamed corn
1 pound fresh okra, sliced or 1 box
   frozen
Salt and pepper to taste
1 12-ounce bottle ketchup

In heavy large pot, brown meat and onions. Add beef broth, bone, and enough water to fill pot scant ¾ full. Bring to boil. Add undrained tomatoes and all other ingredients except okra, salt, pepper, and ketchup. Simmer covered about 1½ hours; then add okra, seasonings, and ketchup and cook for 30-45 minutes more. Taste for seasoning. Put up in meal sized servings and freeze if not immediately consumed! It tastes even better the second day.

Serves 8-10

Ione Lee

Raspberry Wine Fruit Soup

An elegant beginning for a special dinner

2 10-ounce packages frozen
   raspberries in syrup
2 11-ounce cans mandarin orange
   segments
1 cup orange juice

½ cup Burgundy wine
½ cup lemon juice
2 cups pink Chablis wine
¼ cup quick-cooking tapioca
2 tablespoons kirsh liqueur

Drain juice from raspberries and orange segments into 3 quart pan. Set fruit aside. Add orange juice, Burgundy wine, lemon juice, Chablis wine, and tapioca to pan. Stir occasionally over moderately high heat until mixture comes to full boil. Remove from heat. Cool 20 minutes. Add kirsh and fruit. Refrigerate overnight or up to 2 days. Serve in clear bowls or oversized wine glasses. Garnish with whole raspberries.

Serves 8-10

Delle Barnwell

Peach Soup

A delicious way to enjoy Georgia peaches

Soup:
10 fresh peaches
2 cups white wine

1 cup mineral water
1 cup simple syrup

Simple syrup:
1 cup sugar

2 cups water

Simple Syrup: Boil water with sugar until syrupy.

Soup: Dip peaches in boiling water for 1 minute. Remove skins and pits. Place peaches in blender. Add wine, mineral water and simple syrup. Blend until smooth. Chill several hours. Garnish with little cubes of fresh peaches, mint leaves, or chopped pecans.

Serves 12

Chef Gerhard Wind
Westin Peachtree Plaza Hotel

ashleyivey '91

Known as "The City of Roses," Thomasville
has one of 24 Rose Test Gardens in the U.S.

Asparagus Finger Sandwiches

1 15-ounce can asparagus, mashed
1 tablespoon mayonnaise
½ cup chopped pecans
¼ cup chopped onion
Dash soy sauce

Dash garlic salt
Dash seasoned salt
8 ounces cream cheese
Lemon pepper, optional
1 loaf thin bread

Mix all ingredients. Spread on bread

12 large sandwiches   *Carolyn Moon*

Lanie's Crab Sandwiches

½ cup mayonnaise
1 clove garlic, minced
1 pound imitation crab meat
1 cup shredded cheddar cheese
1 cup shredded Monterey Jack cheese

1 6-ounce can ripe olives, sliced in
  half
1 14-ounce can artichoke hearts,
  quartered and chopped
4 split English muffins

Mix mayonnaise, garlic, crab meat, and cheeses. Add olives and artichokes. Place
English muffins on baking sheet. Spoon mixture onto muffins in generous amounts.
Place under broiler, 5 inches from heat. Heat 4-5 minutes or until heated thoroughly.

Serves 8   *Mary Ann Marks*

Salmon on French Bread with Asparagus

1 small loaf French bread
1-2 tablespoons mayonnaise
Bibb lettuce for 2 sandwiches

2 salmon filets, cooked and flaked
Fresh parsley
Dash of lemon pepper

Split small French bread loaves and spread with mayonnaise. Top with Bibb lettuce
and chunks of fresh poached or canned salmon and sprigs of parsley. Sprinkle lightly
with lemon-pepper. Serve with steamed, then chilled, fresh asparagus, marinated in
Cheri's marinade (see recipe). Garnish with strips of pimento and twists of lemon.

Serves 2   *Cheri Dennis*

Mary Jack's Soup Sandwiches

1 loaf white sandwich bread or 16
   slices
1 10¾-ounce can cream of mushroom
   soup

8 ounces sharp cheddar cheese, grated
16 slices bacon

Trim crust from bread. Spread mushroom soup (like mayonnaise) generously on bread. Sprinkle cheese on bread and roll up, jelly roll fashion. Place rolled sandwiches in single layer in container and cover. Refrigerate overnight. On day of serving cook bacon just until limp. Wrap piece of bacon around each sandwich. Secure with toothpick if necessary. Cook in oven until brown. Bacon may be cooked in microwave.

Makes 16 sandwiches   *Mary Ann Marks*

Salad Sandwich

6 Holland rusk rounds
1 tube anchovy paste
6 thin slices red onion
6 thick, unpeeled slices tomato

6 slices hard cooked egg
1 cup Hollandaise
Parsley or watercress, chopped

Spread rusk with layer of anchovy paste. Layer on onion, tomato, and egg. Cover all with 2 tablespoons of Hollandaise. Garnish. Bake 20 minutes at 225 degrees until hot, about 10 minutes. Serve immediately.

Makes 6 servings   *Jeanne Smiley*

Lemon Tea Sandwiches

Very unusual and delicious

3 egg yolks
½ cup sugar
2 tablespoons lemon juice
Rind of 2 lemons

8 ounces cream cheese, softened
1 cup pecans, finely chopped
Mayonnaise
20 thin slices whole wheat bread

Cook egg yolks, sugar, lemon juice, and rind over medium heat until thick, stirring constantly. Add cream cheese and pecans. Stir until smooth. Refrigerate. Remove from refrigerator 30 minutes before making sandwiches. Spread mayonnaise on bread. Spread filling on half the slices of bread and top with other. Trim crusts from sandwiches and cut into triangles or squares for serving.

Serves 10   *Joyce Johnson*

Cucumber Party Sandwiches

2-3 tablespoons garlic and herb or
    ranch dry dressing mix
8 ounces cream cheese, softened
4-6 tablespoons milk

1-2 loaves sandwich bread, decrusted
    and cut into rounds
2 large cucumbers, peeled and thinly
    sliced
Paprika

Add dressing mix to cream cheese. Stir to blend. Add milk to thin to spreadable consistency. Spread bread rounds with thin layer of mixture, top with cucumber slice and sprinkle lightly with paprika.

Note: Use small biscuit cutter to make bread rounds same size as cucumber slices. Bread placed in freezer a few minutes before using is easier to cut, easier to spread, and prolongs freshness of sandwich.

Makes about 4 dozen　　　　　　　　　　　　　　　　　　　　　　*Mary Ann Marks*

The Coheelee Creek Covered Bridge, 1883, near Blakely,
is one of the few remaining in Georgia.

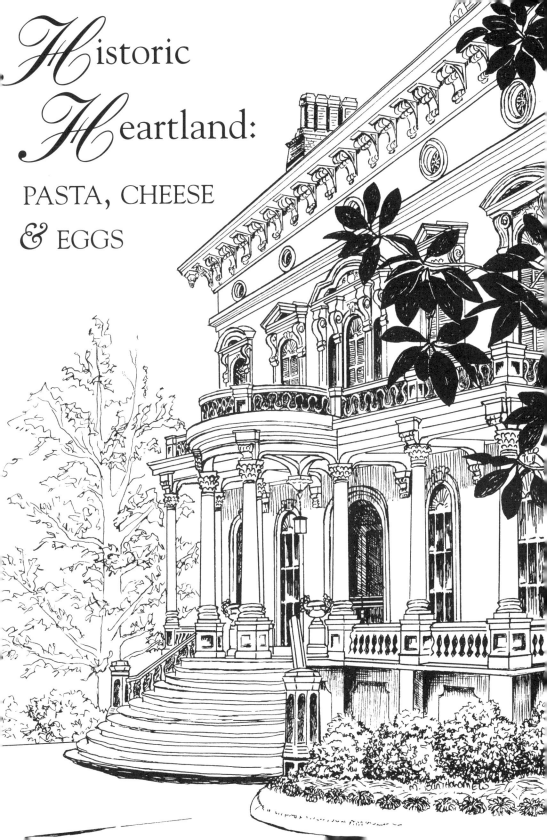

Historic Heartland:

PASTA, CHEESE & EGGS

The Historic Heartland

The Historic Heartland affords an infinite variety of experiences. This central portion of Georgia is rich in Confederate lore and glimpses of Victorian life combined with a vibrant 20th Century lifestyle.

History really comes alive in places such as Athens, home of the University of Georgia, the nation's oldest chartered university; Milledgeville, Georgia's antebellum state capital; Madison, a town with one of the largest collections of historic homes in Georgia; and Macon, a city with more then sixty structures on the National Register.

The Hay House, located in Macon, is an ornate 1855 Italian Renaissance mansion with 24 rooms, exquisite architectural features and priceless furnishings. During the Civil War, the dwelling was used as Confederate headquarters, and legend has it that the Confederate treasury was for a time hidden in its secret room.

Artists:
Margaret Bartholomew — Title Page
Terri Frolich — "The Historic Heartland"

Antipasto Salad

Colorful, tasty Italian dish

2 tablespoons white wine vinegar
2 tablespoons plus 1 teaspoon olive oil
1 tablespoon minced shallots
1 teaspoon dried oregano
⅛ teaspoon crushed red pepper flakes
2 cups cooked cheese tortellini, cooled

1 medium red pepper, cut into thin
   strips
3 ounces provolone cheese, cut into
   cubes
2 ounces beef salami, cut into strips

To prepare dressing whisk together vinegar, oil, shallots, oregano, and pepper flakes. Combine remaining ingredients and add to dressing. Toss to mix well.

Serves 4   *Joan Turcotte*

Seafood Pasta Salad

Delicious when served with lavosh crackers

16 ounces tricolor spiral pasta,
   cooked, drained, and cooled
¾ pound each: Langostinos, shrimp,
   and crab meat, cooked and cleaned

1 cup black olives, sliced
1 cup sweet red pepper, diced
1 cup sweet yellow pepper, diced
½ cup scallions sliced

Dressing:
2 cups mayonnaise
¼ cup lemon juice
½ cup fresh basil leaves, minced

2-3 cloves garlic, crushed
Radish flowers and fresh cilantro
   leaves for garnish

Combine all salad ingredients in large bowl. Combine all dressing ingredients and pour over salad. Toss gently. Refrigerate. When ready to serve garnish with radish flowers and fresh cilantro leaves if desired.

Serves 8-10   *Paula Rymuza*

Greek Pasta Salad

16 ounces noodles, cooked (two
    different shapes)
½ to 1 pound feta cheese
1 cup chopped green peppers
3 spring onions, chopped
1 large tomato, chopped

1 cup safflower oil
¼ cup red wine vinegar
1 tablespoon dill weed
⅛ teaspoon salt and pepper
Cooked chicken or shrimp, optional

Combine noodles with vegetables and cheese. Mix oil, vinegar, dill weed, salt, and pepper and pour over noodles. Marinate overnight. May add chicken or shrimp for main dish.

Serves 6-8   *Jacqueline Clark*

*Sidney Lanier Cottage in Macon, Georgia. Sidney Lanier, who wrote
"The Song of the Chattahoochee" and "The Marshes of Glynn" was
Georgia's best known poet. He was born in Macon in 1842.*

Shrimp Vermicelli

½ cup butter, melted
6 tablespoons flour
2 10¾-ounce cans chicken broth
1 cup grated Swiss cheese
White pepper and garlic powder to taste
Pinch of cayenne pepper
Salt to taste

1 large can sliced mushrooms, drained
1 cup sour cream
2 pounds shrimp, cooked, peeled, and deveined
8 ounce package vermicelli, cooked and drained
Parmesan cheese

Stir flour in butter. Cook at least 2 minutes over low heat. Add chicken broth gradually and cook, stirring constantly until sauce thickens. Add Swiss cheese and season to taste. Add mushrooms and sour cream. Mix well. Add shrimp. Layer vermicelli in oiled lasagna pan. Pour shrimp sauce over this. Cover with Parmesan cheese. Heat in 325 degree oven until bubbly. If reheating, cover tightly with foil and remove foil and brown under broiler for a few seconds.

Note: Remember when cooking shrimp, do not overcook. Put shrimp in vigorously boiling water and after water has returned to rolling boil leave shrimp in water only 30 more seconds. Do not rinse shrimp in the shell when removed from water. Drain in colander and let return to room temperature before you peel them, all the liquid between the body and shell will re-enter the shrimp.

Tester suggests addition of artichoke hearts.

Serves 8-10
Julie Davies

Tonnarelli

Easy and delicious side dish. Used often during Air Force duty day, long before pasta was posh!

½ pound fine egg noodles or vermicelli
1 4-ounce can sliced mushrooms

3 tablespoons butter
1 cup cooked very small green peas
½ cup grated Parmesan cheese

Cook noodles until al dente. Drain. Add drained mushrooms, butter, peas, and Parmesan to hot noodles. Toss until coated with cheese. Serve immediately.

Serves 4
Jeanne Smiley

Chinese Lo Mein

Great as appetizer; perfect as unusual luncheon dish

1 pound vermicelli, cooked, drained, and cooled
4 chicken breast halves, cooked and cut in julienne strips
1 bunch scallions or green onions, chopped
¾ cup chopped walnuts
½ cup vegetable oil

2½ tablespoons oriental sesame oil
¾ cup light soy sauce
1 scant teaspoon hot chili oil, optional
2 tablespoons sesame seeds
Sun-dried tomatoes to taste (about 8 tomato halves) reconstituted according to package directions

Place vermicelli in large bowl. Add chicken, green onions, and walnuts. Mix liquids and sesame seeds. Add to chicken mixture. Add sun-dried tomatoes. Mix by folding gently. Refrigerate, but serve at room temperature. This can also be served as an appetizer without pasta, using toothpicks

Serves 12

Christine Hardcastle

Pasta with Panache

Great bridge or luncheon dish

1 pound raw shrimp
1 pound fresh asparagus
30 large fresh basil leaves (reserve several for garnish)
4 cloves garlic, chopped
2 cups cream
1 cup butter

16 ounces fresh fettucine, cooked and drained
2 cups grated Parmesan cheese
Salt and pepper to taste
Nutmeg to taste
Lemon wedges
Red leaf lettuce

Peel devein, and butterfly shrimp. Cook asparagus and cut into 1 inch pieces. In large sauce pan combine basil, garlic, cream, and butter. Bring to boil and simmer until thickened. Add shrimp and asparagus to cream sauce. Cook 8 or 10 minutes until shrimp are pink. Toss noodles into cream mixture. Add cheese, salt, pepper, and nutmeg. Serve garnished with basil leaves and lemon wedges on bed of red lettuce leaves.

Serves 8

Evalyn Parrish

Pasta with Veal, Peppers, and Basil

Excellent meal with salad and bread

12 ounces spaghetti
3 tablespoons olive oil
¾ pound veal cutlets, sliced crosswise
    into 2-inch wide strips
2 to 3 cloves garlic, minced
¾ teaspoon salt
¾ teaspoon coarsely ground black
    pepper

2 large red and/or green peppers, cut
    into thin strips
1 28-ounce can tomatoes
1 bunch fresh basil or Italian parsley,
    coarsely chopped (about ¾ cup)
Grated Parmesan cheese

Cook spaghetti according to package directions. Drain and return to pot and toss with 1 tablespoon olive oil. Cover and keep warm. Heat 1 tablespoon oil in skillet over high heat. Add veal, garlic, ¼ teaspoon salt and ¼ teaspoon pepper. Cook for 2 or 3 minutes or until lightly browned but still pink in center, stirring frequently. Remove to serving bowl. Reduce heat to medium. To drippings in skillet add remaining tablespoon oil and pepper strips. Sauté for 5 minutes or until peppers are lightly browned. Stir in tomatoes and remaining salt and pepper. Break up tomatoes with spoon. Increase heat to high. Cook 3 to 5 minutes or until mixture is bubbly. Stir in veal and any meat juice accumulated in bowl. Heat through. Pour veal sauce over spaghetti and add basil and toss until well combined. Return to serving bowl and sprinkle with cheese.
Tester suggests using chicken as an alternative.

Serves 4-6   *Julie Davies*

Angel Hair Pasta with Roasted Pepper Sauce

So good you don't even realize it is meatless

1 large red pepper
1 large yellow pepper
1 small bunch green onions, chopped
1 garlic clove, minced
2 tablespoons olive oil

1 16-ounce jar marinara sauce
Salt and pepper to taste
10 leaves fresh basil, chopped
9 ounces angel hair pasta, cooked

Roast red and yellow peppers in oven and slice in 1 inch square pieces. Sauté onions and garlic in oil until tender. Combine all ingredients and simmer 5 minutes. Serve over pasta.

Serves 4   *Ann Mitchell*

Fettuccine Primavera

A colorful side dish to serve with poultry, fish, or beef

⅓ cup pine nuts
2 cups small broccoli florets
3-4 cups sliced zucchini
¼ cup olive oil
1½ teaspoons minced garlic
4 large tomatoes, skinned and
    chopped
¼ teaspoon salt

¼ teaspoon freshly ground pepper
8-10 ounces fettuccine, cooked and
    drained
4 tablespoons butter
½ cup heavy cream
1 cup freshly grated Parmesan cheese
¼ cup minced fresh basil or 1
    teaspoon dried basil

On cookie sheet, toast pine nuts under broiler until light brown, about 2 or 3 minutes. Blanch broccoli for 3 to 4 minutes in boiling water and drain. Blanch zucchini in boiling water for 1 minute and drain. In large skillet, heat olive oil. Add garlic, tomatoes, zucchini, broccoli, salt, and pepper. Sauté briefly, about 2 or 3 minutes. Add fettuccine to skillet along with butter, cream, Parmesan, pine nuts, and basil. Toss gently and serve.

Serves 6   *Susie Jarrett*

Seafood Fettuccine

½ cup butter or margarine
1 medium onion, chopped
3-4 cloves garlic, minced
½ pound shelled, deveined medium
    shrimp
½ pound scallops, rinsed

½ pound lump crabmeat
1 tablespoon cajun spices
1 cup sour cream
12 ounces fettuccine noodles, cooked
    and drained

Melt butter over medium heat. Add onion and garlic. Sauté until soft. Add shrimp. Cook until pink. Add scallops and cook 3 minutes. Add crabmeat. Add cajun spices. Warm through. Add sour cream. Turn heat to low. Do not boil. Serve over hot noodles.

Serves 6-8   *B. J. Worsley*

Paula's Favorite Fettuccine

24 ounces fettuccine noodles, cooked
and drained
⅛ to ¼ pound prosciutto ham, sliced
into thin strips
1 10-ounce package frozen baby green
peas

1 pint half and half
½ pint heavy cream
½ cup Parmesan cheese
Salt and pepper to taste
¼ to ½ teaspoon garlic powder

Over medium heat warm half and half, cream, and cheese. Add noodles, peas, and ham. Toss together and add salt and pepper and garlic powder to taste. When noodles are covered with creamy coating and peas cooked through turn onto warm plate and serve.

Serves 12   *Paula Rymuza*

*The Old State Capitol in Milledgeville, in use from 1807-1867,
has been rebuilt as part of Georgia Military College.*

Fettuccine with Pesto

Perfect side dish for an Italian meal

1 pound fettuccine, cooked and
    drained
4 garlic cloves, peeled
4 ounces pine nuts

½ cup extra virgin olive oil
25 fresh basil leaves
Salt and fresh black pepper to taste
Parmesan cheese, grated

Place fettuccine in large bowl. In food processor or blender place pine nuts, garlic, and olive oil and process until fine. Add basil, salt, and pepper. Grind again until very smooth. Pour mixture over fettuccine. Sprinkle with Parmesan cheese. Toss and serve.

Serves 4-6

Julie Davies

Fettuccine Alfredo

1 pound fresh fettuccine noodles
6 tablespoons butter
¾ cup grated fresh Parmesan cheese

¾ to 1 cup heavy cream at room
    temperature

Cook fettuccine in boiling salted water until tender. Fresh cooks in about 8-10 minutes. Drain well. Toss immediately with butter and add grated cheese. Add cream just before serving. The more cream added, the richer and "soupier" the noodles.

Serves 8-10

JoAnn Crooms

Grandmother's "Real" Macaroni and Cheese

Very much like a soufflé

4 eggs
2 cups grated cheese
2½ cups milk

4 tablespoons margarine, melted
Salt and pepper to taste
1 cup macaroni, cooked and drained

Combine first five ingredients in order listed. Mix with macaroni. Pour into greased 9x13 inch glass baking dish. Cook for 35 minutes at 325 degrees. Serve hot. Great with any meal!

Serves 10

Jan Collins
Maryline Smith

Macaroni and Cheese

1 7-ounce box elbow macaroni
½ cup diced onion
1 4-ounce jar sliced mushrooms
1 2-ounce jar pimentos
1 tablespoon butter

1 10¾-ounce can cream of mushroom
  soup
½ cup mayonnaise
1 pound grated cheese
Bread crumbs

Cook macaroni and drain. Sauté onions, mushrooms, and pimentos in butter. Add macaroni, soup, mayonnaise, and cheeses. Mix well. Turn into greased 2 quart casserole. Top with bread crumbs. Bake at 350 degrees for 30 minutes.

Serves 6-8   *Paul Shanor*

Pizza Casserole

Great dish for teenagers

4 ounces sliced pepperoni
1 medium onion, chopped fine
⅓ cup margarine
6 ounces thin spaghetti, cooked and
  drained
2 8-ounce cans tomato sauce

1 cup grated Swiss cheese
1 pound Mozzarella cheese, sliced thin
1 4-ounce can mushrooms
½ teaspoon oregano
½ teaspoon basil

Boil pepperoni five minutes to remove grease. Drain on paper towel. Sauté onion in 1½ tablespoons margarine until golden brown. Melt remaining margarine and pour into 11x7 inch baking dish. Toss spaghetti in margarine. Cover spaghetti with one can tomato sauce. Add in order listed: ½ the Swiss cheese, ½ the Mozzarella, all the mushrooms and onions. Sprinkle with oregano and basil. Top with remaining Swiss cheese and pepperoni. Add one can tomato sauce spread over top. Add rest of Mozzarella. Bake at 350 degrees for 25 minutes.

Serves 6   *Corrine Laskey*

Easy, Cheesy Onion-Spinach Lasagna

Nutritious, vegetarian dish. No one will complain about absence of meat.

1 8-ounce package whole wheat
  lasagna noodles
3 tablespoons olive oil
3 medium onions, coarsely chopped
3 cloves garlic, chopped fine
2 10-ounce packages frozen chopped
  spinach, thawed

28 ounce jar spaghetti sauce
1 pound grated low-fat mozzarella
  cheese
15 ounces low-fat ricotta cheese
3 ounces grated gourmet Parmesan
  cheese
14 ounce jar spaghetti sauce

Cook lasagna noodles according to package directions, adding 1 tablespoon olive oil to boiling water. Drain. Add cold water to pot and set aside. In large skillet, sauté onions in remaining olive oil until just clear. Add garlic. Cook for 1 minute more. Reduce heat to low. Add spinach, simmer until mixture is dry. Watch carefully. Remove from heat and set aside. Cover bottom of lasagna pan with thin layer of spaghetti sauce. Cover with ½ noodles, then ½ remaining 28-ounce jar of spaghetti sauce, then ½ spinach-onion mixture, ½ ricotta cheese, ½ mozzarella cheese, ½ Parmesan cheese. Repeat layers. Bake at 350 degrees for 45 minutes or until top is bubbly and begins to brown. Heat remaining 14-ounce jar of spaghetti sauce and serve with lasagna to spoon on at table.

Serves 6-8

Judy Mackler

Noodle Kugle

Marvelous for buffets

Step 1:
8 ounces wide noodles, cooked
 and drained
8 ounces cream cheese
½ cup sugar

12 ounces cottage cheese
1 pint sour cream
½ cup butter, melted
4 large eggs

Step 2:
16 ounces apricot preserves
¼ cup melted butter

1 teaspoon vanilla extract
Dash of cinnamon

Mix together all the ingredients in Step 1 and place in a 9x13 inch greased baking dish. Melt together the ingredients in Step 2 and pour on top of noodles and bake at 350 degrees for 1¼ to 1½ hours.

Serves 8-10

Terri Frolich

Arch at University of Georgia
Athens, Georgia

The famous Arch was erected in 1856 in Athens as the symbol of the University of Georgia, the Nation's oldest state chartered university (in 1785).

Grazzini's Vegetarian Lasagna

6 lasagna noodles

1 14-ounce jar thick spaghetti sauce or 2 cups favorite tomato sauce recipe

5-6 large fresh mushrooms

1 medium eggplant, pared and cubed

1 medium zucchini, cubed

¼ cup minced onion

¼ cup sliced black olives, optional

1 1 pound 12 ounce can whole tomatoes, chopped or 4 or 5 fresh tomatoes

1 8-ounce package sliced mozzarella cheese

8 ounces ricotta

¼ cup fresh chopped parsley

1 egg

3 tablespoons Parmesan cheese

Cook lasagna noodles. Grease 13x9 inch pan. Prepare cheese filling (ricotta, egg, parsley, and Parmesan) and set aside. Coat bottom of pan with tomato sauce. Place 3 lasagna noodles on sauce. Mix raw mushrooms, eggplant, zucchini, olives, and tomatoes together and spoon over noodles. Place enough mozzarella slices over vegetables to completely cover. Put remaining 3 noodles over cheese. Add another serving of tomato sauce. Place cheese filling over that. Cover surface with another layer of mozzarella cheese and tomato sauce on top. If desired, sprinkle additional Parmesan lightly on top. Bake uncovered 40-45 minutes at 375 degrees or slightly lower, so cheese doesn't get too dark on top.

Note: Vegetables can be varied, and spinach can be used in the ricotta filling instead of parsley. For variety, a little minced mint in tomato sauce is good and gives a Greek twist to flavor. If this is too much mozzarella, cook 9 noodles and use 3 more in lieu of mozzarella layer on top, being sure to coat well with sauce so they don't dry out.

Serves 6-8   *Jeanne Smiley*

Pasta Leone

2 ounces olive oil
5-6 carrots, diced
5-6 celery stalks, diced
2 green peppers, diced
1 large onion, chopped
4-6 garlic cloves, minced
2 28-ounce cans crushed tomatoes

2 16-ounce cans stewed tomatoes, drained and chopped
1 package Italian sausage links, cut into 1 inch pieces
1 teaspoon red pepper
2 tablespoons Italian seasoning
1 pound mostacciola, cooked and drained

In large skillet, sauté carrots and celery in olive oil for 30 minutes. Add peppers, onion, and garlic. Continue to sauté for 20 minutes or until tender. Add contents to a crockpot. Add tomatoes. In another skillet brown sausage. Drain. Add to crockpot. Add seasonings. Mix well. Simmer for 3 hours. Serve over pasta.

Serves 4   *Edward S. Porubsky, M.D.*

Three Cheese Ham and Pasta Bake

Great way to use the last of a ham

1 pound spiral pasta noodles
4 tablespoons vegetable oil
3 to 4 small zucchini in ¼ inch slices
1 pound fresh mushrooms, sliced
6 green onions, minced
2 cloves garlic, minced
2 tablespoons minced parsley
1 teaspoon oregano
15 ounces ricotta cheese
10 ounces mozzarella cheese, grated

1 cup sour cream
5 ounces grated Parmesan cheese
3 eggs
1 teaspoon Dijon mustard
½ teaspoon salt
½ teaspoon pepper
1 cup bread crumbs, homemade if possible
4 cups cooked ham, diced
3 tablespoons butter

Cook pasta, drain, and toss with 2 tablespoons oil. Set aside. Sauté zucchini, mushrooms, onions, garlic in 2 tablespoons oil for 3 to 4 minutes. Remove from heat. Toss in parsley and oregano. Set aside. Beat ricotta, mozzarella, sour cream, Parmesan, eggs, mustard, salt, and pepper until smooth and well blended. Pour cheese mixture over pasta. Add vegetables and ham and toss gently. Pour into greased 4 quart baking dish. Sprinkle with bread crumbs and dot with butter. Cover and bake at 350 degrees until bubbly, about 30 minutes. Uncover and bake about 10 minutes to brown.

Serves 8-10   *Carol Ann Hardcastle*

Mercer University, founded in 1833, now located in Macon.

Skillet Breakfast

6 slices bacon, diced
1 small green pepper, diced
2 tablespoons diced onion
3 cooked potatoes, peeled and diced

½ cup grated cheddar cheese
6 eggs, lightly beaten and seasoned
    with salt and pepper

In large skillet sauté bacon until crisp. Remove and drain. Drain off all but 3 tablespoons of drippings. Add to drippings green pepper, onion, and potatoes and sprinkle with salt and pepper. Cook, stirring over medium heat, until potatoes are golden. Sprinkle cheese over mixture and stir until cheese melts. Pour eggs into skillet and cook over low heat until set.

Serves 4   *Carol Ann Hardcastle*

Egg Scramble Casserole

2 tablespoons margarine, melted
2 tablespoons flour
2 cups milk
½ teaspoon salt
⅛ teaspoon pepper
8 ounces American processed cheese
1 cup cooked, chopped ham or ½
    pound sausage, cooked and
    drained

¼ cup chopped onion
3 tablespoons melted margarine
12 eggs, beaten
1 4-ounce can mushrooms, drained
1½ cups bread crumbs
⅛ teaspoon paprika

Combine margarine and flour; gradually add milk and cook over low heat until smooth and thick, stirring constantly. Add salt, pepper, and cheese, stirring until cheese melts. Set aside. Sauté ham or sausage and onions in remaining margarine about 5 minutes. Add eggs and mushrooms and cook until set, stirring occasionally to scramble. Fold in cheese sauce and mix well. Spoon mixture into greased 12x8 inch casserole, top with breadcrumbs, sprinkle with paprika, and bake at 350 degrees 30 minutes. Serve immediately.

Serves 8   *Mary Ann Marks*

Cheese Blintz Casserole

Wonderful for brunch or lunch

Filling:

16 ounces softened cream cheese

16 ounces small curd cottage cheese
(or 2 pounds farmers cheese)

¼ cup sugar

Pinch of salt

Juice of 1 lemon

Batter:

1 cup melted butter

½ cup sugar

2 eggs

1 cup sifted flour

3 teaspoons baking powder

Pinch of salt

¼ cup milk

1 teaspoon vanilla

Combine filling ingredients in large bowl. Mix batter ingredients together in small bowl until smooth. Place ½ batter in bottom of greased pan. Spread filling mixture over batter. Top with remaining batter. Bake at 300 degrees for 45 minutes to 1 hour or until set and golden brown. Can be served with sour cream or lemon yogurt.

Serves 12

Karel Forrester

Low-Cal Spinach Quiche

3 eggs, beaten

2 10-ounce packages frozen chopped
spinach, thawed and drained

3 ounces shredded Swiss cheese

2 ounces grated Parmesan cheese

2 cups low-fat cottage cheese

½ teaspoon Dijon mustard

1 teaspoon chopped fresh onion

1 teaspoon cayenne

½ teaspoon salt

Combine all ingredients. Pour into greased baking dish. Bake at 350 degrees for 40 minutes.

Serves 6

Toni Shiver

*This statue of Br'er Rabbit stands in front of the courthouse of Eatonton,
birthplace of Joel Chandler Harris, creator of the Uncle Remus tales.*

Hot Breakfast Treat

Great for overnight guests

2½ cups herb croutons (1 box)
2 cups shredded sharp cheddar cheese
2 pounds medium hot sausage,
   browned
1 4-ounce can sliced mushrooms,
   drained

6 eggs
¾ teaspoon dry mustard
2½ cups low-fat milk
1 can low-sodium mushroom soup

Line greased 9x13 inch casserole with croutons. Sauté sausage until brown. Drain. Sprinkle cheese over croutons. Spread sausage and mushrooms over mixture. Combine remaining ingredients in blender and slowly pour into casserole. Cover and refrigerate overnight. Bake at 300 degrees for 1½ hours. Garnish with red or green pepper strips.

Serves 12

Karel Forrester
Susie McKinnon

Spinach Frittata

1 tablespoon extra-virgin olive oil
2 tablespoon minced onion
¾ cup liquid egg substitute
¼ cup freshly grated Parmesan cheese
½ teaspoon dried oregano, crushed

⅛ teaspoon freshly ground black
   pepper
1 10-ounce package frozen chopped
   spinach, cooked and drained well

Heat oil in 8-inch skillet or omelet pan. Add onion and cook until clear and tender. Combine half the cheese with egg substitute, oregano, pepper, and spinach and mix well. Pour egg mixture into skillet with onion and cook over very low heat until edges ore lightly browned. Sprinkle remaining cheese over top and place under broiler until cheese is lightly browned. To serve, cut into wedges.

Serves 4

Carol Ann Hardcastle

Carolyn's Vegetable Frittata

2 tablespoons melted margarine
½ cup chopped fresh mushrooms
1 bunch green onions, chopped, white
    and light green
¼ cup each chopped red and yellow
    peppers
3 tablespoons margarine

½ cup shredded cheddar cheese
7 eggs
5 tablespoons milk
Salt and pepper to taste
1 cup shredded low fat mozzarella
    cheese

Sauté mushrooms, onion, and peppers briefly in melted margarine. Add to beaten eggs, milk, salt, pepper, and cheddar cheese. Melt 3 tablespoons margarine on medium low heat in non-stick rounded skillet. Add egg mixture and cover. Check often, moving cooked eggs to center and allowing uncooked eggs to flow to outer edge. Use rubber spatula to lift up cooked and allow uncooked to flow underneath. Cook until almost set, sprinkle with shredded mozzarella, cover, and allow cheese to melt. To serve cut into wedges.

Note: High heat toughens eggs. This method makes them tender and light. Any vegetable does well or bacon or ham, etc.

Serves 4　　　　　　　　　　　　　　　　　　　　　　　　　　*Carolyn Hoose*

The Woodruff House in Macon, now part of Mercer University.

Chili Rellenos Casserole

2½ pounds Monterey Jack cheese
3 4-ounce cans chili peppers, diced
3 eggs

2 cups milk
½ cup flour
½ teaspoon salt

Grate cheese or thinly slice. Remove seeds and membranes from chilies. Beat eggs, add flour, salt, and milk. Mix well. Layer cheese and chilies alternately in 8x12 inch baking dish. Pour eggs and milk mixture over chilies and cheese. Bake at 350 degrees for 45-55 minutes until set and golden brown. Serve hot or at room temperature.

Serves 8   *Jeanne Smiley*

Ham and Broccoli Strata

16 slices bread, decrusted
8 slices sharp cheese
2 cups diced ham
1 10-ounce package frozen chopped
   broccoli, cooked and drained
6 eggs, beaten

3½ cups milk
½ teaspoon dry mustard
1 teaspoon salt
½ cup melted butter
2 cups crushed corn flakes

Place 8 bread slices in 9x13 inch baking pan. Cover with slices of cheese, ham, and cooked broccoli. Place remaining bread over broccoli. Mix eggs, milk, mustard, and salt. Pour mixture over bread. Cover and refrigerate overnight. Before cooking mix butter and corn flakes. Sprinkle over top. Bake at 350 degrees for 1½ hours.

Serves 8-10   *Cindy Souther*

Quiche Without Crust

2 cups white bread crumbs
3 tablespoons margarine, melted
8 eggs
1½ cups milk

½ teaspoon salt
⅛ teaspoon nutmeg
2 cups grated Swiss cheese
1 cup chopped cooked ham

Place bread crumbs in 10 inch round baking dish. Pour margarine over crumbs, toss and spread evenly over bottom of pan. In large bowl beat eggs just until blended. Add milk, salt, nutmeg, cheese, and ham. Mix well. Pour egg mixture over bread crumbs. Bake at 350 degrees 35-40 minutes or until golden brown and fluffy.

Serves 8   *Mary Ann Marks*

Cheese-Green Chili Pie

1 unbaked 9-inch pastry shell, chilled
4 eggs
1 cup heavy cream
½ cup milk
½ teaspoon salt

⅛ teaspoon hot pepper sauce
1 cup sharp cheddar cheese
1 4-ounce can chopped green chilies
    (mild, medium, or hot)

Pre-bake pastry shell at 450 degrees until light brown, about 10 minutes. Beat together eggs, cream, milk, salt, and hot pepper sauce. Add chopped chilies. Sprinkle cheese on bottom of pie crust. Pour cream mixture over cheese. Bake at 325 degrees until set or knife tip inserted comes out clean.
Note: Monterey Jack or Swiss cheese may be used instead of cheddar.

Serves 6   *Elizabeth Smiley*

Jason's Ultimate Egg O'Bagel

A teenager's dream

2 slices bacon or 1 slice Canadian
    bacon
1 bagel

1 egg
2 slices cheese

Cook bacon and set aside. Toast bagel in halves. Top with one slice cheese on each half. Scramble egg, then put egg and bacon inside the two bagel halves, making a bagel sandwich. Try this with sausage patty or thin-sliced ham.

Makes 1 sandwich   *Jason Rymuza*

Fort Benjamin Hawkins is marked by a reconstructed blockhouse of the style built when the Federal government established the first modern settlement here in 1806.

Mountain Majesty: ENTRÉES

Mountain Majesty

Georgia's northeast mountains offer up a patchwork quilt of mountains and valleys, wildflowers and waterways, state parks and rustic lodges, quaint towns and apple orchards, mountain crafts and mountain music.

Each season of the year has its own special beauty in these, the Blue Ridge Mountains. In the spring, dogwoods, azaleas and a dazzling array of wildflowers dot the mountainside. Summer brings the spectacular rhododendron and mountain laurel blossoms to reflect in the serene waters of mountain lakes. Fall's fireworks of riotous colors paint the leaves of mountain trees in red and orange and gold. In winter, the pines, the spruces, and the cedars take center stage.

Recreation areas abound in these parts. Fishing, boating, swimming, waterskiing, hiking, camping, rafting, and horseback riding are just some of the sports to be enjoyed in the Georgia mountains. Whatever it is that one seeks to nourish and renew the mind, body, and soul — whether it be recreation, relaxation, or inspiration — it can likely be found in this highland haven.

Artists:
Margaret Bartholomew — Title Page
Mary George Poss — "Mountain Majesty"

Sausage Wild Rice Casserole

Spicy winter-time casserole

1 pound bulk sausage
1 6-ounce box wild and long grain rice
¼ cup flour
½ cup cream
1 10-ounce can condensed chicken
    broth

1 teaspoon salt
Pinch of oregano, thyme, marjoram
2 4-ounce cans mushrooms or ½
    pound fresh mushrooms
2 onions, chopped
½ cup toasted almonds

Brown crumbled sausage. Drain and reserve most of meat juice. Cook rice according to directions. Make white sauce with meat juice, flour, cream, and broth. Add salt and seasonings. Add mushrooms, onions, rice, and sausage. Mix well. Place in greased 3 quart casserole. Bake at 350 degrees for 30-40 minutes. Top with almonds after baking.

Serves 8-10
Mary Ellen Pendergrast

Pork Chops with Apple Glaze

4-8 pork chops
1 tablespoon flour
1 teaspoon dry mustard
1 teaspoon salt

¼ teaspoon pepper
2 cups sweetened applesauce
¼ cup brown sugar
¼ teaspoon ground cinnamon

Rub chops with mixture of flour, mustard, salt, and pepper. Spread with apple glaze made by combining remaining ingredients. Cover and bake in a 300 degree oven about 45 minutes to an hour.

Serves 4-8
Betsy Fowler

Pork Chops and Gravy

Easy and consistently good

6 pork chops (center cut best)
2 tablespoons cooking oil
1 10¾-ounce can cream of mushroom
    soup or cream of chicken soup

¾ can water
Salt and pepper

Brown seasoned chops in small amount of oil. Place chops in baking dish. Add cream of mushroom soup and water. Cover with foil and cook at 350 degrees one hour. May need more water at end of cooking. Makes a delicious gravy for rice.

Serves 3-4
Mary Jane Bolton

Original Georgia Brunswick Stew

Legend has it that the first Brunswick Stew was made in Brunswick, Georgia, to feed the Confederate troops. This worthy dish has since spread to all parts of the South, each state having its own version.

8 pork chops
4 ears corn
6 ripe tomatoes, peeled and chopped

½ cup butter
2 cups soft bread crumbs
Salt and pepper to taste

Sauce:
¼ cup melted butter
½ cup vinegar
¼ cup water
1 teaspoon salt

1 teaspoon Worcestershire
½ teaspoon pepper
½ teaspoon mustard
Hot pepper sauce to taste

Boil pork in water to cover until meat falls from bones. Grind or chop meat. Return it to broth it was cooked in. Cut corn from ears and add with tomatoes. Simmer about ½ hour. Add bread crumbs and butter. If too thick add water and season to taste. Mix sauce ingredients and serve with stew.

Serves 10   *Toni Shiver*

Stuffed Apple Pork Chops

Perfect winter meal for family or guests

4 double pork loin chops
1 large apple, chopped
½ cup chopped celery
3 tablespoons butter
½ cup water

3 tablespoons raisins
Salt and pepper to taste
¾ cup dry unseasoned croutons
1 egg, lightly beaten

Have butcher cut chops 1½ inches thick and cut pocket in each one. To prepare stuffing sauté apple and celery in butter and water for 5 minutes. Add raisins. Cook about ½ minute. Remove from heat. Add salt and pepper to taste. Stir in croutons and egg. Stuff pocket in each chop. Secure with small skewers or toothpick. Sear chops quickly in oiled skillet. Turn chops carefully so that stuffing stays in chop. After browning cover pan. Simmer 1 hour or place chops in baking dish and bake covered at 325 degrees for 1¼ hours or until tender. Remove cover for last 15 minutes.

Serves 4   *Pat Tanner*

Easy Holiday Ham

Try it and you'll be a believer!

Whole ham, size does not matter, but
preferably smoked

7 cups water
Large enamel roasting pan with lid

Oven temperature and times "must" be strictly adhered to. Preheat oven to 500 degrees. Place ham and 7 cups cold water in large enamel roasting pan. Cover with lid. Place in oven for 15 minutes. Turn off oven. 3 hours later, turn oven back on to 500 degrees for 15 minutes. Turn off oven and let remain in oven overnight (or all day for evening serving). Ham is ready the next morning or noon whichever you wish. ABSOLUTELY DO NOT OPEN OVEN AT ANY TIME BEFORE THE NEXT MORNING.

Note: Works equally well with a fresh ham or a smoked or fresh turkey.

Yields a whole ham

Angelia Ulrich

Mountain crafts.

Cuban Roasted Fresh Pork Leg

1 large garlic clove, crushed
1 teaspoon salt
1 teaspoon pepper
½ teaspoon cumin
1 teaspoon oregano

2-3 tablespoons lime or lemon juice
1 large onion, sliced
2 bay leaves
1 large fresh leg of pork (or fresh
    pork ham or tenderloin)

Combine all ingredients except bay leaves, onion, and pork and make into a paste. Make many small slits in meat and rub paste into meat. Spread onion slices over meat. Cover and refrigerate at least 3 hours, better overnight. Place 2 bay leaves under meat in pan. Roast 35-40 minutes per pound in 350 degree oven.

Serves 8   *Renee Hernandez*

Black Spareribs

Have lots of napkins on hand. Too good to waste a drop!

3-4 pounds pork back ribs
¼ cup lemon juice

Salt and pepper

Sauce:
½ cup of each of the following:
Brown sugar
Vinegar
Ketchup

Worcestershire sauce
Water
2 tablespoons chili powder

Place ribs in a 9x13 inch baking dish. Sprinkle with lemon juice. Salt and pepper to taste. Bake at 350 degrees uncovered for 1 hour. Turn ribs. Cover loosely with aluminum foil and continue baking approximately 30-45 more minutes until juices run clear. Mix sauce ingredients in saucepan. Bring to boil over medium heat. Reduce heat and simmer, stirring frequently until thick, about 1½ hours. Do not boil. When ribs are done, remove from oven and cover ribs completely with sauce. Return ribs to oven and continue baking another 15 minutes. Serve with extra sauce.

Serves 5-6   *Terri Jackson*

Veal Scallopini

Simple and tastes gourmet

1 pound ¼ inch thick veal cutlets,
    trimmed
3 tablespoons flour
½ teaspoon salt
½ teaspoon freshly ground pepper

Vegetable cooking spray
4 teaspoons vegetable oil
1 cup Chablis or other dry white wine
4 tablespoons lemon juice
Lemon twists

Place veal on waxed paper. Flatten to ⅛ inch thickness, using meat mallet or rolling pin. Cut into 2 inch pieces. Combine flour, salt, and pepper. Dredge veal in flour mixture. Coat large skillet with cooking spray. Add oil and place over medium to high heat until hot. Add veal. Cook 1 minute on each side or until lightly browned. Remove veal from skillet and set aside. Pour wine and lemon juice into skillet. Bring to boil. Return veal to skillet, turning to coat with sauce. Reduce heat and simmer 1 to 2 minutes or until sauce is slightly thickened and veal is thoroughly heated. Garnish with lemon twists if desired.

Serves 4   *Jan Collins*

Vitello Tonnato

Distinct flavor for an unusual dish

2 tablespoons olive oil
3½ pounds boneless leg of veal
1 large onion, sliced
2 cups chopped carrots
2 celery ribs, chopped
2 cloves garlic, minced
1 can anchovy filets
1 can tuna
1 cup white wine, dry

3 sprigs parsley
2 bay leaves
Pinch of thyme
½ teaspoon salt
Black pepper to taste
1 cup mayonnaise
Lemon juice
Capers and parsley for garnish

Heat oil in Dutch oven. Add veal. Brown lightly on all sides over high heat. Add onion, carrots, celery, and garlic. Lower heat. Add anchovy, tuna, wine, parsley, bay leaves, thyme, salt, and pepper. Cover and cook for 2 hours on low. Remove meat from kettle and chill. Cook contents of kettle until reduced by half. Purée in blender. Chill. Blend with mayonnaise. Sprinkle with lemon juice. To serve, slice meat very thin and serve on cold rice with capers and chopped parsley. Serve sauce separately.

Serves 4-6   *Paul Shanor*

Smoked Leg of Lamb

5-6 pound leg of lamb
½ cup lemon juice
2 tablespoons garlic powder
1 tablespoon black pepper

4 strips bacon
1 medium green pepper
1 lemon sliced

Sauce:
6 tablespoons butter melted
Juice of 3 lemons

2 tablespoons Worcestershire sauce
1 tablespoon water

Rub lamb with lemon juice, garlic powder, and black pepper. Place bacon across lamb leg along with green pepper and lemon slices. Place directly on smoker rack and smoke approximately 4 hours.

Sauce: Heat all sauce ingredients on medium heat in one quart saucepan. Serve with lamb as a garnish.

Serves 6-8

Charles Hodges, M.D.

Herbed Leg of Lamb

Gourmet Club's favorite

1 5-pound leg of lamb
1 clove garlic (or more)
1 teaspoon salt
½ teaspoon oregano
¼ teaspoon thyme
¼ teaspoon ginger

½ teaspoon black pepper
8 canned Elberta peach halves
1 cup dry red wine
1 tablespoon currant jelly (or more)
1 tablespoon mint jelly (or more)
1 jigger of gin, if desired

Cut slit at base of roast, near bone. Insert garlic clove. Mix dry ingredients and rub thoroughly over meat. Place meat on rack in roasting pan. Cook in 300 degree oven, uncovered, about 2 hours for well done; less for medium rare. Twenty minutes before done, surround meat with peach halves. Return to oven. Baste peaches and meat frequently with cooking juices and wine. Remove lamb and peaches to serving platter. Fill center of peaches with jellies alternating color for a decorative presentation. Remove garlic clove from lamb. Let stand several minutes before carving. Strain fat from juices, add 2 tablespoons currant jelly and heat until melted. Serve hot with thinly sliced lamb. Flame with gin if desired.

Serves 8

William L. Barnwell, M.D.

Lamb with Feta, Tomatoes, and Olives in Parchment

Original recipe published in Gourmet Magazine

1 tablespoon vegetable oil plus additional for brushing parchment

4 1-inch thick lean lamb shoulder chops or leg steaks

½ cup dry white wine

4 20x15 inch pieces of parchment paper

1 teaspoon minced garlic

¼ pound Feta, cut into 8 slices

3 plum tomatoes cut into 16 slices

24 black olives (preferably Kalamata), sliced lengthwise

1 teaspoon fresh rosemary leaves, chopped or ½ teaspoon dried, crumbled

4 sprigs fresh rosemary for garnish, if desired

In large heavy skillet heat oil until hot but not smoking. Pat lamb dry and season with salt and pepper. Brown in hot oil, turning once, for 3 minutes. Transfer to plate. Remove fat from skillet, add wine and deglaze skillet over high heat, scraping up brown bits. Boil wine until reduced to about 2 tablespoons. Add any lamb juices accumulated on plate. Brush a 20x15 inch area of work surface with additional oil. Arrange 1 of parchment pieces on top of oiled surface and brush lightly with oil. Arrange second piece of parchment on top of first, brushing lightly with oil. Repeat procedure with remaining parchment pieces. Fold top piece of parchment in half by bringing short ends together. Unfold and place one chop on parchment just to right of fold line. Rub chop with ¼ teaspoon garlic and arrange decoratively on it 2 slices Feta, 4 slices tomato and 10-12 slices olives. Sprinkle with ¼ teaspoon rosemary, pour ¼ deglazing liquid over it, and fold other half of parchment over chop. Beginning with a folded corner, twist and fold the edges together, forming a half-heart shape and seal end tightly by twisting. Make papillotes with remaining ingredients in the same manner. Papillotes may be prepared up to this point one hour in advance. Bake papillotes on baking sheet in preheated 400 degree oven 10 minutes. Cut open, garnish each papillote with rosemary sprig if desired.

Serves 4   *William L. Barnwell, M.D.*

Elegant Rack of Lamb

A showy presentation

1 double rack of lamb (two racks joined together. Have butcher hack the backbone in center away and remove thin lean layer of meat with fat on top of rack.)

1 tablespoon peanut, corn, or vegetable oil.
Salt and freshly ground pepper to taste

Topping:
4 tablespoons fine untoasted fresh bread crumbs

2 tablespoons chopped parsley
½ teaspoon minced garlic

Cut fat from top of ribs, leaving thin layer over meaty loin at top of the ribs. Arrange racks of lamb, meaty side down in shallow baking dish. Sprinkle with oil, salt, and pepper to taste. Place 3 inches from broiler. Cook 4½ to 5 minutes. Turn racks meaty side up. Return to broiler for 2½ minutes. Remove and sprinkle top with bread crumb mixture. Turn oven to 475 degrees. Bake 4-5 minutes or longer for well done lamb. If not brown enough run under broiler. Carve between each two ribs and serve.

Serves 4-6

Roy W. Vandiver, M.D.

Sky Valley in Dillard is Georgia's only ski resort, elevation 3,200 feet.

Moussaka

Greek favorite

Meat sauce:

2 tablespoons butter
1 cup finely chopped onion
1 clove garlic, crushed
1½ pound ground chuck or lamb
½ teaspoon dried oregano leaves
1 teaspoon dried basil leaves
½ teaspoon ground cinnamon
1 teaspoon salt
⅛ teaspoon pepper
1 tablespoon sugar

¼ cup fresh parsley, chopped
2 8-ounce cans tomato sauce
½ cup red wine
3 medium eggplants
½ cup melted butter
Salt to taste
½ cup grated Parmesan cheese
½ cup grated cheddar cheese
2 tablespoons dry bread crumbs

Cream Sauce:

2 tablespoons butter
2 tablespoons flour
½ teaspoon salt
⅛ teaspoon pepper

⅛ teaspoon nutmeg
2 cups milk
2 eggs

In 3½ quart Dutch oven, melt butter. Sauté onion, garlic, and meat stirring until brown. Add herbs, spices, tomato sauce, and wine. Bring to boil stirring. Reduce heat. Simmer uncovered for 30 minutes. Halve eggplants lengthwise. Slice into ½ inch slices. Place on bottom of broiler pan. Sprinkle lightly with salt and brush with butter. Broil 4 inches from heat about 4 minutes per side until golden. Set aside.

Cream Sauce: In saucepan melt butter. Remove from heat. Add flour, salt, pepper, and nutmeg. Return to heat. Add milk gradually. Bring to boil, stirring until mixture is thick. Remove from heat. Beat eggs with whisk and add to hot sauce, stirring well. Set aside.

In bottom of 3 quart baking dish, layer half of eggplant, overlapping slightly. Sprinkle with 2 tablespoons each grated Parmesan and cheddar cheeses. Stir crumbs into meat sauce. Spoon meat sauce over eggplant, then 2 tablespoons of cheeses. Layer rest of eggplant slices, overlapping as before. Pour cream sauce over all. Sprinkle top with remaining cheese. Bake at 350 degrees for 35-40 minutes.

Serves 10-12   *Noula Kokenes*

Bistec a la Criolla

A South American Recipe - Try It!

2 pounds beef tenderloin cut in 8 thin
  slices
Juice of 1 lemon
Dash of black pepper
Dash of cumin powder
2 tablespoons vinegar

2 ripe tomatoes cut in small pieces
2 onions, sliced
½ teaspoon ground garlic
Dash of oregano
Salt to taste
2 tablespoons vegetable oil

Season meat with lemon juice, pepper, cumin, and vinegar. Set aside. Mix tomatoes, onions, garlic, oregano, and salt. Sauté for 10 minutes over medium heat. Set aside. In large frying pan heat 2 tablespoons vegetable oil. Sauté bistec (or thin steaks) about 2 minutes each side. Add mix of tomatoes, onions, garlic, oregano, and salt. Cover and cook 5-7 minutes over medium heat.

Variation: Bistec on a Horse. Ideal for breakfast! The same Bistec a la Criolla can be served with two sunny eggs and sauce on top of meat. Can be served with white rice.

Serves 6-8 *Cecilia Baute*

Grilled Beef Tenderloin

Onions grilled on top add a special touch

5-7 pound beef tenderloin, untrimmed
Lemon pepper
2 cups soy sauce
½ cup bourbon or sherry cooking
  wine

2 large cloves garlic, crushed
3-4 strips bacon
1 large onion, sliced

Heavily coat tenderloin with lemon pepper. Place in 10x15 inch pan. Mix soy sauce, bourbon or sherry, and garlic. Pour over meat. Marinate for at least 2 hours or overnight, turning meat at least once. Heat coals on grill and divide them by pushing ½ of them to each side of grill (this is the indirect heat method). Place meat on grill. Baste with marinade. Place bacon strips and onion slices on top and close cover. Cook until desired doneness.

Serves 8-10 *Robert O. House, M.D.*

Beef Wellington

Elegant dinner entrée

3-4 pound beef tenderloin
2 tablespoons butter

Salt and pepper to taste

Duxelle:
¼ cup butter
1 pound fresh mushrooms, chopped
½ cup chopped onion

½ cup dry sherry
¼ cup chopped parsley

Pie Crust for 1 pie
1 egg

1 tablespoon water

Sherry Sauce:
2 cups beef stock
½ cup dry sherry
½ cup chopped onion
1 carrot, finely chopped
1 stalk celery, finely chopped

2 sprigs parsley
1 bay leaf
⅛ teaspoon thyme leaves
3 tablespoons dry sherry
2 tablespoons butter

Place tenderloin on rack in shallow pan. Spread butter on all sides. Sprinkle with salt and pepper. Bake 20 minutes at 425 degrees. Remove and cool. Pat dry and set aside. (This may be done a day ahead and kept in refrigerator.) Mix Duxelle by cooking butter, mushrooms, onion, sherry, and parsley in saucepan until liquid is absorbed. Set aside. Roll pie crust into a 24x18 inch rectangle. Place tenderloin on edge of longer side of pastry. Spread duxelle over remaining surface of pastry, leaving a one inch margin on each side. Roll tenderloin and pastry. Seal seam and ends. Mix egg and water and brush over top and sides of pastry. Place seam side down on baking sheet. Reduce oven to 400 degrees. Bake 30 minutes or until pastry is golden brown. In saucepan, combine stock, ½ cup sherry, onion, carrot, celery, parsley, bay leaf, and thyme. Simmer 30 minutes. Strain and discard vegetables. Stir in remaining sherry and simmer 5 minutes longer. Stir in remaining butter, a little at a time. Serve sauce with tenderloin.

Serves 8

Lois Ann Grishkin

Beef Stroganoff

This recipe was served to Helen Corbitt, the famous Neiman Marcus chef, when she visited our home. I was so nervous cooking for her that I left out the sour cream. She thanked me for "the delicious gypsy stew"!

2 pounds sliced and cubed tenderloin
3 tablespoons oil
5 tablespoons chopped onions
1 pound fresh mushrooms
1 teaspoon salt
1 teaspoon pepper
1 teaspoon paprika
1 teaspoon flour

1 6-ounce can tomato paste
1 10½ ounce can beef consommé
1 tablespoon soy sauce
1 teaspoon steak sauce
3 tablespoons red wine
1 teaspoon A-1 meat sauce
3 tablespoons or more sour cream

Sauté meat in oil on high heat. Pour off juice, but save. Add onions and mushrooms to the meat and sauté. Add salt, pepper, paprika, flour, tomato paste, and reserved juice from meat. Add consommé. Add soy sauce, steak sauce, wine, and meat sauce. Simmer for 5 minutes. Stir in sour cream. Serve over rice or noodles.

Serves 6-8   *Jan Collins*

Bachelor Beef

Great for singles and short order cooks

Chopped steak (as many as desired)
Garlic salt
Lemon pepper

Slice white bread
Margarine, melted

Rub steak on both sides with garlic salt and lemon pepper. Cook in margarine until done. Remove from skillet. Place one piece of bread per piece of meat in skillet. Sauté on both sides. Place steak pieces on top of bread. Cook 1 more minute and serve.

William C. Collins, M.D.

Marinated Flank Steak

Preparation is done quickly. Leftovers make wonderful sandwiches

2 1¼-pound flank steaks
½ cup soy sauce
¼ cup Pickapeppa sauce
3 tablespoons vegetable oil

3 tablespoons Burgundy or other dry
   red wine
3 tablespoons red wine vinegar
2½ tablespoons brown sugar
2 cloves garlic, minced

Prick both sides of steaks with fork and place in large shallow pan. Combine remaining ingredients; pour over steak. Cover. Marinate 24 hours in refrigerator, turning occasionally. Remove steaks from marinade. Grill over hot coals 4 to 5 minutes on each side, or until desired degree of doneness. To serve; slice steak across grain in thin slices.

Serves 6-8   *Lynn Gussack*

Helen, a replicated Bavarian Alpine village, is now a year-round resort with events such as its annual Balloon Race in the spring.

January Pot Roast Relevee

4-5 pound chuck roast
2 tablespoons oil

Salt and pepper
1 cup red wine (or more)

Relevee:
3 tablespoons horseradish sauce
2 teaspoons horseradish
2 teaspoons mustard
¼ teaspoon dry mustard
¼ teaspoon ground oregano

¼ teaspoon crushed thyme leaves
¼ teaspoon crushed basil leaves
¼ teaspoon celery seeds
¼ teaspoon garlic powder
1 tablespoon red wine

Vegetables:
8 stalks celery, halved
4 large onions, halved

5 medium potatoes, halved
2 cloves garlic, minced

Brown meat on both sides in hot oil in stove top pot. Season with salt and pepper to taste. Add 1 cup wine. Make a paste of Relevee ingredients to produce highly seasoned herbed sauce. Apply a coating of Relevee to top of roast. Simmer 3-4 hours. Turn roast occasionally and apply more sauce as desired. About one hour before total cooking time is completed add vegetables and minced garlic. When ready to serve you may wish to thicken liquid in pot for a delicious gravy, or serve pot roast au jus.

Serves 8-10   *Vincent Masters, M.D.*

Apple Pot Roast

4 pound chuck blade bone pot roast
2 tablespoons vegetable oil
1½ teaspoons salt
¾ teaspoon ground ginger
5 whole cloves
1 bay leaf

¼ teaspoon black pepper
1 cup apple juice
½ cup dry red wine
4 medium red delicious apples, cored
    and quartered with skins
2 large sliced onions

In Dutch oven brown roast on both sides in hot oil. Add next seven ingredients. Bring to boil. Reduce heat. Cover and simmer 2 hours. Add apple and onion slices. Cover. Return to simmer and cook ½ hour longer. Remove meat to heated platter. Surround with apples and onions.

Serves 6   *Virginia Logan*

Beef Stew Crowned with Biscuits

4 tablespoons oil
1 clove garlic, split
2 large onions, sliced thin
⅓ cup flour
1¼ teaspoons salt
¼ teaspoon black pepper
2½ pounds stewing beef, cut into
    1½ inch cubes
½ teaspoon dill weed
1 cup burgundy

1 10-ounce can beef consommé
1 10-ounce package frozen artichoke
    hearts, thawed or 1 8- ounce can
4 tablespoons butter
18 fresh mushrooms, halved or
    quartered
2 8-ounce containers refrigerated
    biscuits
Melted butter
Parmesan cheese

Heat oil in heavy skillet. Sauté garlic and onions until golden. Remove from skillet. Mix flour, salt, and pepper. Dredge meat in mixture and brown well in same oil. Add more oil if needed. Return onion to pot. Add dill weed, wine, and consommé. Cover; simmer 1½ hours or until tender. If using frozen artichokes cook one minute less than package directions. Add to meat. Sauté mushrooms in butter and add to meat. Mix gently. Correct seasoning. Pour into 2½ quart casserole. Crown casserole with biscuits. Bake 15 or 20 minutes in 400 degree oven. Five minutes before done brush biscuits with butter and sprinkle with Parmesan cheese. Bake extra biscuits for dunking.

Serves 6   *Susan Hayes*

Oven Beef Stew

A cold weather favorite. Just add a loaf of French bread for a great meal

2½ pounds lean stew meat, cut into
    1-inch cubes
1 28-ounce can undrained tomatoes
1 cup coarsely chopped celery
4 medium carrots, sliced
3 medium potatoes, cubed
3 medium onions, chopped
1 10-ounce package frozen English
    peas

4 tablespoons quick-cooking tapioca
2 beef bouillon cubes
1 tablespoon salt
1 tablespoon sugar
Freshly ground pepper to taste
¼ teaspoon ground thyme
¼ teaspoon rosemary leaves
¼ teaspoon ground marjoram
¼ cup red wine

Combine all ingredients in 5 quart casserole. Cook covered at 250 degrees 5 hours. Stir well after 3½ hours. Continue cooking until done.

Serves 6   *Pennie Zumbro*

The historic Glen-Ella Springs Hotel, built in the late 19th century as an inn, has been fully restored with 16 rooms and suites and dining facilities.

New Style Lasagna

A favorite dish for family and informal gatherings

1½ pound ground round
1 teaspoon salt
¼ teaspoon pepper
Lasagna noodles

3½ cups spaghetti sauce
1 pound ricotta cheese
8 ounces shredded mozzarella cheese
Parmesan cheese

Brown beef and season with salt and pepper. Drain. Line bottom of greased 9x13 inch casserole with uncooked lasagna noodles. Spread with one cup spaghetti sauce. Add a layer of beef, a layer of ricotta cheese, and a layer of mozzarella cheese. Continue process with a second layer. Top with spaghetti sauce. Cover tightly and bake at 350 degrees for 1 to 1½ hours. Top with Parmesan cheese while hot.

Serves 8-10

Julie Dimond

Lasagna Florentine

2 pounds ground turkey or ground beef
2 32-ounce jars spaghetti sauce
2 12-ounce packages frozen spinach soufflé, thawed
1 10-ounce package frozen chopped spinach, cooked and well drained

24 ounces low or non-fat small curd cottage cheese
2 eggs, well beaten
1 16-ounce box lasagna noodles, cooked and drained
16 ounces mozzarella cheese, grated
1 cup grated Parmesan cheese

Brown meat over medium heat and drain well. Add spaghetti sauce. Simmer at least 30 minutes, stirring occasionally. Set aside. Combine spinach soufflé, spinach, cottage cheese, and eggs. Mix well and set aside. In 3 8-inch square pans or 2 13x9 inch pans layer as follows: noodles, meat sauce, spinach, cottage cheese mixture, mozzarella cheese. Repeat layers. Finish with layer of noodles and meat sauce. Top with Parmesan cheese. Bake at 375 degrees 45 minutes or until bubbly.

Note: May be frozen before baking. When ready to use allow to thaw overnight in refrigerator.

Note: To prevent lasagna noodles from sticking during cooking, add 2 tablespoons olive oil to water before heating to boil.

Serves 18   *Margaret Bartholomew*

Linda's Mozzarella Bake

Great family favorite

1½ pounds lean ground beef
2 8-ounce cans tomato sauce
½ teaspoon minced onion
⅛ teaspoon garlic salt
⅛ teaspoon pepper
1 egg beaten
8 ounces sour cream

12 ounces cottage cheese
8 ounces grated mozzarella cheese
⅛ teaspoon salt
3 ounces grated Parmesan cheese
5 ounces thin spaghetti, cooked and drained

Brown ground beef in large skillet. Drain. Add tomato sauce and seasonings. Simmer over low heat for 15-20 minutes. Beat egg in large bowl. Add sour cream, cottage cheese, mozzarella cheese, and salt. Blend well. Stir in noodles. Place half the noodle mixture in greased 9x13 inch baking dish. Top with half the ground beef mixture. Repeat layers. Sprinkle Parmesan thickly over top. Bake at 350 degrees for 20-30 minutes until bubbly.

Serves 6-8   *Linda Browne*

Chili for a Crowd

Excellent served with a salad, sourdough bread or cornbread

½ cup olive oil
1¾ pounds yellow onions, chopped
2 pounds sweet Italian sausage,
  removed from casing
8 pounds ground beef chuck
1½ tablespoons fresh black pepper
24 ounces tomato paste
Garlic to taste
3 tablespoons minced parsley
3 ounces cumin seed
4 ounces chili powder
½ cup Dijon mustard

4 tablespoons salt
4 tablespoons basil
4 tablespoons oregano
6 pounds Italian plum tomatoes,
  drained
½ cup Burgundy wine
¼ cup lemon juice
½ cup chopped fresh dill
½ cup chopped Italian parsley
48 ounces kidney beans, drained
22 ounces pitted black olives, drained

Heat oil in large soup pot. Add onions and cook about 10 minutes. Crumble sausage and chuck and cook until browned. Drain off fat. Over low heat stir in pepper, tomato paste, garlic, cumin seed, chili powder, mustard, salt, basil, and oregano. Add drained tomatoes, burgundy, lemon juice, dill, parsley, and kidney beans. Stir well and simmer uncovered for about 15 minutes. Correct seasoning. Add olives and simmer 5 more minutes. Heat through. Serve with sour cream, chopped onions, and grated cheddar cheese on side.

Serves 24

Julie Davies

Chili Con Carne

Very good and very easy

2 tablespoons fat or salad oil
1 pound ground beef
1 teaspoon salt
2-3 tablespoons chili powder
1 8-ounce can tomato sauce

1 medium onion, grated or finely
  chopped
1 15-ounce can red kidney beans,
  liquid and all
2 tablespoons vinegar
½ teaspoon garlic powder, if desired

Heat fat in large heavy skillet. Quickly brown meat, stirring with fork. Add remaining ingredients. Mix well. Cover, simmer, stirring occasionally, 30-45 minutes.

Serves 6

Belle Brightwell

Baked Bean Casserole

Excellent for a crowd of hungry children

1 pound ground beef
1 large onion, chopped
2 20-ounce cans pork and beans
1 12-ounce bottle chili sauce

2 tablespoons Worcestershire
Salt and pepper to taste
½ pound sharp cheddar cheese,
  optional

Brown meat and onions. Pour off any grease. Add remaining ingredients except cheese. Mix. Bake in 3 quart casserole topped with cheese at 250 degrees for 2 hours.

Serves 10-12   *Katherine White*

A collection of authentic early Appalachian structures reconstructed in Mountain City by the Foxfire Program.

Family-Style Meatballs

1½ pounds ground chuck
1 egg
⅔ cup Pepperidge Farm cornbread
    dressing mix
1 teaspoon sage
¼ cup milk

2 tablespoons dry onion soup mix
2 tablespoons bacon drippings
2 tablespoons flour
2 tablespoons dry onion soup mix
2 cups water
Salt and pepper to taste

Combine first six ingredients. Mix well. Shape into large meatballs. Brown in bacon drippings. Remove meat balls. Add flour to drippings and cook until flour is dark brown. Add remaining soup mix and water. Season to taste. Return meatballs to gravy. Cover and simmer for 1 hour.

Serves 6

Holly Glass

Old Fashioned Meat Loaf

Advice from Ann Landers: Nation's most popular meat loaf

2 pounds ground round steak
2 eggs
1½ cups bread crumbs
¾ cup ketchup
1 teaspoon Accent

½ cup warm water
1 package onion soup mix
2 strips bacon
1 8-ounce can tomato sauce

Mix first 7 ingredients thoroughly. Put into loaf pan. Cover with bacon. Pour tomato sauce over top. Bake at 350 degrees for 1 hour.

Serves 6

Jan Collins

"Kofta" - Egyptian Hamburger

Great with Tabouli Salad

1 pound ground round
1 medium onion, chopped
1 cup fresh chopped parsley
½ teaspoon cumin

½ teaspoon dried dill weed
Pinch garlic powder
Salt and pepper to taste

Mix all ingredients. Form into patties. Grill, bake, or fry. May serve in pita pockets.

Serves 2-4

Afaf Zaki, M.D.

Meat Loaf with Vegetables

Easy and delicious every-day dinner dish

1½ pounds ground beef or 1 pound
    ground beef and ½ pound ground
    pork
3 tablespoons chopped onion
½ cup chopped green pepper
1 16-ounce can mixed vegetables,
    drained

3 slices bread made into crumbs
¼ cup ketchup
1 egg
¼ cup chopped parsley
¼ teaspoon black pepper

Coating:
½ cup ketchup
1 tablespoon brown sugar

¼ teaspoon onion powder or onion
    salt

Mix all ingredients in large bowl. Place in 5x9x3 inch loaf pan. Mix coating ingredients and spread evenly over top. Bake at 350 degrees for 1 hour.

Serves 6　　　　　　　　　　　　　　　　　　　　　　　　　　　*Ingrid Vega*

Hamburger Pie

Teenagers' favorite

1 cup biscuit baking mix
¼ cup cold water
1 pound ground beef
½ teaspoon salt
½ teaspoon ground oregano
¼ teaspoon pepper
½ cup fine dry bread crumbs
1 8-ounce can tomato sauce

¼ cup chopped onion
¼ cup chopped green pepper
1 egg
¼ cup milk
2 cups shredded cheese
½ teaspoon salt
½ teaspoon dry mustard

Mix baking mix and water until moist, then beat 20 times. Knead 5 times and make a pie shell. Cook ground beef, onion, and green pepper until done. Drain. Stir in salt, oregano, pepper, dry crumbs, tomato sauce, and pour into pie shell. Mix cheese, milk, salt, egg, and dry mustard together. Place on top of meat mixture. Bake at 375 degrees for 30 minutes or until golden brown.

Serves 8　　　　　　　　　　　　　　　　　　　　　　　　　　　*Jean Crabbe*

Chicken Breast Wellington

10 ounce package frozen patty shells, thawed

6 ounce box long grain and wild rice mix (original recipe)

Grated peel of 1 orange

8 boned chicken breast halves

1 egg white

Sauce:

12 ounce jar red currant jelly

½ teaspoon Dijon mustard

1 tablespoon orange juice

2 tablespoons white wine

Thaw patty shells in refrigerator. Cook rice according to package directions. Add orange peel. Set aside to cool. Pound chicken breasts to flatten. Sprinkle with salt and pepper. Beat egg white until soft peaks form. Fold into rice mixture. On floured surface roll out patty shells into 8-inch circles. Place 1 chicken breast in center of each circle. Add ¼ cup rice mixture to each and roll each jelly roll style folding edges up. Place seam down on baking sheet. Cover with foil and refrigerate overnight. When ready to bake, remove from refrigerator, remove foil, and bake in 375 degree oven 35-45 minutes until golden brown. For sauce, heat jelly in small saucepan and gradually stir in mustard, orange juice, and wine. Pass warm sauce at the table.

Serves 8   *JoAnn Crooms*

Chicken Ham Wellington

Great way to use left over ham

1 package frozen patty shells or frozen puff pastry

6 chicken breast halves, boned and skinned

6 slices or ¾ cup ground country ham

¼ cup grated Parmesan cheese

1 10¾-ounce can cream of chicken soup (optional)

Milk

Partially thaw and roll out patty shells (or pastry) into 6 rectangles large enough to cover chicken breasts. Place one chicken breast on each rectangle and top with 1 slice or 2 tablespoons ham and 2 teaspoons cheese. Fold pastry over chicken and seal well using a small amount of water to seal edges of pastry. Place in greased 9x13 inch dish and bake at 375 degrees for 45 minutes. If desired, heat chicken soup with small amount of milk and serve as sauce over chicken packages.

Serves 6   *Ann Claiborne Christian*

Canadian Company Chicken

12 boned and skinned chicken breast
  halves
½ cup flour
2 teaspoons curry powder
½ teaspoon salt
½ teaspoon pepper
½ teaspoon garlic powder

½ cup butter or margarine
1 cup sliced onions
1 cup ketchup
1 cup water
¼ cup raisins
1 cup chopped green pepper
½ cup toasted almonds

Combine flour, curry powder, salt, pepper, and garlic powder in a plastic bag. Add chicken pieces, a few at a time, and shake well to coat. Reserve remaining flour mixture. Melt butter in large skillet and sauté chicken until brown. Remove chicken and keep warm. Sauté onions in same pan in remaining butter until transparent. Add 1 tablespoon reserved flour mixture and stir to form a paste. Add ketchup, water, and raisins. Mix well. Return chicken to pan, cover and simmer 45 minutes. Add green pepper and cook another 10 minutes. Sprinkle with almonds.

Makes 6-8 servings   *Martha Schwartz*

Chicken Cacciatore

Wonderful to serve guests

8 skinned chicken breast halves
½ to 1 cup cooking oil
2 cups chopped onions
½ cup chopped fresh green pepper
2 cups sliced fresh mushrooms
1 pound can Italian tomatoes with
  basil, chopped

1 pound can tomato purée
1 bay leaf
Salt and pepper to taste
Several cloves of garlic minced
½ to 1 teaspoon oregano, or to taste
½ to 1 teaspoon basil, or to taste

Brown chicken with garlic in cooking oil. Remove chicken. Add onion, green pepper, and mushrooms. Sauté until tender. Add tomatoes, purée, and seasonings. Place chicken in sauce. Cook over low heat until tender, about 45 minutes. Can be prepared the day before and reheated. Seasonings are much better the second day.

Serves 8   *JoAnn Crooms*

Sesame Lime Chicken

A nice oriental touch

2 tablespoons fresh ginger, finely chopped
2 cloves garlic, minced
1 small onion, finely chopped
¼ cup lime juice, fresh or reconstituted

⅓ cup soy sauce
2 tablespoons honey
1 tablespoon grated lime or lemon peel
6 large chicken pieces, skinned
3 tablespoons sesame seeds

Combine ginger, garlic, onion, lime juice, soy sauce, honey, and peel. Add chicken pieces and coat well. Marinate 2 hours. Remove chicken from marinade and arrange in one layer in 8x12-inch baking dish. Sprinkle with sesame seeds. Bake 35-45 minutes at 375 degrees or until chicken is cooked. Bring marinade to a boil and simmer for 5 minutes. Serve as gravy for chicken. Serve with rice. Garnish with parsley.

Serves 6

Rita Kaufman

Lemon Basil Chicken

½ cup margarine or butter
6 to 8 boneless chicken breast halves
1 cup or 1 can chicken broth
3 tablespoons chopped fresh basil or 1 tablespoon dried basil

2 teaspoons grated lemon peel
Juice from 1 lemon
Thinly sliced lemon for garnish, if desired

In large frying pan, melt 2 tablespoons of margarine or butter over medium heat. Add chicken and cook 4 to 5 minutes until lightly browned. Add broth, basil, lemon peel, and juice; simmer covered until chicken is no longer pink when cut in thickest part (10-12 minutes). Remove to serving dish and keep warm. Boil pan juices, uncovered, over high heat until reduced to about half. Reduce heat to medium, add accumulated chicken juices, the remaining 2 tablespoons margarine, and stir until melted. If sauce is too thin to coat a spoon, simmer uncovered shaking the pan until thicker. Pour around chicken. Garnish with basil leaves and thinly sliced lemon.

Serves 6

Cathy Ridley

Sherried Chicken Breasts

12 boned chicken breast halves
12 slices Swiss cheese
2 10-ounce cans cream of chicken
    soup

1 cup dry sherry
1½ cups dry herb stuffing mix
½ cup margarine, melted

Arrange chicken in greased 9x13 inch baking dish. Place cheese slices over chicken. Mix soup and sherry and pour over chicken. Sprinkle top thoroughly with stuffing mix. Drizzle with melted margarine. Bake, uncovered, for 1½ hours at 300 degrees or until chicken is tender.

Serves 12   *Kathryn Fox Winokur*

Lemon Barbecue Chicken

A family favorite

¼ cup margarine
½ cup oil
1 teaspoon salt
¼ teaspoon pepper

¼ teaspoon paprika
1 cup flour
1 2½-pound frying chicken, cut up

Lemon Barbecue Sauce:
1 clove garlic
½ teaspoon salt
¼ cup oil
½ cup lemon juice

2 tablespoons finely chopped onions
1 teaspoon pepper
½ teaspoon dried thyme

Melt margarine and ¼ cup oil in shallow baking pan in a 400 degree oven. Combine salt, pepper, paprika, and flour in shallow dish large enough to hold chicken parts. Dip chicken pieces in melted margarine mixture, then in flour mixture. Arrange skin side down in single layer in the baking pan and bake for 30 minutes. Remove chicken from oven, turn pieces skin side up and pour Lemon Barbecue Sauce over. Bake 30 minutes longer or until tender.

Lemon Barbecue Sauce: Mash garlic with salt. Combine garlic mixture with oil, lemon juice, onions, pepper, and thyme in small bowl and blend well. Makes about 1 cup sauce.

Serves 4   *Courtenay Collins*

Chicken in Orange Almond Sauce

Good served over saffron rice

1 fryer cut up
¾ teaspoon salt, divided
¼ cup melted butter or margarine
2 tablespoons flour
Dash ground ginger

⅛ teaspoon ground cinnamon
1 ½ cups orange juice
½ cup slivered almonds
½ cup white raisins
1 cup orange sections

Sprinkle chicken with ½ teaspoon salt. Brown in butter in large non-stick skillet over low heat. Drain chicken. Pour off all but 2 tablespoons pan drippings. Blend flour, spices, and ¼ teaspoon salt into pan drippings. Cook over low heat, stirring constantly until bubbly. Gradually add orange juice. Cook until smooth and thickened. Stir in slivered almonds and raisins. Add chicken to sauce. Cover and cook over low heat 30 minutes or until chicken is tender. Just before serving, add orange sections.

Serves 4

Fran Kirsh

Chicken Celestine

3 whole skinned and boned chicken
   breasts
Juice of 1 lemon
¼ cup oil
1 tablespoon margarine
½ onion, chopped
2 cups sliced fresh mushrooms
½ clove garlic, minced

½ cup dry white wine
½ cup chicken broth
Salt and pepper to taste
Dried rosemary
1 tablespoon margarine
2 tablespoons flour
¼ cup minced chives

Cut chicken into bite-sized pieces. Marinate in lemon juice for 5 minutes. Sauté chicken in oil and 1 tablespoon margarine in a large skillet until brown. Remove chicken from pan and keep warm. Add onion and mushrooms to drippings in pan and sauté for 4 minutes. Add garlic, wine, and chicken broth. Return chicken to pan. Sprinkle with salt, pepper, and rosemary to taste. In a small pan melt 1 tablespoon margarine. Add flour. Stir to blend. Add to chicken to thicken broth. Sprinkle with chives. Serve over rice.

Serves 4

Sidneye Henderson

Ranch Chicken Casserole

Famous Texas Recipe

1 package flour tortillas (16)
2 whole boiling chickens, cooked,
    deboned and diced (reserve stock)
1 large onion, chopped
1 10-ounce can tomatoes and chilies

2 10¾-ounce cans cream of
    mushroom soup
1 10¾-ounce can cream of chicken
    soup
1 pound cheddar cheese, grated
Chili powder to taste

Line large casserole with half the tortillas, each dipped in warm chicken stock. Combine chicken, onion, tomatoes, and soups. Put half this mixture on top of tortillas. Add half of cheese. Sprinkle with chili powder, if desired. Repeat layers. Bake uncovered at 350 degrees for 45 minutes.

Serves 12   *Nancy Carr*

Chicken Fajitas

4 skinned, boneless chicken breasts
    cut into ½-inch strips
2 tablespoons olive oil
3 cups purple onions cut into ¼-inch
    strips
1 red pepper cut into ½-inch strips
1 green or yellow pepper cut into
    ½-inch strips

2 cloves garlic, crushed
2 tablespoons balsamic vinegar
Juice of 1 lime
16 cherry tomatoes or 1 cup coarsely
    chopped tomato
3 tablespoons chopped parsley
¼ cup finely chopped cilantro
Salt and pepper to taste

In a skillet over medium-high heat sauté chicken pieces in 2 tablespoons oil for 5-10 minutes. Remove from skillet and set aside. Add to skillet garlic, onions, and peppers. Stir-fry for 3 minutes or until crisp tender. Add chicken pieces, vinegar, lime juice, and tomatoes. Continue cooking for 2 minutes, tossing frequently. Remove from heat, add parsley, cilantro, and salt and pepper to taste. Serve over steamed rice, or traditionally, with tortillas and jalapeño peppers.

Serves 4   *Donna Slappey*

Oven-Fried Herb Chicken

½ cup low-fat yogurt
1 tablespoon lemon juice
1 tablespoon Worcestershire
2 tablespoons poultry seasoning
2 teaspoons paprika

½ teaspoon pepper
8 boned, skinless chicken breast
  halves
1 cup herb seasoned bread crumbs
Vegetable cooking spray

Whisk together yogurt, lemon juice, Worcestershire, poultry seasoning, paprika, and pepper. Dip chicken in yogurt mixture, then in bread crumbs. Place in 9x13-inch baking pan coated with vegetable cooking spray. Bake uncovered at 350 degrees for approximately 40 minutes.

Serves 8   *Nancy Story*

Poulet à la Borger

Great buffet dish - Heart healthy

6 skinned chicken thighs (or 4 breast
  halves)
1 tablespoon olive oil
Garlic powder, salt, and pepper to
  taste
⅓ cup flour
½ cup cornflakes or bread crumbs

⅓ cup chopped onion
⅓ cup chopped green, yellow, or red
  pepper
⅓ cup sliced mushrooms (optional)
1 14-ounce jar chunky Spaghetti
  Sauce
⅓ cup rosé or white wine

Combine garlic powder, salt, pepper, flour, and breadcrumbs. Dip moist skinned chicken in mixture. Brown in olive oil in large skillet over medium heat on both sides until golden about 10 minutes. Add chopped onion, pepper, and mushrooms. Brown an additional 2-3 minutes. Add spaghetti sauce and wine. Stir. Simmer, covered, turning chicken pieces several times for 30 minutes. Serve over cooked pasta or rice.

Serves 4   *Kathy Gross*

Italian Chicken

4 chicken breast halves, skinned and
    boned
3 tablespoons flour
1 egg beaten
⅓ cup fine, dry breadcrumbs
2 tablespoons vegetable oil
2 tablespoons margarine, melted

2 tablespoons olive oil
1 tablespoon lemon juice
½ teaspoon salt
½ teaspoon dried whole basil
½ teaspoon dried whole oregano
¼ teaspoon garlic powder

Dredge each chicken breast half in flour, dip into egg, and coat with breadcrumbs.
Cook chicken in oil over medium-high heat about 2 minutes on each side or until
golden brown. Place chicken in 9-inch square baking dish. Set aside. Combine
remaining ingredients. Pour over chicken. Cover and bake at 350 degrees for 30
minutes.

Serves 4   *Glenda Thompson*

Lake Lanier, located near Gainesville, is a 38,000-acre lake with 550 miles of shoreline.

Crusty Chicken Breasts

½ cup mayonnaise
3 tablespoons prepared mustard
4 ounces melted butter or margarine

8 boned chicken breast halves
1 8-ounce package herb stuffing mix, crushed

Thoroughly mix mayonnaise, mustard, and butter. Dip chicken breasts in mixture and roll in stuffing. Place breasts in an 8x12 inch baking dish. If there is stuffing left, stir with remaining butter mixture and sprinkle around chicken. Bake covered for 1 hour at 350 degrees; remove cover and bake an additional 30 minutes.

Serves 6-8

Sheryl Patwardhan

Chicken Avocado Melt

Not only delicious, but also a beautiful dish to serve

4 broiler-fryer chicken breast halves, boned, skinned
2 tablespoons cornstarch
1 teaspoon ground cumin
1 teaspoon garlic salt
1 egg, lightly beaten
1 tablespoon water
⅓ cup corn meal
3 tablespoons cooking oil

1 firm, ripe avocado, peeled, sliced
1½ cups shredded Monterey Jack cheese
½ cup sour cream, divided
¼ cup sliced green onion tops
¼ cup chopped sweet red pepper
Cherry tomatoes
Parsley sprigs

On hard surface, pound chicken to ¼ inch thickness. In shallow dish, mix together cornstarch, cumin, and garlic salt; add chicken, dredging to coat. In small bowl, mix egg and water. In another small bowl, place cornmeal. Dip chicken, first in egg, then in cornmeal, turning to coat. In large frying pan, place oil and heat to medium temperature. Add chicken and cook two minutes on each side. Remove chicken to shallow baking pan; place avocado slices over chicken and sprinkle with cheese. Bake in 350 degree oven for about 15 minutes or until fork can be inserted in chicken with ease and cheese melts. Top chicken with sour cream; sprinkle with onion and pepper. Garnish with cherry tomatoes and parsley.

Serves 4

Louise Dodd

Sherried Chicken with Dumplings

Great winter dish

½ cup flour
1 teaspoon paprika
1 teaspoon salt
½ teaspoon pepper
4 boned chicken breasts, halved (8 pieces)
¼ cup vegetable oil

1 small jar cooked onions (or 1 small onion, sliced and sautéed)
1 4-ounce can sliced mushrooms, drained
1 10¾-ounce can cream of chicken soup
½ soup can water
½ soup can dry sherry

Poppy Seed Dumplings:
2 cups biscuit mix
1 teaspoon poultry seasoning
1 teaspoon celery seed

1 teaspoon poppy seeds
¼ cup vegetable oil
1 cup milk

Gravy:
1 cup sour cream

1 cup cream of chicken soup

Mix flour, paprika, salt, and pepper. Dredge chicken in flour mixture. Brown chicken in hot oil. Place in 9x13-inch casserole. Distribute onions and mushrooms around chicken. Add soup to browned mixture in skillet. Add water and sherry. Bring to boil. Pour over chicken. Bake 45 minutes at 350 degrees. Serve with Poppy Seed Dumplings or wild rice with Gravy.

Poppy Seed Dumplings: Mix all ingredients well. Drop by spoonsful onto meat 20-25 minutes before done. Increase heat to 425 degrees and bake until golden brown.

Gravy: Mix sour cream and soup. Heat slowly. Do not allow to boil. Serve separately.

Serves 8   *Cathy Cundy*

*"The Mark of the Potter" — A shop of contemporary crafts
located in Grandpa Watts' Mill on the Soquee River.*

Chicken Stuff

A family favorite

1 green pepper, chopped
1 cup chopped celery
1 onion, chopped
8 slices loaf bread, broken into small
    pieces
2 cups cooked, diced chicken

½ cup mayonnaise
Salt and pepper to taste
4 eggs
3 cups milk
1 10¾-ounce can mushroom soup
½ pound cheddar cheese, grated

Sauté pepper, onion, and celery. Place half the bread in bottom of a 13x9 inch baking dish. Mix chicken, mayonnaise, salt, pepper, and sautéed mixture; spread over bread. Top with remaining bread. Beat eggs. Add milk to eggs and pour over all. Spoon mushroom soup over top. Sprinkle with cheese. Bake at 325 degrees for 1 hour. You may mix chicken, mayonnaise, salt, pepper, and sautéed ingredients up to two days ahead of time and refrigerate. Assemble when needed.

Serves 10

Allyce North

Chicken Artichoke Casserole

1 cup butter or margarine
½ cup flour
3½ cups milk
¼ teaspoon cayenne
1 clove garlic
⅛-¼ pound sharp cheddar cheese, cubed

3-6 ounces Gruyère cheese, cubed
1 8-ounce can button mushrooms
4 to 6 chicken breast halves, cooked and cubed
2 8½-ounce cans artichoke hearts, drained and chopped

Topping:
1 cup corn flakes

2 tablespoons melted butter

Make roux of butter and flour. Add milk, stirring constantly until thick and smooth. Add seasonings and cheeses. Stir until cheese melts and sauce bubbles. Add mushrooms to sauce. In 9x13 inch ungreased pan, layer cubed chicken and artichoke hearts. Pour sauce over top. Sprinkle buttered corn flakes on top. Bake uncovered at 350 degrees for 30 minutes.

Serves 4

Judy Hill
Linda Karempelis

Chicken Delight

1 onion chopped
2 tablespoons butter
¼ cup chopped green pepper
2 cups cooked pasta of your choice
1 10¾-ounce can cream of chicken soup
1 cup sour cream
¼ cup milk

½ teaspoon salt
1 8-ounce can water chestnuts
1 4-ounce can mushrooms, drained
⅛ teaspoon pepper
2 cups cooked, diced chicken
¼ cup blanched slivered almonds
1 tablespoon dried parsley

Sauté onions and pepper in butter. Combine these with remaining ingredients, except almonds and parsley. Pour into 2 quart casserole. Top with almonds and parsley. Bake at 325 degrees for 35-40 minutes.

Serves 6

Ann Claiborne Christian

Buntin Boys' Chicken Pie

Delicious! Great to take to a friend

2 carrots, sliced
2 stalks celery, sliced
1 tablespoon butter or margarine
1 14¾-ounce can chicken broth
1 10¾-ounce can cream of chicken
    soup

2 cups cooked, chopped chicken
1 cup self-rising flour
½ cup butter, melted
1 cup milk

Sauté carrots and celery in butter. Add broth, soup, and chicken. Place in 13x9-inch baking dish. Mix flour and butter. Blend until smooth, but not browned. Stir in milk and blend well. Pour mixture evenly over chicken mixture. Bake at 350 degrees 40 minutes.

Serves 4 to 6

Frances Buntin

Sour Cream Chop Suey

1 cup sliced onions
¼ cup butter
1 cup shredded carrots
3 cups diced celery
1 green pepper, chopped fine
1 teaspoon salt

1 cup chicken broth
½ pound mushrooms, sliced
2 cups cooked diced chicken
¼ cup each flour and broth (or water)
2 tablespoons soy sauce
1 cup sour cream

Sauté onions in butter for 5 minutes. Add carrots, celery, pepper, salt, and broth. Cook to boiling. Cover and simmer on low heat for 10 minutes. Add mushrooms and chicken. Heat to boiling. Blend flour, broth, and soy sauce until smooth. Stir into mixture. Cook until thick and clear. Add sour cream. Heat through. Serve over rice or Chinese noodles.

Serves 6

Julie von Haam

Stuffed Cornish Hens

2 frozen Cornish hens, thawed
1 cup orange juice
½ teaspoon salt
½ teaspoon lemon pepper
1 6-ounce package dried apricots

½ cup currants or raisins
¼ cup melted butter
¼ cup apricot preserves
2 cherry tomatoes
2-3 sprigs fresh parsley

Rinse hens well with water, then rinse hens, including cavity, in orange juice. Sprinkle hens inside and out with salt and pepper. Combine apricots and currants and use mixture to stuff hens. Brush hens with melted butter and place in 9x13-inch greased baking pan. Bake at 350 degrees for 1 hour, basting every 15 minutes. Ten minutes before end of cooking period, remove hens from oven and increase temperature to 400 degrees. Coat both hens with apricot preserves, return to oven and cook 10 minutes longer. To serve garnish with cherry tomatoes and parsley.

Serves 2   *Nancy Watts*

Turkey Stroganoff

A family favorite

½ cup chopped onion
¼ cup margarine
1½ pounds ground turkey
1 teaspoon salt
1 teaspoon pepper
¼ teaspoon paprika
1 tablespoon flour

1½ cups sliced fresh mushrooms or
   canned sliced mushrooms
1 10-ounce can cream of mushroom
   soup
1 cup buttermilk
Cooked rice

Brown onions in hot margarine. Add turkey, salt, pepper, and paprika. Cook until turkey is done. Add flour. Stir well. Add mushrooms, soup, and buttermilk. Cook over medium heat 5-10 minutes. Serve over rice.

Serves 4-6   *Toni Shiver*

Shrimp Creole I

1 large onion, chopped
½ green pepper, chopped
2 cloves garlic, minced
1 stalk celery, chopped
½ cup margarine, melted
1 6-ounce can tomato paste or 1 8-ounce can tomato sauce
¼ teaspoon thyme

¼ teaspoon basil
1 bay leaf
1 cup water (see note)
Creole seasoning or salt and cayenne to taste
1 pound shrimp, peeled and deveined (save shrimp shells - see note)

Sauté first four ingredients in margarine for five minutes. Add tomato paste. Stir. Add spices and water. Stir. Cook for 2 hours, stirring occasionally. More water may be added if mixture becomes too thick. About 10 minutes before serving, add raw shrimp seasoned with creole seasoning. Cook until shrimp are pink and tender. Do not overcook! Serve over spaghetti or rice.

Note: Tester suggests a seafood broth may be substituted for the water. To make broth, simmer shrimp shells, celery, and onions in water to cover for about 20-30 minutes. Strain. This will add more flavor.

Serves 4-6   *Maureen Roshto*

Shrimp Creole II

6 slices bacon
1 large onion, chopped
2 green peppers, diced
3 stalks celery, sliced
4 ripe fresh tomatoes, chopped or 1 28-ounce can plum Italian tomatoes
1 10¾-ounce can zesty tomato soup
1-2 dashes hot pepper sauce

1 tablespoon Worcestershire
1 teaspoon oregano
⅛ cup sugar
1 tablespoon salt
¼ tablespoon pepper
½ bottle chili sauce
3 pounds shrimp, peeled and deveined
Cooked rice

In 4-quart pot sauté bacon. Drain well and set aside. Sauté onion, peppers, and celery in 3 tablespoons bacon drippings until tender. Add tomatoes, tomato soup, sauces, spices, and sugar. Stir well. Bring very gently to slow simmer. Crumble bacon and add to mixture and cover. Simmer very slowly over low heat one hour. When ready to serve, add shrimp to sauce. Return to simmer but do not boil. Simmer approximately 10 minutes or until shrimp is cooked and tender. Do not overcook shrimp. Serve over hot white rice.

Serves 6   *Terri Jackson*

Spicy Shrimp Creole

1 cup onions, chopped
1 cup celery, chopped
2 cloves garlic, minced
⅛ cup oil
2 16-ounce cans tomatoes
2 8-ounce cans tomato sauce
2 medium green peppers, chopped
2 teaspoons sugar
2 tablespoons Worcestershire

2-3 dashes hot pepper sauce
4 teaspoons cornstarch
2 pounds medium sized shrimp,
　　cooked, peeled, and deveined
1 teaspoon chili powder
⅛ teaspoon red pepper flakes
1½ teaspoons salt, optional
4 cups cooked rice

Sauté onions, celery, and garlic in oil until tender but not brown. Mash tomatoes with juice from can and add. Add tomato sauce, pepper, and all seasonings except salt. Simmer 45 minutes. Taste for flavor. Add salt only if needed. Mix cornstarch with 2 tablespoons cold water. Stir into sauce. Cook 3 minutes. Simmer for 5 minutes. Add shrimp. Simmer 5 minutes. Serve over white rice.

Serves 8　　　　　　　　　　　　　　　　　　　　　　　　*Anna Kathryn Brown*

Hall's Boat House is a landmark on scenic Lake Rabun, a lake originally created in 1915 from waters of the Tallulah River to generate electricity.

Cajun Gumbo

A wonderful meal with a salad and crusty French bread

1 cup flour
1 cup margarine
1 green pepper chopped
1 large bunch celery with leaves,
  chopped
1 large bunch green onions, chopped,
  tops included
4 tablespoons chopped parsley
1½ quarts chicken broth, fresh if
  possible

1 cup margarine
4 cups fresh or frozen chopped okra
3 cups onions, chopped
2 pounds shrimp, peeled and deveined
1 tablespoon Worcestershire sauce
1 pound crab meat
1 bay leaf
Salt and pepper to taste
4 cups cooked rice

In a large heavy pot melt margarine. Add flour to make a roux. This is made by stirring the flour constantly until a very dark color is achieved. Add pepper, celery, green onions, and parsley and cook until wilted. Add broth gradually, stirring constantly. Simmer mixture. Melt margarine in separate pan. Add chopped okra and onions and sauté until "stickiness" disappears. Add to roux mixture. Cook shrimp in boiling water to cover until pink. Drain and set aside. Add seasoning to roux mixture and stir occasionally. Simmer mixture about 2 hours, stirring occasionally or until consistency of heavy cream. Add shrimp about 15 minutes before serving. Add crab meat about 10 minutes before serving. Serve in soup bowl with spoonful of rice.

Serves 10   *Carol Ann Hardcastle*

Shrimp in Sour Cream

Outstandingly simple and delicious

1 cup sliced fresh mushrooms
2 tablespoons chopped green onions
2 tablespoons margarine, melted
1 tablespoon flour

1 10¾-ounce can cream of shrimp
  soup, undiluted
1 pound shrimp, peeled and deveined
1 cup sour cream
⅛ teaspoon white pepper

Sauté mushrooms and onions in margarine until tender, but not brown. Blend in flour. Add soup. Cook until thickened. Add shrimp and cook until pink, about 5 minutes. Add sour cream and pepper. Heat thoroughly. Do not boil. Serve in patty shells or on toast points, rice, or fresh pasta.

Serves 6   *Nancy Carr*

Kiawah Island Shrimp with Cheese Rice

Beach specialty

½ cup chopped bacon
2 cloves garlic, chopped,
⅔ cup chopped celery
1 large onion, chopped
1 medium green pepper, chopped
½ cup olive oil
1 28-ounce can Spanish tomatoes
2 6-ounce cans tomato paste

1 cup water
1½ teaspoons sugar
2 teaspoons Worcestershire
½ teaspoon hot pepper sauce
Salt and pepper to taste
½ to 1 pound Polish Sausage, sautéed
2½ pounds shrimp, cooked, peeled
    and deveined

Rice:
4 cups water
2 cups rice
2 teaspoons salt

1 onion, chopped
1 cup grated sharp cheddar cheese

In large skillet, cook until clear: bacon, garlic, celery, onion, pepper, and olive oil. Add tomatoes, tomato paste, water, sugar, Worcestershire, pepper sauce, salt, and pepper. Boil and simmer mixture three hours. Ten minutes before serving add shrimp and sausage. Serve over Cheese Rice.

Cheese Rice: Bring water to boil. Add rice, salt, and onion. Bring to boil again, cover, reduce heat to low and cook for 20 minutes. When rice is done, stir in cheese.

Serves 6-8   *William Collins, M.D.*

Shrimp Wiggle

Old-fashioned Low Country dish

1 pound medium shrimp, deveined
    and peeled
4 tablespoons Worcestershire sauce
½ pound bacon, diced
1 large onion, minced

3-4 tablespoons flour
2 cups cooked white rice
Cayenne pepper to taste
Salt to taste

Marinate shrimp in Worcestershire sauce while proceeding with recipe. Fry bacon in large skillet. Set aside. Sauté onion in bacon drippings. Remove shrimp, reserving marinade, and lightly coat shrimp with flour and cook in skillet until pink. Add rice, reserved marinade, and bacon. Stir fry one minute. Do not over-cook shrimp! Season with cayenne pepper and salt.

Serves 6   *Courtney Flexon*

Shrimp Harpin

2 pounds medium shrimp, cooked, peeled, and deveined
1 tablespoon lemon juice
1 tablespoon oil
1 cup regular rice
¼ cup minced green pepper
¼ cup minced onion
2 tablespoons butter, melted
1 10½-ounce can tomato soup
1 cup whipping cream
½ cup sherry
1 teaspoon salt
⅛ teaspoon mace
⅛ teaspoon pepper
Dash cayenne pepper
¼ cup sliced almonds
Paprika

Place shrimp in 2-quart casserole. Sprinkle with lemon juice and oil. (This can be done the day before.) Cook 1 cup rice and add to shrimp in casserole. Sauté green pepper and onions in butter. Add remaining ingredients except almonds and paprika. Pour over shrimp and rice. Top with almonds and paprika. Bake uncovered at 350 degrees for 45 minutes.

Serves 6   *Ellen Mansberger*

Garlic Shrimp with Peppers

3 tablespoons olive oil
1¼ pounds shrimp, peeled and deveined
2 large cloves garlic, crushed
1½ cups peppers, stemmed, seeded, and sliced into strips (use any combination you like of green, red, and yellow peppers)
9 ounces fresh angel hair pasta
⅛ cup fresh lemon juice (about 1 medium lemon)
2½ tablespoons butter, not margarine
Salt and pepper to taste

In large skillet heat olive oil over medium high heat. Cook shrimp and garlic until shrimp turn pink on one side. Turn shrimp and add peppers. Cook only until shrimp are pink and tender and peppers are still crisp. Do not overcook shrimp. Meanwhile bring large pot of salted water to boil and cook pasta until tender. Remove from heat, add lemon juice and stir in butter until incorporated. Return to low heat and re-warm. Season to taste with salt and pepper. Drain pasta, place on serving platter, top with shrimp and pepper mixture and serve immediately.

Serves 4   *JoAnn Crooms*

Shrimp and Mushrooms in Dill Sauce

Serve with cooked rice, salad, and bread for a delicious meal.

¼ pound mushrooms, thinly sliced
1 pound medium shrimp, peeled and
  deveined
1 tablespoon butter melted
Salt and freshly ground black pepper
  to taste

3 tablespoons Cognac
1 cup plus 3 tablespoons heavy cream
1 egg yolk
⅛ teaspoon cayenne
1 tablespoon lemon juice
¼ cup finely minced fresh dill

Cook mushrooms in butter until wilted about 2 minutes, stirring. Add shrimp, seasoning with salt and pepper to taste. Cook about 3 minutes, stirring frequently. Sprinkle with Cognac and ignite with match. Remove shrimp with a slotted spoon and set aside. Add one cup cream. Cook over high heat about 6 minutes to reduce liquid. Blend remaining 3 tablespoons cream with egg yolk and stir into sauce. Cook briefly, stirring rapidly. Add the shrimp. Salt to taste. Add remaining ingredients and serve piping hot over rice or linguine.

Serves 4-6   *Julie Davies*

Shrimp and Lobster Casserole

Almost a one-dish meal. Just add salad. Always a crowd pleaser.

6 to 8 4-ounce lobster tails, cooked
  and chopped
1½ pounds shrimp, peeled, cooked,
  deveined, and chopped
½ cup margarine or butter, melted
1 cup chopped onion
1½ cups chopped celery
1 cup chopped green pepper

1 6-ounce box wild rice mix, cooked
  and drained
5 tablespoons chopped pimento
3 10½-ounce cans mushroom soup
1 10½-ounce can cheese soup/sauce
2 8-ounce cans sliced mushrooms
2 packages toasted almonds
16 ounces cheese, grated
½ cup dry white wine, optional

Mix all ingredients except almonds and cheese. Pour into 2 8x12 inch casseroles or 1 10x15 casserole. Sprinkle almonds and cheese on top. Bake at 350 degrees for 45 minutes.

Serves 12   *Maureen Vandiver*

Shrimp Casserole I

A secret recipe

2 pounds shrimp, peeled and deveined
4 tablespoons butter
2 10¾-ounce cans cream of
  mushroom soup
1 cup slivered almonds
3 cups cooked rice
1 cup heavy cream
1 cup sherry or milk

¼ teaspoon pepper
1 teaspoon salt
Grated peel of 2 lemons
¼ cup parsley flakes
¼ of a green pepper julienned
¼ cup slivered almonds
½ cup sherry

Sauté shrimp in butter until pink. Add next nine ingredients. Mix. Pour into 3 quart casserole. Bake at 325 degrees for 30 minutes. When done sprinkle with parsley, pepper, almonds, and sherry.

Serves 8   *Ingrid Brunt*

Shrimp Casserole II

1½ pounds shrimp, cooked, peeled,
  and deveined
1 cup mayonnaise
1 2-ounce jar pimento, diced
1 clove garlic, minced
3 hard-cooked eggs, diced
2 10¾-ounce cans cream of
  mushroom soup, low-salt if
  possible

Salt and pepper to taste
Dash of seasoned salt
2 teaspoons Worcestershire
Bread crumbs (homemade or canned)
½ cup almonds, sliced
Margarine

Combine first 9 ingredients. Mix well. Pour into large 9x13 inch greased casserole. Cover with bread crumbs, sprinkle with almonds, and dot with margarine. Bake uncovered at 350 degrees 20 minutes or until heated through.

Serves 4-6   *Ann Smith*

Shrimp and Wild Rice Casserole

1½ cups chopped onions
¾ cup chopped green onions
1½ cups sliced fresh mushrooms
¾ cup butter or margarine, melted
3 tablespoons Worcestershire
Dash hot pepper sauce

2 6-ounce packages wild rice, cooked
1 14-ounce can quartered artichoke
    hearts
1 8-ounce can sliced water chestnuts
2 pounds shrimp, cooked, peeled,
    deveined, and cut in half if large

Sauté onions and mushrooms in butter until soft. Add seasonings. Add rice. Fold in artichoke hearts, water chestnuts, and shrimp. Spoon into buttered 2½ quart casserole. Bake at 300 degrees 30 minutes or until heated through.

Serves 10-12

Carol Ann Hardcastle

Royal Seafood Casserole

3 pounds shrimp cooked, peeled, and
    deveined
2 10¾-ounce cans cream of shrimp
    soup, undiluted
1½ cups celery, diced
1 small onion, grated
2 8-ounce cans water chestnuts, sliced
    and drained
1½ cups rice, cooked

12 ounces crabmeat
½ cup milk
¼ cup sherry or white wine (more if
    desired)
½ cup mayonnaise
Salt, pepper, and nutmeg to taste
½ cup sliced almonds
Paprika

Mix all ingredients except almonds and paprika. Bake in a 9x13 inch casserole at 350 degrees about 40 minutes. Garnish with almonds and paprika.

Serves 10-12

Margie Evans
Martha Hancock
Patty Ramage

C-Lark Seafood Casserole

4 tablespoons butter or margarine
4 tablespoons flour
1 cup milk
1 cup chicken stock
½ teaspoon salt
2 cups grated cheddar cheese

1 cup sour cream
1 pound raw, peeled shrimp
1 pound fish fillets, scallops or
    crabmeat
1 6-ounce can mushrooms, optional
½ cup toasted almond slivers

Make a cream sauce by cooking butter with flour over low heat, stirring constantly for a minute or two. Add milk and chicken stock gradually, stirring constantly. Cook about 10 minutes or until thick and smooth. Add salt and grated cheese, mix well, and cool. Fold in sour cream. Pour half of cream sauce in 2-quart casserole, add seafood and mushrooms, if desired, and cover with remaining half of cream sauce. Cook at 300 degrees for 20 minutes. Before serving sprinkle with almonds.

Serves 6   *Sue Clark*

Curried Seafood Casserole

1 small onion, diced
3 tablespoons margarine, melted
3 tablespoons flour
1 cup milk
1 cup half-and-half
1-2 teaspoons curry powder
1 teaspoon prepared mustard
1 teaspoon Worcestershire
2 teaspoons lemon juice
2 tablespoons sherry

1 cup sharp cheddar cheese, grated
 Salt and pepper to taste
1 14-ounce can artichoke hearts
1 1-pound can crabmeat with shell
    fragments discarded
2 pounds shrimp, cooked, peeled and
    deveined
¼ cup sharp cheddar cheese, grated
    for topping

Sauté onions in margarine until clear and soft but not brown. Stir in flour. Gradually add milk and half-and-half to make a white sauce. When thickened, add all spices, lemon juice, Worcestershire, sherry, and 1 cup cheese. Stir until cheese melts. Add salt and pepper. In a large casserole dish, layer artichoke hearts, crab, and shrimp. Pour sauce over layers and top with remaining cheese. Bake at 350 degrees for 20 minutes.

Serves 10-12   *Barbara Tippins*

Seafood Casserole

Traditional "Masters" Wednesday night dinner for 20 years

2 pounds shrimp, cooked, peeled, and deveined
1 pound crab claw meat
1 cup raw rice, cooked
1 15-ounce can early peas, drained
½ cup chopped green pepper
½ cup chopped celery
½ cup chopped onion
1 cup mayonnaise
Worcestershire to taste
Salt and pepper to taste
16 saltine crackers, crushed

Mix all ingredients except saltines. Pour into 9x13 inch casserole and sprinkle with crushed saltines. Bake at 350 degrees about 45 minutes.

Serves 6-8   *Lynn Amie*

Dahlonega, the site of America's first major gold rush in 1828.

Baked Red Snapper

Makes a beautiful presentation

2½ cups chopped green onions
1 stalk celery, chopped
2 13-ounce cans mushrooms, stems
    and pieces
Olive oil for sautéing
¼ cup olive oil
1 large red snapper 6-10 pounds

Salt to taste
Cayenne to taste
2 tablespoons dried parsley flakes
3 cups sauterne wine
4 dashes wine vinegar
1 tablespoon Worcestershire

Sauté onions, celery, and mushrooms in olive oil. Pour ¼ cup olive oil in baking pan. Sprinkle fish with salt and cayenne and place in pan. Spread sautéed onions, celery, and mushrooms over fish. Sprinkle with parsley. Rinse frying pan used for sautéing with wine, vinegar, and Worcestershire. Pour over fish. Bake at 375 degrees basting occasionally until fish flakes when tested with fork, about 40 minutes.

Serves 8-10   *Cecilia Baute*

Baked Striped Bass

1 3-5 pound striped bass
2 ripe tomatoes, peeled and sliced thin
1 large Vidalia onion sliced thin
3 tablespoons chopped parsley

1 tablespoon chopped fresh dill
1 cup dry red wine
Butter, salt, and pepper
Oil or vegetable spray

Remove backbone of bass. Oil fish inside and out. Stuff with onions, tomatoes, parsley, and dill. Salt and pepper to taste. Place fish in a flat non-metal baking dish. Dot with lots of butter. Bake at 400 degrees for 6 minutes. Add wine. Continue to bake 6 minutes per pound. Baste 3 times during cooking. Remove fish to warm plate and pour the wine sauce over it. If sauce is not thick enough it may be reduced in a saucepan.

Serves 4-6   *Pat Tanner*

Dr. Woodward's Grilled Fish

Delicious and easy.

2 tablespoons butter, melted
2 teaspoons Old Bay seasoning
1 teaspoon garlic salt
1 teaspoon black pepper

3 tablespoons lemon juice
4-8 fillets of fish of your choice,
    trout, Spanish mackerel, etc.

Combine first 5 ingredients. Pour over fish. Grill 10-15 minutes, until flakes when tested with fork.

Serves 4
Bolan Woodward, M.D.

Dijon Grilled Tuna for the Microwave

Great dish to make ahead and cook when company arrives

½ cup olive oil
2 tablespoons coarse Dijon mustard
2 tablespoons fresh chopped parsley

1 tablespoon lime juice
2 medium garlic cloves, crushed
4 1-inch thick tuna steaks

Combine first five ingredients to make a marinade. Coat tuna steaks on all sides with marinade and place in a baking dish. Cover with remaining marinade. Let stand 2 hours at room temperature or overnight in refrigerator. Preheat a microwave browning tray 5 minutes on high. Drain marinade off tuna steaks. Place steaks on tray and microwave on high 2 minutes. Cooking time may vary depending upon power of oven. Turn and microwave on high 1½ minutes or until center is done. Place on warm platter. Heat marinade juices on high 1 minute. Pour over steaks.

Serves 4
Martha Schwartz

Catfish Special

Wonderful easy quick main dish. Good enough for company.

2 catfish fillets
¼ cup Caesar salad dressing

10 buttery crackers, crumbled
¼ cup shredded sharp cheddar cheese

Place fillets in single layer in baking dish. Pour dressing over fish. Sprinkle with cracker crumbs. Bake at 400 degrees for 10 minutes. Top with cheese. Bake 5 minutes more or until fish flakes easily with fork.

Serves 2
Allyce North

Fish Fillets with Tomato Wine Sauce

4 fish fillets, about 6 ounces each, sea
    bass, trout, or red snapper
4 teaspoons butter or margarine
Salt and pepper to taste
1 tablespoon butter or margarine
1 large shallot or 1 small onion, diced
½ cup white wine

½ cup dry sherry
4 fresh tomatoes, peeled and diced
    (may substitute 3 tablespoons
    sundried tomatoes marinated in oil
    and minced)
1 cup heavy cream
1 teaspoon basil

In shallow 2 quart baking dish, place fish fillets. Dot each with 1 teaspoon butter. Season lightly with salt and pepper. Cover dish with foil and bake 15 minutes at 400 degrees. Meanwhile, sauté shallot or onion in butter for 2 minutes. Add wine and sherry. Bring to boil and simmer about 5 minutes until liquid is reduced to about ¼ cup. Stir in tomatoes. Add cream. Simmer about 5 more minutes until sauce is reduced to about ¾ cup. Add basil. Place fish on warm platter with sauce and serve immediately.

Serves 4   *Sarah Schilling*

Easy Tasty Fish Fillets

6-ounce fish fillets, 1 or 2 per person
1 tablespoon flour
Salt and pepper to taste
1 tablespoon butter
¼ cup olive oil

1 bunch green onions, chopped,
    including tops
1 tablespoon capers
½ cup white wine
Lemon wedges

Sprinkle fillets with flour, salt, and pepper. Melt butter in skillet and add olive oil. Sauté fish until lightly browned. Remove to a warm dish. Add onions and capers to skillet, with scrapings. Sauté briefly. Add wine. Stir. Return fillets for a minute or two. Serve, pouring juices over fish. Garnish with lemon wedges.

Serves 4-6   *Pat Minor*

Dr. Schwartz's Lime-Fennel Salmon for the Grill

An elegant use of the grill

Marinade:
2 tablespoons minced fresh parsley
1 tablespoon chopped fresh fennel or
    1 teaspoon dried
¼ cup salad oil

2 minced shallots
¼ cup lime juice
Pepper to taste

Fish:
4 7-ounce salmon steaks
1 tablespoon chopped fresh fennel or
    1 teaspoon dried

Oil to grease grill
Foil-lined fish basket, optional

Mix all ingredients for marinade and pour over fish. Place salmon steaks in shallow dish. Turn fish after 30 minutes and marinate 15 minutes more. To grill, sprinkle 1 tablespoon fennel over hot coals. Place fish on oiled grill (or place fish basket on grill) for 5 minutes. Brush steaks with remaining marinade and turn. Cook 3 more minutes or until fish flakes when tested with a fork. Arrange steaks on individual plates and serve with thin slices of red onion.

Serves 4

Meyer P. Schwartz, M.D.

Salmon Sauté

Good, tasty, and easy

1 tablespoon olive oil
6 4-ounce salmon fillets or steaks
2 cloves garlic, minced
½ red onion, chopped
4 plum tomatoes, chopped

3 tablespoons fresh basil, chopped or
    1½ tablespoons dried
1 tablespoon capers
Fresh ground black pepper to taste

Heat oil in large nonstick skillet. Sauté salmon on each side for 2 or 3 minutes. Remove fish from skillet. Add garlic, onion, and tomatoes. Sauté 2 minutes, or until vegetables are tender. Add salmon, basil, capers, and pepper. Cover and cook over low heat 20 minutes or until salmon is done.

Serves 6

Tammy Williamson

Salmon Steak Kyoto

Absolutely delicious

4 salmon steaks or 2 pounds salmon
  fillets

Marinade:
⅓ cup orange juice (frozen   1 teaspoon lemon juice
  concentrate)   ½ teaspoon Dijon mustard
2 tablespoons oil   1 tablespoon chopped green onion
2 tablespoons tomato juice   ½ teaspoon fresh minced ginger root

Mix marinade ingredients and pour over salmon in 2 quart baking dish. Refrigerate at least one hour, longer if possible. When ready to grill, pour marinade into saucepan. Cook marinade on low heat while steaks are being grilled. Grill steaks on medium heat 20 minutes. Serve with marinade sauce or pour over steaks and keep warm in low oven.

Serves 4   *Judy Domescik*

Oysters Mosca

This recipe is served at a wonderful restaurant just outside of New Orleans

1 large onion, chopped   Salt and pepper to taste
½ cup butter, melted   4 dozen oysters, drained, reserving
3 cloves garlic, minced   liquid
2 tablespoons chopped fresh parsley 1 cup bread crumbs
½ teaspoon thyme   2 slices fried and crumbled bacon
¾ teaspoon oregano   Grated Parmesan cheese
⅛ teaspoon red pepper

Sauté onion in butter until clear. Add garlic, parsley and seasonings. Add oysters and cook until edges of oysters curl. Add liquid. Fold in bread crumbs and bacon. Bake at 350 degrees 15 or 20 minutes. Sprinkle with cheese. Serve hot. May serve in ramekins as first course.

Serves 4   *Julie Davies*

La Prade's, Lake Burton, was built in 1916 as a camp, then became a fishing retreat. It now offers lodging and dining in a rustic setting.

Oyster Casserole

36 saltine crackers
1½ -2 pints oysters
6 tablespoons butter

1½ -2 pounds cheddar cheese, grated
¾ cup milk

In 2 quart casserole layer crackers, then oysters and dot with butter and cheese. Repeat until desired amount, always ending with cheese. Pour milk over all. Bake at 325 degrees until brown, about 25 minutes. May be reheated in microwave. Ingredients do not have to be exact. Just make sure the layers are the same and that the last layer is cheese.

Serves 8

Charlotte Hagen

Eggplant Neptune

2 teaspoons butter
2 8-ounce cans chopped clams,
    including juice
2 buds of garlic, pressed
1 large eggplant, peeled and cut into
    ½ inch cubes

¼ cup minced parsley
¼ cup minced fresh chives or green
    onion tops
¼ cup grated Parmesan cheese
¼ cup more minced parsley

In heavy iron skillet place butter and liquid from cans of clams. Add garlic and cook slowly. Add eggplant and cook, stirring occasionally for 15 minutes. Add first ¼ cup parsley and chives. Cook 5 minutes. Add clams, Parmesan cheese, and remaining parsley. Mix well. Serve at once. Further cooking will make the clams tough!

Serves 4   *Emily Haltiwanger*

Crab Imperial

Serve as appetizer in small shell dishes, or as entrée
with brown rice and fresh seasonal vegetables

1 pound backfin or special crabmeat
1 cup mayonnaise
⅛ teaspoon dry mustard
Pinch of white pepper
1 egg, lightly beaten

¼ teaspoon Dijon mustard
¼ teaspoon lemon juice
2 tablespoons pimiento, chopped fine
¼ cup grated Parmesan cheese

Remove all shell from crabmeat. Combine mayonnaise, mustard, and pepper. Mix well. Add egg, mustard, lemon juice, and pimiento. Gently fold in crabmeat and spoon into 8x8-inch casserole. Top with cheese. Bake 20 minutes at 350 degrees or until golden and bubbly. Serve immediately.

Serves 6-8   *Tina James*

Meeting Street Crabmeat

Adds a special touch to an elegant dinner party

4 tablespoons butter
4 tablespoons flour
½ pint cream or milk
Salt and pepper to taste
4 tablespoons sherry

1 pound white crab meat (may
   substitute shrimp or lobster for
   part of crabmeat)
¾ cup sharp grated cheese

Make cream sauce of butter, flour, and cream. Add salt, pepper, and sherry. Remove from heat. Add crabmeat. Pour into buttered 2 quart casserole. Sprinkle with grated cheese. Bake at 350 degrees 20 to 30 minutes.

Serves 6

Jan Collins

Crab Fondue

Add green salad, crusty rolls, and light dessert for a great luncheon

2 7½-ounce cans crab or 1 pound
   frozen crab
8 slices bread, crust removed
½ cup mayonnaise
1 cup chopped celery
1 green pepper, chopped

1 medium onion, chopped
½ teaspoon salt
3 cups milk
4 eggs, slightly beaten
1 can cream of mushroom soup
½ cup grated sharp cheddar cheese

Drain and dice crab, removing any pieces of shell. Dice 4 slices of bread into bottom of 9x13 inch casserole. Mix crab, mayonnaise, celery, green pepper, onion, and salt. Spread over diced bread. Place remaining bread over crab. Mix eggs with milk and pour over crab and bread. Refrigerate several hours or overnight. Bake at 325 degrees for 15 minutes. Pour undiluted soup over top of casserole. Sprinkle with cheese. Return to oven and bake 1 hour at 325 degrees.

Serves 8-10

Barbara Tippins

Crab Casserole

2 cups half-and-half
3 14-ounce cans artichoke hearts,
    drained and halved
1 8-ounce can buttered chopped
    mushrooms
1 pound lump crabmeat
½ cup butter

4 tablespoons flour
½ teaspoon pepper
½ teaspoon salt
¼ teaspoon hot pepper sauce
½ teaspoon ground mace
3 tablespoon dry sauterne

Warm half-and-half with artichokes and mushrooms over low heat. Remove artichokes and mushrooms and arrange in large buttered casserole. Add crabmeat. Melt butter in saucepan. Stir in flour, pepper, salt, hot pepper sauce, mace, and sauterne. Gradually stir in warm half-and-half to make a sauce. Cover casserole with sauce and cover with foil. Bake at 325 degrees for 20-25 minutes until sauce bubbles. Do not overcook. Serve over rice.

Serves 10

Ingrid Brunt

Coquilles St. Jacques

16 ounces scallops
1 cup dry white wine
1 small onion, chopped or 1 whole
    shallot, chopped
1 4-ounce can chopped mushrooms

4 tablespoons butter
1 cup flour
1 cup milk
¾ cup grated Swiss cheese
Salt and pepper to taste

Poach scallops in wine. (Bring wine to boil and boil scallops for 4 or 5 minutes). Set aside. Sauté onions in 2 tablespoons of butter. Add mushrooms and sauté 2 minutes more. Set aside. Make a Bechamel sauce by melting remaining 2 tablespoons butter, adding flour, and mixing well over low heat. Add milk slowly, stirring constantly to make a heavy sauce. Add ½ cup wine in which scallops were poached. Discard remainder of wine. Mix. Add grated cheese. Mix. Add mixture of onions and mushrooms. Salt and pepper to taste. Cut scallops in fourths and add to sauce. Pour in shells or individual au gratin dishes. Grate additional cheese on top. Broil until brown and bubbly. Serve immediately. Your might serve in patty shells.

Serves 4

Julie Davies
Andrea Jones

Bountiful Plains: VEGETABLES

The Bountiful Plains

The Bountiful Plains serve as Georgia's cornucopia. This fertile land yields the famous Vidalia sweet onion, along with peanuts and pecans, peaches and blueberries, tomatoes, sweet potatoes and corn, soybeans, cotton, and tobacco.

Lumber for markets around the world is provided by the millions of tall pines grown in this region. The popular Claxton fruitcake — the one that tastes "homemade" — is produced in the town of that name by the Parker family.

To celebrate the abundant harvests of this section, many communities present festivals that occur throughout the year. Dublin's St. Patrick's Day, Jesup's Dogwood Festival, Glennville and Vidalia's Onion Festival, Hawkinsville's Harness Festival, Claxton's Rattlesnake round-up, and Ocilla's Sweet Potato Festival are some of the ways communities in the Bountiful Plains entertain their homefolks and visitors alike.

Artists:
Margaret Bartholomew — Title Page
Dee Jackson — "The Bountiful Plains"

Asparagus and Pea Casserole

1 15½-ounce can asparagus spears
   (premium kind)
1 15-ounce can green peas
½ cup low-fat milk
6 tablespoons flour
¼ cup margarine

½ teaspoon salt
¼ teaspoon pepper
1 cup grated low-fat cheddar cheese
2 tablespoons pimiento
1 hard-boiled egg, sliced
⅔ cup bread crumbs

Drain vegetables, reserving 1½ cups liquid. In medium saucepan, stir together milk and flour until smooth. Add vegetable liquid, margarine, seasonings, and cheese. Cook until mixture thickens, stirring constantly. Remove from heat. Add pimiento. In a 1½ quart casserole layer peas and asparagus and egg slices. Pour sauce on top. Sprinkle with bread crumbs. Bake at 350 degrees about 30 minutes.

Serves 6 to 8   *Grace Walden*

Green Beans with Cashews

2 pounds fresh green beans, broken
Boiling water
4 tablespoons butter or margarine,
   melted
1 cup chopped thin onions

¾ cup salted cashews (3 ounces)
Juice of one lemon
½ teaspoon chopped parsley
Salt and pepper to taste

Cook beans in salted water until tender but crisp, about 10 minutes. Drain. Rinse under cold water to stop cooking. Before serving sauté onions in butter in large skillet until tender. Add green beans and cashews. Cook and stir for 2 minutes. Stir in lemon juice and parsley. Season to taste with salt and pepper.

Serves 8   *Cecilia Baute*

Green Bean Bundles

Unusual presentation

2 pounds fresh green beans
1 pound thick sliced bacon, each slice
    cut into 3 lengthwise strips
4 quarts chicken broth

1 teaspoon salt
1½ teaspoons minced fresh basil
½ teaspoon pepper

Wash and trim whole beans. Bundle 12-15 beans together and place on top of a bacon strip. Tie bacon around bundle in a knot or bow. Continue making bundles until all beans are used. Bring broth and seasonings to a boil in 5-quart dutch oven. Using slotted spoon, slip bean bundles into broth. Cover and simmer until crisp tender, about 25 minutes. Amazingly they stay in bundles. Hint: Chill bacon in freezer 10 minutes to facilitate bow-tying.

Serves 6

Linda Flournoy

Company Green Beans

3 16-ounce packages frozen French
    style green beans
4 tablespoons butter or margarine,
    melted
3 tablespoons onion, finely minced

3 tablespoons flour
Salt and pepper to taste
2 8-ounce containers sour cream
Parmesan cheese, freshly grated

Cook green beans according to directions on package. Drain well. Spread beans in a 3-quart flat casserole dish. Sauté onions in butter for 2 or 3 minutes until clear. Add flour, salt, and pepper. Stir over low heat until thick. Remove from heat, add sour cream. Mix thoroughly. Pour over beans. Coat all beans. Sprinkle generously with freshly grated Parmesan cheese. Heat in 350 degree oven about 30 minutes.

Serves 12

Mary Ann Marks

New Orleans Red Beans

Very tasty! Goes well with Sausage, French Bread and Salad

1 24-ounce bag dried red beans
3 strips bacon
6 green onions, chopped
1 stalk celery, chopped
1 small green pepper, chopped
1 clove garlic, minced
1 tablespoon salt

1 teaspoon dry mustard
1 teaspoon chili powder
½ teaspoon cayenne
Dash parsley and thyme
1 tablespoon flour
1 cup beef stock or beef cube plus 1
    cup water

Soak beans in water overnight to hydrate them. Drain. Place beans in a large pot, cover with water and bring to boil, then turn to simmer. Fry bacon until crisp; drain. Crumble and add to beans. Sauté onions, celery, pepper, and garlic in bacon grease until tender. Add to beans with salt and all spices. Cook beans until tender, approximately 1½ to 2 hours. Add water when necessary to cover beans. Partially cover pot with lid. After beans have cooked for 1 hour mix one tablespoon of flour to one cup of beef stock and add to beans to thicken. Continue cooking. Serve over rice.

Serves 8 to 10   *Maureen Roshto*

Louisiana Red Beans

You'll love this one

1 pound dried red beans, washed,
    drained, and soaked in water
    overnight and drained
3 cups water
2 cloves garlic, chopped
½ cup chopped celery

1 large bay leaf, crushed
1 medium onion, chopped
½ cup cooking oil
Salt and pepper to taste
1 pound smoked sausage, sliced
2 tablespoons parsley, chopped

Place beans in dutch oven in cold water. Add garlic, celery, bay leaf, onion, and oil. Bring to boil. Reduce heat. Simmer 2 hours. Add water as needed, stirring occasionally. Add salt, pepper, sausage, parsley and continue cooking over low heat for approximately 1 hour. Serve over rice.

Serves 6 to 8   *Evelyn Utke*

Rice-Broccoli Casserole

1 package frozen chopped broccoli
1 cup cooked rice
1 10¾-ounce can cream of mushroom
  soup

4 tablespoons margarine
1 tablespoon chopped onion
1 cup grated cheddar cheese

Cook broccoli according to package directions and drain well. Mix broccoli with other ingredients and place in greased 1½ quart casserole. Top with grated cheese and bake at 350 degrees for 35 minutes.

Serves 4   *Glenda Bates*

The old-fashioned outhouse, rural Georgia.

Broccoli Soufflé

Serve this in a clear glass soufflé dish

½ cup mayonnaise or plain yogurt
¼ cup flour
1 ½ cups milk
1 teaspoon salt
3 ounces grated Parmesan cheese

1 10-ounce package frozen chopped
   broccoli, thawed and drained
4 eggs, separated
4 slices cooked crumbled bacon,
   optional

Combine mayonnaise and flour; mix well. Gradually add milk. Cook stirring constantly over low heat until thickened. Add salt and cheese. Continue cooking until cheese melts. Cool slightly; stir in broccoli and lightly beaten egg whites. Pour mixture into 1½ quart buttered casserole. With tip of spoon make slight indentation around top of soufflé to form a top hat. Bake 1 hour and 15 minutes. Garnish with bacon if desired. Serve immediately. May substitute spinach for broccoli.

Serves 6 *Lynn Pearson*

Broccoli with Chowder Sauce

Very eye-catching because of colors and arrangements

1 bunch fresh broccoli (may use
   frozen)
1 can New England Clam chowder

8 ounces sour cream
½ to 1 cup grated sharp cheddar
   cheese

Cook broccoli until tender but crisp. Arrange broccoli stalks end to end in a rectangular baking dish so that florets are on outside of dish. Make a sauce by mixing chowder and sour cream. Pour sauce down center of broccoli. Sprinkle grated cheddar cheese on top of sauce. Heat in 350 degree oven until bubbly and cheese is melted (10-15 minutes), being careful not to scorch broccoli. Broccoli may be microwaved before assembling dish, or dish may be microwaved to heat after assembly. Usually 2 to 3 minutes on high.

Serves 6 to 8 *Cam DeLoach*

Martha's Cabbage Casserole

½ cup margarine, melted
1½ cups crushed corn flakes
4 cups shredded cabbage
½ cup chopped onion
½ cup milk

1 10¾-ounce can cream of celery
  soup
½ cup mayonnaise
¼ teaspoon salt and pepper
2 cups grated cheddar cheese
½ to 1 cup bread crumbs

Put a half inch of cornflakes in a 2 quart casserole. Cover with margarine. Place cabbage and chopped onion over this. Combine soup, milk, and mayonnaise and pour over vegetables. Sprinkle cheese over top. Place bread crumbs over top of cheese. Bake at 350 degrees for 45 minutes.

Serves 6-8   *Sally Swann*

Irish Claddagh, Dublin, Georgia.

Lemon-Glazed Carrots

1 pound carrots, washed, peeled, and
  cut diagonally
1 teaspoon salt
Boiling water to cover carrots

3 tablespoons margarine, melted
2 tablespoons sugar
4 thin slices lemon

Cook carrots in salted water until tender. Drain. In heavy skillet over medium heat melt margarine. Stir in sugar. Add lemon slices and carrots. Gently toss until carrots are glazed, 5-10 minutes. Do not overcook. Note: Carrots may be cooked in microwave and then glazed in skillet.

Serves 4   *Martha Ann Laslie*

It Can't Be Carrots Soufflé

Good enough for dessert

2 cups diced carrots, cooked and
  drained
½ cup sugar
¼ cup margarine

1 teaspoon vanilla (may use almond
  for a different flavor)
2 eggs
½ cup milk

Place all ingredients in blender and blend until mixture is thick and smooth. Pour into buttered one quart soufflé dish. Bake at 450 degrees for 30 minutes.

Serves 4   *Jamie Trotter*

Carrot Casserole

10-12 large cooked carrots
4 tablespoons butter
½ cup grated cheese
¾ cup chopped green pepper

½ cup half and half cream
Salt and pepper to taste
Buttered bread crumbs

Mash carrots. Add remaining ingredients. Pour into greased 2 quart casserole. Sprinkle lightly with buttered bread crumbs. Bake at 350 degrees for about 30 minutes.

Serves 8   *Joyce Johnson*

Corn Casserole I

A soufflé type dish. Best when served immediately

½ cup corn oil margarine
¼ cup plain flour
⅔ cup low-fat milk
1 16-ounce can creamed corn, drained

3 egg whites
½ cup egg substitute
½ teaspoon salt
½ cup grated low-fat cheese

Melt margarine in top of double boiler; add flour and stir. Add milk and creamed corn and cook until thick. Remove from heat. Mix egg whites and egg substitute and add to corn mixture. Add salt and cheese. Pour into a greased 2 quart casserole dish and bake at 350 degrees for 20-30 minutes.

Serves 6   *Grace Walden*

Corn Casserole II

2 10-ounce packages frozen Shoe Peg
    corn, thawed
8 ounces sour cream

1 small onion, chopped
1 10½-ounce can cream of celery
    soup

Topping:
1 stack round buttery crackers,
    crushed

¼ cup butter, melted
3 tablespoons slivered almonds

Mix corn, sour cream, onion, and soup. Pour into 1½ quart casserole. Add topping. Bake at 350 degrees for 30-45 minutes or until bubbly.

Serves 6-8   *Lucy Skinner*

Eggplant Soufflé

1 medium eggplant, peeled and cubed
3 tablespoons butter or margarine
1 small onion, minced
10 saltines, crushed

1 4-ounce can mushrooms, drained
1 egg, beaten
½ cup milk

Cook eggplant in boiling water until tender, about 8-10 minutes. Drain well. Add butter and onion to eggplant. Mix well. Add saltines and mushrooms. Mix egg with milk and gently fold into eggplant mixture. Pour into buttered 1½ quart dish. May top with additional cracker crumbs or grated cheddar cheese. Bake at 350 degrees about 30 minutes. Serve immediately.

Serves 6   *Mary Ann Marks*

Lou Griffin's Famous Mushroom Casserole

Auxiliary brunch favorite

12 slices day old white bread, crusts
   removed and cubed
5 beaten eggs
2½ cups milk
1 teaspoon salt
¼ teaspoon pepper
½ teaspoon dry mustard
Pinch of red pepper
½ pound sharp cheddar cheese, grated
   and divided

½ cup melted butter, divided
1 pound fresh mushrooms
2 tablespoons butter
Dash Worcestershire
1 teaspoon prepared mustard
1 teaspoon lemon juice
1 10¾-ounce can cream of mushroom
   soup
Paprika

Place half of bread cubes in bottom of buttered 2 quart baking dish. Beat together eggs, milk, salt, pepper, dry mustard, and red pepper. Pour half of mixture over bread cubes. Top with ¼ pound cheese and ¼ cup butter. Separately, sauté stems and caps of mushrooms in 2 tablespoons butter. Season with Worcestershire, prepared mustard, and lemon juice. Layer stems over cheese. Add remaining bread cubes, egg mixture, ¼ pound cheese, ¼ cup butter. Top with mushroom caps. Refrigerate 8 hours to 2 days. Top with mushroom soup. Sprinkle with paprika. Bake at 350 degrees for 45 minutes.

Serves 8 to 10   *Richmond County Auxiliary*

Vidalia Onion Pie

A Georgia tradition

2 pounds Vidalia onions, peeled and thinly sliced
½ cup butter or margarine, melted
3 eggs, beaten
1 cup sour cream
¼ teaspoon salt
½ teaspoon pepper
Dash hot pepper sauce
1 9-inch unbaked pastry shell
¼ cup grated Parmesan cheese

Sauté onions in butter. Combine eggs and sour cream. Add to onion mixture. Stir in seasonings. Pour mixture into pie shell. Top with cheese. Bake in preheated 450 degree oven for 20 minutes. Turn heat down to 325 degrees and bake 20 minutes more or until brown.

Serves 6-8   *Jan Collins*

Vidalia Onions

6 medium Vidalia onions, cored
6 beef bouillon cubes
6 pats butter
6 strips bacon, cut in half

Place onions in 2 quart casserole dish. Into each onion center, place a bouillon cube and pat of butter and criss-cross with strips of bacon. Cover and cook at 325 degrees for 40 minutes. Baste several times. Remove cover to brown and crisp bacon at end of cooking time.

Serves 6   *Jan Collins*

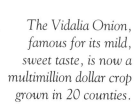

The Vidalia Onion, famous for its mild, sweet taste, is now a multimillion dollar crop grown in 20 counties.

Onion Pie

A classic treatment of our wonderful Vidalia Onion

1 tube crushed round buttery crackers
¼ cup butter or margarine, melted
2 cups sliced onions (Vidalia if
    possible)
2 tablespoons butter or margarine
¾ cup milk

2 eggs
½ teaspoon salt
¼ teaspoon pepper
½ cup grated sharp cheddar cheese
Paprika for garnish

Mix crushed crackers with melted butter. Pat into 9 inch pie plate. Sauté sliced onions in 2 tablespoons butter until opaque. Spoon onto crust. Beat eggs, milk, salt, and pepper until well-mixed. Pour this mixture over onions. Sprinkle with grated cheese and paprika. Bake at 350 degrees 30-35 minutes or until toothpick inserted in center comes out clean. Should be lightly browned on top.

Serves 6   *Valerie Carter*

Cheese Scalloped Onions

Especially good with Vidalia Onions

6 cups thinly sliced onion rings
¼ cup butter or margarine
¼ cup flour

2 cups milk
½ teaspoon salt
2 cups shredded sharp cheddar cheese

Place onions rings in ungreased 1½ quart casserole. Melt butter in saucepan; blend in flour. Gradually stir in milk and cheese. Cook, stirring constantly until thick. Add salt. Pour sauce over onions. Top with additional grated cheese if desired. Bake uncovered at 350 degrees for 1 hour or until onions are tender.

Serves 6   *Nancy Steinchen*

Grilled Vidalia Onion Packages

8 Vidalia onions, cleaned and
    quartered but not cut through
    bottom
Butter
Garlic powder

Chervil or other herbs of choice
Parmesan (optional)
2 teaspoons white wine or champagne
    (optional)

Place onions on squares of aluminum foil. Put 1 tablespoon butter on top of onion. Sprinkle garlic, herbs, and cheese as desired. Add wine if desired. Seal foil packages. Place on grill or bake in 350 degree oven. Cook about 15-20 minutes.

Serves 8   *Paula Rymuza*

Stewed Okra and Tomatoes

3 pounds fresh okra, thinly sliced
⅓ cup bacon drippings
2 cups finely chopped onions
1 clove garlic, minced
½ cup finely chopped celery
1 cup finely chopped green pepper
1 bay leaf

2 pounds ripe tomatoes, peeled and
    cut in small pieces
1 teaspoon salt
⅛ teaspoon thyme
3 to 4 dashes hot pepper sauce
Pepper to taste
½ pound bacon, crisply fried and
    crumbled

Fry okra in bacon drippings, stirring often, until there is no sign of ropiness, or about 30 minutes. Add onions, garlic, celery, green pepper, and bay leaf. Cook until onions are clear, about 15 minutes. Add tomatoes and cook 10 minutes. Add salt, thyme, hot sauce, and pepper. Simmer, covered for 30 minutes. Remove bay leaf. Serve garnished with bacon.

Serves 8

Mary Williams

Potatoes Chantilly

Received honorable mention in cooking contest

4-5 medium all-purpose potatoes,
    peeled, diced, and cooked
¾ cup hot milk

½ cup heavy cream
½ cup shredded sharp cheddar cheese
Salt to taste

Mash potatoes with milk. Pile potatoes into greased 1½ quart round baking dish. Make a volcano-shaped crater in center by pushing potatoes down and to the sides. Whip cream. Fold in cheese. Add salt to taste. Pour into center and over top of potatoes. Bake at 350 degrees for 20 minutes, or until lightly browned. Whipped cream will puff up during baking and flatten by serving time. Serve immediately. Note: Potatoes may be cooked, shaped into bowl, covered, and refrigerated overnight. When ready to cook, bring to room temperature, add cream and cheese mixture and bake an additional 10 minutes.

Serves 6

Angelia Ulrich

Potatoes and Cheese

A good do-ahead dish for a hungry crowd

8 ounces sour cream
8 ounces cream cheese
½ cup margarine melted

1 to 2 cups grated cheddar cheese
8 medium baking potatoes, peeled,
   cubed, and cooked

Combine sour cream, cream cheese, and margarine. Fold in potatoes and place in greased casserole. Sprinkle cheese on top. Bake at 350 degrees until mixture bubbles and cheese is melted.

Serves 12   *Marty Hagood*

Cheesy New Potatoes

A good hearty dish for a family meal

12 medium new potatoes, unpeeled,
   cubed, cooked, and drained
½ cup butter or margarine, melted
¼ teaspoon pepper

1 cup fully cooked bacon pieces (6-8
   slices)
2 cups grated sharp cheddar cheese
¼ cup chopped fresh parsley,
   optional

Fold butter and pepper into potatoes. Spoon half the potatoes into a greased 3 quart casserole. Top with half the bacon and cheese. Repeat layers. Bake at 350 degrees for 20 minutes. Garnish with parsley.

Serves 8 to 10   *Nancy Story*

Scalloped Potatoes

Exceptional

1 large garlic clove, minced
½ teaspoon crushed red pepper
3 tablespoons butter, melted
1¼ cups milk
1½ cups whipping cream
½ teaspoon salt

¼ teaspoon pepper
2½ pounds red potatoes, unpeeled and
   sliced
1 cup shredded Gruyère cheese
¼ cup grated Parmesan cheese

Sauté garlic and red pepper in butter for 2 minutes. Add milk and next 3 ingredients, stirring well. Add potatoes. Bring mixture to boil over medium heat. Spoon mixture into greased 12x8 inch baking dish. Sprinkle with cheese. Bake at 350 degrees for 1 hour. Let stand for 30 minutes before serving.

Serves 8   *Leslie McLeod*

Garlic Roasted Potatoes

¼ cup olive oil

1 clove garlic, finely minced

8 red-skinned new potatoes, scrubbed
   clean and dried

1 clove garlic cut in half

Salt and pepper

Mix olive oil with minced garlic and set aside. Slice a small piece off one end of each potato so they will sit flat. Liberally rub each potato with cut clove of garlic. Insert a skewer lengthwise in potato ¼ inch from bottom. Cut ⅛ inch slices to this point. You should have a number of thin slices which remain attached to bottom of potato. Brush the potatoes with garlic-olive oil and sprinkle with salt and pepper. Bake on a greased baking sheet at 400 degrees for 30 minutes. Baste with more garlic-olive oil and bake another 20 minutes until tender and golden brown. Tester suggests basil is excellent added to basting oil.

Serves 4

Alice Horney

The Chatter Tree or Holland House, Statesboro, Georgia.

Sweet Potatoes Rhumba

1 16-ounce can sweet potatoes
½ pint heavy cream
½ teaspoon nutmeg
½ cup sugar
Pinch of salt
½ cup rum or 1 tablespoon rum
    flavoring

3 to 4 oranges halved and hollowed
    out
2 tablespoons butter or margarine,
    melted
6-8 maraschino cherries (optional)

Drain sweet potatoes of liquid. Mash well or blend in blender until smooth. Add next five ingredients and mix well. Hollow out fruit of orange halves until only white rind is present. Fill each orange half with sweet potato mixture. Brush with melted butter. Garnish each with one maraschino cherry. Bake at 350 degrees on foil covered baking sheet about 40 minutes or until heated through.

Note: For a more festive look, edges of orange rinds may be zig-zagged.

Serves 6 to 8   *Lynn Pearson*

Holiday Sweet Potato Soufflé

Excellent with poultry

3 cups mashed sweet potatoes (4
    sweet potatoes)
½ teaspoon salt
2 eggs, beaten

½ cup milk
1 cup sugar
1 teaspoon vanilla
5 tablespoons margarine, softened

Topping:
1 cup brown sugar
1 cup chopped pecans

⅓ cup flour
5 tablespoons margarine, melted

Mix first 7 ingredients and pour into baking dish. Mix last 4 ingredients thoroughly for the topping. Sprinkle over potato mixture. Bake at 350 degrees for 35 minutes. Note: Cook the sweet potatoes in the microwave for 10-12 minutes until soft. Remove skins and mash. To "mash" the potatoes use a beater, the soufflé will be fluffy and light.

Serves 8   *Jan Collins*
     Paula Rymuza
     Grace Walden

Rice Casserole

Excellent side dish for any beef entrée

1 cup raw rice
1 10¾-ounce can French onion soup
   (not cream style)

1 10¾-ounce can beef bouillon or
   consommé
½ cup margarine

Mix rice and soups together in 2 quart casserole. Cut up margarine and place on top. Bake at 350 degrees for 1 hour.

Variation: Add 1 4-ounce can drained mushrooms. As casserole cooks, mushrooms rise to top and look very pretty.

Serves 6

Bonnie Bedingfield
Sandra Jackson
Gladys Williams

Easy Wild Rice Casserole

1 cup wild rice
½ cup butter or margarine
2 tablespoons chopped green pepper
1 medium onion, chopped
4 ounces canned sliced mushrooms

1 cup chopped pecans
½ cup regular rice
4 cups chicken broth
Salt and pepper to taste

Wash wild rice. Cover with boiling water and let soak for 1 hour or cover with cold water and let soak overnight. Drain well. Melt butter in large pot. Add pepper, onion, and mushrooms. Sauté for 5 minutes. Add pecans. Cook one minute longer. Add rices. Mix well. Add chicken broth, salt, and pepper. Mix thoroughly. Place in a greased 9x13 inch casserole and cover tightly with foil. Bake at 350 degrees for 1 hour. Check at 50 minutes. Remove foil last 10 minutes.

Serves 8 to 10

Roberta Letton

Olive Rice Casserole

Simple and easy, but the inclusion of olives makes
it a bit different from other rice casseroles

1 cup long grain rice, uncooked
2 10¾-ounce cans beef consommé
6 tablespoons melted margarine

1 small onion, chopped
1 small can mushrooms, drained
1 small jar stuffed olives, sliced

Mix all ingredients and pour into 2 quart casserole. Cover with foil or lid and bake at 350 degrees for 30 minutes. Uncover and continue to cook for an additional 30 minutes.

Serves 6   *Nancy Herron*

Men's Favorite Rice Casserole

An excellent choice as the one "hot" dish for a cold buffet supper

4 tablespoons butter or margarine
1 cup chopped onion
4 cups freshly cooked rice, not instant
2 cups sour cream
1 cup cream style cottage cheese
1 large bay leaf, crumbled

½ teaspoon salt
⅛ teaspoon pepper
3 4-ounce cans chopped green chilies, drained
2 cups grated sharp cheddar cheese
Chopped parsley

Melt butter in large skillet. Sauté onion until golden. Remove from heat; stir in hot rice, sour cream, cottage cheese, bay leaf, salt, and pepper; toss lightly to mix well. In a greased 8x12 inch baking dish layer half the rice mixture, then half the chilies, then sprinkle with half the cheese. Repeat. Bake uncovered 25 minutes, or until bubbly and hot. Sprinkle with chopped parsley.

Serves 8   *Ruthie Hester*

Easy and Delicious Vegetable Spanish Yellow Rice

1 green pepper, chopped
1 large onion, chopped
2 garlic cloves, chopped
Olive oil

1 can tomatoes (cut tomatoes in halves or thirds and save juice)
1 can corn, drained
1 6-ounce package yellow or Spanish rice

Cover bottom of heavy pot with enough olive oil to sauté onion, green peppers, and garlic. When onions begin to brown add tomatoes, rice, and drained corn. Stir. Add liquid according to instructions on rice package. Bring to boil and cook over high for 1 minute, cover tightly and simmer 20 minutes.

Serves 8   *Renee Hernandez*

Bulloch County Courthouse, Statesboro, Georgia

Mediterranean Spinach

1-2 tablespoons pine nuts
2 tablespoons olive oil
1 pound fresh spinach, washed

¼ cup raisins, plumped in warm water
1-2 tablespoons fresh, grated
    Parmesan cheese

In large frying pan toast pine nuts in olive oil. Set aside. Cook spinach, covered, in a dry saucepan over low heat until wilted about 3-5 minutes. Drain well and slice or chop spinach; add to pan containing toasted pine nuts and oil, along with drained raisins. Heat briefly; tossing. Sprinkle with Parmesan and serve immediately.

Serves 4   *Betsy Fowler*

Turnips Filled with Spinach

8 medium sized white turnips
1 8-ounce package fresh spinach
1 tablespoon butter

¼ cup whipping cream
Salt and pepper
1 tablespoon butter, melted

Peel and steam turnips until fork tender. Cool and cut out center. Wash spinach and remove stems. Chop fine. Melt butter, add spinach and fork stir over high heat 30 seconds. Add cream and cook until cream is reduced. Season with salt and pepper. Fill cavity in turnip. Place in baking dish. Pour melted butter over and heat in a 350 degree oven for 10 minutes.

Serves 8   *Helen Corbitt Cooking School sponsored by AMAA*

Spinach Soufflé

3 eggs, beaten
3 tablespoons flour
⅛ teaspoon nutmeg
¼ teaspoon pepper
¼ teaspoon salt
1 teaspoon lemon juice

1 9-ounce package frozen chopped
    spinach, defrosted but not drained
1 cup low fat cottage cheese
⅓ pound grated cheddar cheese
⅓ cup melted margarine
Additional shredded cheese for
    topping

Whisk eggs with flour, nutmeg, salt, pepper, and lemon juice. Add spinach, 2 cheeses, and margarine. Put in greased 1½ quart casserole. Bake at 350 degrees 50-60 minutes or until set. During last 5 minutes of baking sprinkle with additional cheese. To freeze, cook 40 minutes, cool and freeze. Later put frozen casserole in 350 degree oven and bake 50-60 minutes. Can be prepared in morning, refrigerated, then cook later.

Serves 8   *Carolyn Hoose*

Spinach-Artichoke Casserole

2 10-ounce packages frozen chopped
   spinach, cooked and drained
½ cup finely chopped onion
½ cup margarine

1 cup sour cream
1 14-ounce can artichoke hearts,
   quartered
½ cup grated Parmesan cheese

Sauté onion in margarine. Mix onion, spinach, sour cream, and artichoke hearts and pour into 8x12 inch casserole dish. Sprinkle with Parmesan cheese. Bake at 350 degrees for 20-30 minutes. Tester suggests adding 2 teaspoons lemon juice when mixing.

Serves 6-8   *Nancy Wolff*

Southern Summer Squash

10-12 medium sized squash, cleaned
   and sliced
1 large onion, coarsely chopped
4 tablespoons butter or margarine

1 beaten egg
15 to 20 crumbled round buttery
   crackers
4 ounces sliced or shredded cheese

Cook squash and onion in water until tender. Drain. Add butter, egg, and crackers. Put in greased 2 quart casserole and top with cheese. Bake at 325 degrees for 30 minutes.

Serves 6   *Jan Collins*

Jean's Posh Squash

2 pounds yellow squash, sliced and
   cooked
1 cup mayonnaise
2 eggs, beaten
Salt and pepper to taste
1 cup Parmesan cheese

1 small bunch green onions, chopped
   (include some of tops)
¼ cup chopped green pepper
Bread crumbs
¼ to ½ cup melted butter or
   margarine

Cook squash in small amount of water until tender. Drain. Combine mayonnaise, beaten eggs, salt, pepper, and Parmesan cheese. Mix well. Add onions and pepper to squash mixture. Place in a 2 quart casserole and top with bread crumbs and butter. Cook 30-40 minutes uncovered until golden brown and set.

Serves 6   *Jeanne Smiley*

Butternut Squash Casserole

2 cups cooked butternut squash,
    drained and mashed
3 eggs
6 tablespoons butter, melted
1 cup milk
¾ to 1 cup sugar

½ teaspoon ground ginger
½ teaspoon coconut extract and/or 2
    tablespoons flake coconut
¼ teaspoon salt
Buttered cracker crumbs

Combine all ingredients except cracker crumbs. Place in greased 1 ½ quart baking dish. Set casserole in a pan of water and bake at 350 degrees for 45 minutes or until set. Before removing from oven cover with crumbs and brown.

Serves 8

Evelyne Bronikowski

Tomato Casserole

1 cup chopped green pepper
1 cup chopped onions
1 cup chopped celery
4 tablespoons butter
2 28-ounce cans tomatoes

1 cup sugar
Salt and pepper to taste
4 tablespoons vinegar
4 tablespoons cornstarch
Bread crumbs, optional

Sauté pepper, onion, celery in butter. Add tomatoes and sugar. Bring to boil. Mix vinegar and cornstarch. Stir into hot mixture gradually. Simmer mixture 5 to 10 minutes. Pour into 9x13-inch casserole. Top with breadcrumbs. Bake at 375 degrees for 40 minutes.

Serves 8

Betty Claire Neill

Grilled Vegetables with Basil Mayonnaise

Original recipe featured on cover of Gourmet Magazine

Basil Mayonnaise:

1 large egg at room temperature
5 teaspoons fresh lemon juice
1 teaspoon Dijon-style mustard
¾ cup packed fresh basil leaves

¼ teaspoon salt
¼ teaspoon white pepper
1 cup olive oil, vegetable oil, or
    combination of both

Vegetables:

4 carrots including 1 inch of green
    tops
2 red onions, halved lengthwise
2 yellow summer squash, halved
    lengthwise
8 radishes including ½ inch of green
    tops
8 small tomatoes including stems
1 red pepper, quartered and seeded

2 red or yellow Italian sweet peppers,
    halved lengthwise and seeded
¼ pound small okra (about 8)
2 heads Bibb lettuce, halved
    lengthwise, rinsed well and patted
    dry with paper towels
Olive oil or vegetable oil for brushing
    vegetables

Basil Mayonnaise: In food processor or blender at high speed, blend egg, lemon juice, mustard, basil, salt, and white pepper. Add oil slowly, blending mixture until mayonnaise is emulsified. May be made 1 day in advance and kept covered and chilled.

Vegetables: Cook carrots and onions in boiling salted water 5 minutes. Transfer to colander and refresh under cold water. Pat vegetables dry. In boiling salted water, cook squash for 1 minute, add radishes, and cook for 3 minutes. Drain vegetables, refresh and dry. Brush carrots, onions, squash, radishes, tomatoes, red peppers, Italian peppers, okra, and lettuce with oil. Arrange vegetables in a grill basket and grill on a rack set 5-6 inches over glowing coals, turning basket once. Grill for 5-8 minutes or until tender. Serve with basil mayonnaise.

Serves 4-6   *William L. Barnwell, M.D.*

In the 1820's, Georgia was the world's largest cotton producer, and cotton is still one of the five most important cash field crops in the state.

Sweetie's Zucchini

A unique combination of flavors

6 zucchini
1 cup mayonnaise
3 tablespoons crumbled bleu cheese
½ teaspoon garlic salt

½ cup grated Parmesan cheese
Dash of cayenne
½ teaspoon salt
1 teaspoon oregano

Parboil whole zucchini in salted water until just tender (5-8 minutes). Drain. Cut zucchini in half, lengthwise. Cool slightly. Combine mayonnaise, bleu cheese, garlic salt, Parmesan cheese, and cayenne. Blend well. Sprinkle zucchini halves with salt. Spread mayonnaise mixture on cut halves. Sprinkle with oregano. Bake for 20 minutes at 350 degrees.

Serves 6-8

Nancy Story

Zucchini Provençale

1 medium onion, sliced
1 clove garlic, minced
¼ cup salad oil
2 pounds zucchini, sliced
4 tomatoes, cut up

1 green pepper, chopped
Salt and pepper to taste
Minced parsley
Parmesan cheese

In skillet, sauté onion and garlic in salad oil. Add zucchini, tomatoes, green pepper, and salt and pepper to taste. Cook until tender. Sprinkle with parsley and Parmesan cheese before serving.

Serves 8

Jan Collins

Golden Isles:
ACCOMPANIMENTS

The Golden Isles

The "Golden Isles," so-called because of cream-colored sand and year-round sunshine, are steeped in history, romance, and intrigue. Probably no area of Georgia has inspired as much prose and poetry as the Golden Isles. The marshes, the sea, and the people have stirred the writers' muse since Oglethorpe landed on the south bank of the Savannah River in 1733.

Scenic wonders beckon the artist and tourist alike. Historic Savannah, founded as England's last colony in the New World, is called by some the most beautiful city in North America. Following the coast south of Savannah are the 15 barrier islands of the Golden Isles, with St. Simons, Jekyll, and Sea Island being the most visited.

The lighthouse on St. Simons Island, one of the oldest continuously working lighthouses in the country, is a popular landmark. Built in 1871, it followed a lighthouse on this site dating from 1804 that was destroyed by Confederate troops during the Civil War.

Artists:
Margaret Bartholomew — Title Page
Blanche Nettles — "The Golden Isles"

Carolina Spoon Bread

Popular North Carolina recipe

1 cup yellow corn meal
3 cups milk, divided
1 teaspoon baking powder
1 teaspoon salt (optional)

2 tablespoons vegetable oil
3 well-beaten egg yolks
3 stiff-beaten egg whites

Cook cornmeal and two cups milk until consistency of mush. Remove from heat. Add baking powder, salt, oil, and 1 cup milk. Add egg yolks. Fold in egg whites. Bake in greased 2 quart baking dish at 325 degrees for 1 hour. Serve immediately in baking dish and spoon onto plates. Add butter or margarine.

Serves 8 *Tina James*

Southern Spoon Bread

Traditionally served in Maryland with shad roe and asparagus

1 cup boiling water
½ cup white corn meal
½ cup milk
½ teaspoon salt

1½ teaspoons baking powder
1 tablespoon butter, softened
2 eggs, well beaten

Pour water over corn meal. Beat in milk, salt, baking powder, butter, and 2 eggs. Pour into buttered 1 quart casserole. Bake at 400 degrees until set, about 20-25 minutes. Serve immediately with butter and/or syrup.

Serves 3 *Cheri Dennis*

Grandma Marek's Dressing

Fabulous with fresh Cranberry-Banana Sauce

2 eggs
2 cups seasoned bread crumbs
½ cup melted margarine
2 tablespoons parsley flakes

¼ cup chopped onion
¼ cup chopped celery
Salt and pepper to taste
2 cups milk

Beat eggs in large bowl; add bread crumbs, margarine, parsley, onion, and celery. Mix well. Add salt and pepper to taste. Slowly stir in milk and mix well. Stuff 2 chickens or a large turkey and cook according to poultry directions. Remove from poultry before serving.

Amy Swindle

Corn Bread Dressing

A family tradition

Egg Bread:

2 cups self-rising meal
2 tablespoons shortening
1 cup boiling water

½ cup flour
¾ to 1¼ cups buttermilk
1 egg

Dressing:

Egg Bread
½ loaf white bread
1 onion, chopped
2 stalks celery, chopped and cooked

Chicken or turkey stock
2 beaten eggs
2 teaspoons baking powder

Prepare the recipe for egg bread the day before. Crumble egg bread and loaf bread. Add onion and celery. Add stock to make a soft consistency. Add eggs and baking powder. Place in 9x13-inch pan and bake for 1 hour at 350 degrees.

Serves 10

Jan Collins
Talitha Russell

Judy Jay's Scrumptious Turkey Stuffing

Especially recommended for brides who have agreed
to do the honors with no previous experience!

6 cups herbed stuffing mix
8 cups cornbread, crumbled
1 teaspoon salt
1 teaspoon coarse ground black
  pepper
2 teaspoons poultry seasoning
1 teaspoon sage
1 teaspoon thyme leaves

4½ cups diced celery
4 cups diced onion
2½ cups pecan halves
1 medium apple, chopped
¼ pound butter, melted
4 eggs, beaten
1 cup milk
¼ cup sherry

Combine first seven dry ingredients. Add next four chopped ingredients. Toss. Add next four liquid ingredients. Thoroughly mix all ingredients. Makes enough stuffing for a 25 pound turkey, plus some! Extra stuffing may be baked covered in a separate pan at 350 degrees for 30-40 minutes.

Judy Jay Masters

Italian Ambassador's Wild Rice Stuffing

A sophisticated change from usual poultry stuffing

2 cups raw wild rice
Tepid water - enough to cover rice
½ cup olive oil
1 cup finely diced celery
1 cup chopped onion
1 cup condensed beef consommé

½ cup dry sherry wine
1 cup sliced fresh mushrooms
½ cup chopped green pepper
½ tablespoon chopped parsley
2 teaspoons salt
1 teaspoon Angostura bitters

Wash uncooked wild rice and soak for one hour in tepid water. Heat olive oil in heavy skillet. Stirring constantly, add drained wild rice, celery, and onion. When blended, add consommé and sherry. Stir in mushrooms, pepper, parsley, salt, and bitters. Cover tightly and allow to simmer for ½ hour or until rice is done. This dressing is best and the flavor is improved if the mixture is cooled and kept overnight in refrigerator.

Stuffing for 1 turkey or 10 Cornish hens   *Bunkie Rivkin*

*The Cloister on Sea Island, opened in 1928, is a handsome Spanish-style inn
that has earned the reputation as one of America's finest resorts.*

Liz's Baked Apples

An excellent accompaniment to meats

5 Granny Smith apples, peeled and
    sliced or 2 20-ounce cans sliced
    apples
8 ounces sharp cheddar cheese, grated

1 cup sugar
½ cup butter
¾ cup flour

Place sliced apples in lightly greased 9x9 inch casserole dish. Sprinkle grated cheese on top of apples. Combine softened butter with sugar and flour. Make a coarse mixture. Spread on top of casserole. Bake uncovered at 350 degrees for 30 minutes or until golden brown and bubbly.

Serves 6

Sandra Burns
Florrie Funk
Ruth Goldsmith

Gingered Papayas

The color and flavor makes this a unique accompaniment for almost any entrée

4 firm ripe papayas
8 tablespoons butter
4 tablespoons lime juice

1 teaspoon ground ginger
8 thin slices of lime
Dash of cayenne

Cut papayas in half, lengthwise, and scoop out seeds. Arrange in a glass baking dish with ⅛ inch warm water in bottom. In each papaya hollow, place 1 tablespoon butter, ½ tablespoon lime juice, and ⅛ teaspoon ground ginger. Bake at 350 degrees for 30 minutes, basting 10 minutes before done. Place a slice of lime at edge of each papaya half. Add a dash of cayenne and serve warm.

Serves 8

Janice Baldwin

Pineapple Casserole

An interesting mixture of tastes - good with meats or crisp vegetables

1 20-ounce can pineapple chunks
½ cup sugar

3 tablespoons flour
1 cup shredded sharp cheddar cheese

Drain pineapple, reserving 3 tablespoons juice. Combine sugar and flour. Stir in pineapple juice. Add cheese and pineapple chunks. Mix well. Spoon into 1 quart baking dish. Bake at 350 degrees for 20-30 minutes.
Variation: Try doubling the cheese and top with cracker crumbs mixed with melted butter.

Serves 4-6

Ashley Swann

Mrs. Miller's Persian Pineapple

A family favorite. Excellent with ham or poultry

2 eggs, or equivalent egg-substitute
½ cup sugar
¼ pound corn oil margarine

5 slices white bread, crust removed
1 20-ounce can crushed pineapple

Beat 2 eggs with sugar lightly. Melt margarine. Break bread into small pieces and add to margarine, stirring until bread is well-coated. Add this mixture to sugar and egg mixture. Stir. Add crushed pineapple. Stir (do not beat). Pour in greased 9x9 inch baking dish and bake at 350 degrees for 30 minutes.

Note: If preparing larger quantity, use large oblong casserole, not deep dish.

Serves 6   *Grace Walden*

Kate Riggins' Cranberry Casserole

Great for holiday buffets

2 large Granny Smith apples, cored
**   and sliced with peeling**
2 cups fresh cranberries, washed
1 cup sugar

½ cup butter or margarine, melted
1 cup old-fashioned oats
1 cup chopped pecans

Place sliced apples on bottom of ungreased 2 quart baking dish; add cranberries on top. Sprinkle with sugar. Make paste of melted butter, oats, and pecans. Spread over cranberries. Cover tightly. Cook at 350 degrees for 1 hour. Remove cover. If too runny, cook uncovered 10 minutes longer.

Serves 8   *Mary Ann Marks*

Hot Salsa

1 red or green pepper
1-3 seeded jalapeño peppers (to taste)
1 medium onion
2 cloves garlic
1 10-ounce can tomatoes and chilies

1 medium tomato cut into small cubes
½ teaspoon salt
¼ teaspoon fresh ground pepper
Chopped cucumber, optional
Green and ripe olives, optional

Chop peppers, onion, and garlic in food processor. Add to tomatoes and chilies along with fresh tomatoes. Add salt and pepper to taste. Store covered in refrigerator. Should salsa be too watery to dip with Tortilla chips, drain off some tomato juice.

Makes 3-4 cups   *Betsy Fowler*

Jalapeño Green Sauce

Adds pepper flavor and spicy sensation to your favorite dishes

2 quarts jalapeño peppers
¼ cup white vinegar

1 tablespoon salt

Wash peppers and remove most of the seeds and white membrane. (Wear gloves to protect hands from being burned by chili oil. You can use the whole pepper to make this sauce, but with the seeds and membranes it is hotter and lacks the vibrant green color.) Place peppers in food processor or blender in batches. Liquefy until there is about a quart of puréed peppers. Add vinegar and salt and combine well. Spoon into jars and store in the refrigerator for up to a year.

Makes 1 quart   *John Ed Fowler, M.D.*

D.B.'s Bar-B-Que Sauce

Fraternity cook's secret recipe

1 32 ounce bottle ketchup
2 cups water
½ cup light or dark brown sugar
¼ cup Worcestershire
1 teaspoon garlic salt
2 tablespoons vinegar
2 dashes hot pepper sauce

1 teaspoon dry mustard
1 teaspoon chili powder
1 tablespoon plus 2 teaspoons liquid
    smoke
¼ teaspoon cayenne
1¼ teaspoons black pepper

Put all ingredients into a big pot and mix well. Bring to a boil while stirring frequently. After mixture comes to a boil turn to simmer for 45 minutes.

Makes 1½ quarts   *David Brunt*

Sanddollars on Jekyll Island.

Riviera Marinade for Steak

Good for Shish-Kabobs

1 cup dry red wine
1 cup salad oil
2 tablespoons vinegar
1 tablespoon grated lemon peel
1 crushed garlic clove

1 teaspoon salt
1 teaspoon pepper
½ teaspoon dry mustard
¼ teaspoon thyme
¼ teaspoon basil

Combine all ingredients and mix thoroughly. Marinate tender cuts of steak or shish-kabobs 30-60 minutes. Baste with additional mixture.

Makes 8 servings   *Lynn Pearson*

Teriyaki Sauce Marinade

A nice no-fat marinade

Marinade:
1 cup soy sauce
½ cup water
¼ cup rice wine or 3 teaspoons sugar
⅓ cup brown sugar

½ cup sugar
1 tablespoon minced garlic
1 tablespoon minced fresh ginger

Gravy:
2 tablespoons butter   2 tablespoons flour

Combine ingredients in saucepan. Heat until sugar dissolves. Cool before using. Cook meat as desired (grill, bake, etc.). Gravy may be made from remaining marinade to serve with meat. Melt butter in saucepan, add flour and cook, stirring constantly for 2 minutes. Gradually add marinade until gravy is thickness desired.

Enough for 3-4 pounds of meat   *Laurie Amerson*

Tybee Island Lighthouse

*Located within Fort Screven on Tybee Island, this is one of the
first public structures in Georgia, dating from Colonial times.*

Dilled Cucumbers

Wonderful with grilled meats

3 large cucumbers, sliced thin
3 tablespoons coarse salt
1½ cups wine vinegar

½ cup sugar
1 tablespoon white pepper
2 cups chopped fresh dill

Slice unpared cucumbers (washed well to remove any wax) or use hydroponic cucumbers sliced as thin as possible. Pour coarse salt over slices, weigh down with a plate and let stand for 3 hours. Then pour off juice and mix it with wine vinegar, sugar, pepper, and dill. Pour over cucumbers and refrigerate four hours.

Serves 4

Russell B. Smiley, M.D.

Norwegian Dilled Cucumbers and Onions

Served as a side dish in most Scandinavian homes

1 large long "English" cucumber
    peeled and sliced thinly
1 medium thinly sliced onion
½ cup sugar

½ cup cider vinegar
Salt and pepper to taste
½ teaspoon dill weed

Cover cucumbers and onions in salted ice water about ½ hour. Drain and squeeze out excess water. Mix sugar, vinegar, salt, pepper, and dill. Pour over cucumbers and onions. Marinate several hours or overnight.

Serves 4-6

Carolyn Hoose

Cucumber Relish

Wonderful on hot dogs

12 large cucumbers
2 large onions
2 tablespoons salt
3 cups vinegar

1 teaspoon dry mustard
2 teaspoons tumeric, optional
4 cups sugar

Grind cucumbers and onions, or chop in food processor. Let stand 1 hour and drain. Add all other ingredients and cook on medium heat for 25 minutes. Pack in pint jars and seal.

Makes 6-8 pints

Jana Hill

Shrimp Gravy

A family recipe for over 50 years

1 cup finger sized white bacon
¾ cup chopped onion
½ cup flour
3 cups deveined white raw shrimp,
    (small shrimp preferred, they're
    sweeter. If large shrimp are used,
    cut in pieces)

2¼ cups water
¾ cup half-and-half
Salt and pepper to taste

On low to medium heat fry bacon in deep iron skillet until bacon is done. Set bacon aside. Use grease to fry onion until tender. Sprinkle flour in while stirring. Will make a white paste. Stir in water, half-and-half and shrimp. Season to taste. Mix well. Cover and cook on low 15-20 minutes. Do not overcook or shrimp will be tough. If too thick add water to consistency desired. Serve over rice, potatoes, or English muffins. Very different

Serves 4-6   *Charlotte Hagen*

Shrimp Boat, Darian, Georgia.

Salad Dressing

A thoroughly original concoction

1 cup vinegar
1¼ cups oil
¼ cup plus 2 tablespoons water
1 teaspoon paprika
1¼ teaspoons garlic salt
⅛ teaspoon oregano

1 tablespoon lemon juice
3 tablespoons sugar
1¼ teaspoons Worcestershire
Pepper to taste
Parmesan cheese to taste

Mix ingredients well. Refrigerate.

Mary Williams

Homemade Ranch Dressing

Better than the best you can buy

Dry Mix:
1 teaspoon garlic powder
2 teaspoons dried parsley

1 teaspoon black pepper
½ teaspoon onion powder

Ranch Dressing:
1 cup real mayonnaise
1 cup buttermilk

3⅛ teaspoons Dry Mix

Dry Mix: Mix all ingredients and store in airtight container. Stir or shake well before using.

Ranch Dressing: Mix dry and wet ingredients thoroughly by shaking well in a quart jar. Store in refrigerator until ready for use. When mixed, will keep in refrigerator for weeks.

Variations: Add 1 tablespoon dried chives, 1 teaspoon Italian Seasoning, and a dash of cayenne, or 2-4 ounces bleu cheese.

Makes 1 pint   *Tina James*

Celery Seed Dressing

⅓ cup sugar
1 teaspoon dry mustard
1 teaspoon salt
1 teaspoon grated onion

2 teaspoons celery seed
1 teaspoon vinegar
1 cup oil
3 tablespoons vinegar

Place first five ingredients in bowl. Mix in 1 teaspoon vinegar. Slowly add oil and remaining vinegar alternately while mixer is running. Mix until thick and smooth.

Mary Williams

Vinaigrette Dressing or Marinade

A little oriental touch

¼ teaspoon minced garlic
½ teaspoon lemon pepper
¼ teaspoon ground ginger
2 teaspoons chopped parsley (fresh or dehydrated)

Pinch of salt
⅛ cup soy sauce (low sodium)
⅛ cup champagne vinegar or tarragon wine vinegar
¼ cup oil

Blend all ingredients with a whisk, adding oil slowly last. Set aside until ready to use. Whisk again immediately before pouring on salad. It is a terrific marinade for cold vegetables. As a meat marinade pour over beef or poultry 3-4 hours prior to cooking. As a vegetable marinade pour over vegetables no more than an hour before serving.

1 salad for 6   *Cheri Dennis*

Roquefort Dressing

Wonderful on salads or with raw vegetables

2 tablespoons tarragon vinegar
4 tablespoons ketchup
½ cup olive oil

Large chunk chopped Roquefort cheese
2 teaspoons grated onion or 1 teaspoon minced garlic

Combine ingredients and mix well. Refrigerate. Keeps several weeks in refrigerator.

Carol Ann Hardcastle

Cathedral of St. John the Baptist, located within the Historic District of Savannah, is the oldest Roman Catholic Church in Georgia.

Heavenly Salad Dressing or Vegetable Dip

⅓ cup chopped white onions
2 cups mayonnaise
½ cup minced parsley
2 cloves garlic, minced
2 teaspoons anchovy paste

1 cup sour cream
½ cup wine vinegar (without garlic)
2 teaspoons lemon juice
½ pound bleu cheese

Add ingredients to blender and blend on high for one minute. Refrigerate. Keeps several weeks.

Makes 3 pints   *Carol Ann Hardcastle*

The Best Poppy Seed Dressing

Passed from friend to friend

¾ cup sugar
⅓ cup vinegar
1 teaspoon salt
1 teaspoon dry mustard

1 tablespoon finely chopped onion
1 cup vegetable oil
1½ tablespoons poppy seeds

Place first four ingredients in food processor on medium speed. Slowly add remaining ingredients and process for 2 full minutes. Ready to serve. Good for fresh fruit or spinach salad.

Makes 2 cups   *Sandra Brown*
                                                      Ruth Ann Price

Dee Dee's Slaw Dressing

2 eggs
¾ cup sugar
2 tablespoons flour
1 teaspoon salt
½ teaspoon dry mustard

Black and red pepper to taste
½ stick butter
1 cup vinegar
Celery seed to taste

Beat eggs and set aside. Mix sugar and dry ingredients. Heat vinegar and butter until butter has melted. Add dry ingredients to eggs and slowly add vinegar. When well mixed, cook over medium heat stirring constantly until thick. Add celery seed. Store in jar in refrigerator. Mix 3 parts dressing with 1 part mayonnaise when mixing with shredded cabbage. Add a chopped apple for color and flavor.

Makes about 2 cups   *Ann Claiborne Christian*

J. T.'s Steak Salt

1 heaping tablespoon hickory smoked
   salt
1 heaping tablespoon charcoal salt

1 teaspoon garlic salt
1 8-ounce jar seasoned salt

Mix and store in airtight jar. Sprinkle on hamburgers or steak a few minutes before
cooking.

Ingrid Brunt

*The Owens-Thomas House Museum, located on Lafayette Square
in the Historic District of Savannah, 1816-1819.*

Capital City: BREADS

The Capital City

Atlanta has been aptly called the "Capital City of the New South." Staying true to her beginnings as a railroad town, Atlanta now serves as the transportation hub of the nation. The home of Coca-Cola, "Gone with the Wind," CNN, the Atlanta Braves, Super Bowl XXVII, and the 1996 Summer Olympics, Atlanta is an exciting metropolis that combines the charm of the past with the energy of the present, and the vision of the future.

Like her symbol the Phoenix, that mythical bird that rose from the ashes, Atlanta continues to soar to greater and greater heights. Her skyline has been resculpted with magnificent new architecture, while more and more of the handsome old buildings have been saved and restored.

*The regal **State Capitol**, built in 1889 of neoclassical design, is crowned with a dome sheeted in gold, brought by wagon trail from Dahlonega, the site of America's first major gold rush in 1828.*

Artists:
Margaret Bartholomew — Title Page
Bebe Davidson — "The Capital City"

Pain Perdu

Special treat for overnight guests

6 1½-inch thick slices of day old
    French bread, cut diagonally
2 eggs, beaten
2 cups half-and-half
¼ cup sugar
1 tablespoon grated lemon peel

½ teaspoon vanilla
¼ teaspoon salt
¼ teaspoon grated nutmeg
2 tablespoons butter
2 tablespoons oil
Powdered sugar

Arrange bread in 3 quart baking dish. Whisk remaining ingredients except butter and oil and pour over bread. Let soak 5 minutes. Turn slices over. Cover and refrigerate overnight.

Melt butter and oil in large skillet. (Additional butter and oil needed if using 2 skillets.) Over medium heat fry bread until golden and crusty, approximately 5 minutes per slice. Sprinkle with powdered sugar and serve with syrup.

Serves 6

Ingrid Brunt

The Georgian Hotel, originally opened in 1911, was a favorite lodging for visiting celebrities. It has recently been restored to its former grandeur.

Sticky Buns

1 25-ounce package of frozen roll
   dough in pieces
¼ to ½ cup chopped raisins
¼ to ½ cup chopped pecans
1 scant cup dark brown sugar

1 to 2 teaspoons cinnamon
¼ of a 3½-ounce box instant
   butterscotch pudding
¾ cup butter

Sprinkle pecans and raisins evenly over greased bundt pan. Sprinkle pieces of roll dough around bottom of pan. Sprinkle with pudding. Bring to boil the brown sugar, butter, and cinnamon and cook until syrupy. Pour mixture over dough. Cover pan with a plate and let rise overnight. Bake at 375 degrees for 20-30 minutes or until brown on top. Invert on plate after baking and separate using forks back to back.

Serves 10

Ann Martin

The Dorothy Chapman Fuqua Conservatory at the Atlanta Botanical Garden recreates environments ranging from an arid desert to a lush tropical jungle.

Barbara's Sticky Buns

1 can butterflake refrigerated biscuits
3 tablespoons margarine
⅓ cup brown sugar

¾ cup granola-type cereal
Pancake syrup

Melt margarine in round cake pan. Sprinkle brown sugar over margarine. Sprinkle cereal next. Separate biscuits and place in pan, turning each over before cooking. Sprinkle with more cereal and drizzle syrup over all. Bake at 450 degrees 10-12 minutes or until golden brown.

Serves 4-6   *Barbara Kanto*

Sourdough Pancakes

Old West prospectors carried "starter" in their saddlebags

Starter:
4 cups water
1 cup flour

1 package prepared dry yeast
4 tablespoons sugar

Night before:
2 cups flour

2 cups water

To make pancakes:
1 tablespoon baking powder
1 egg
½ teaspoon salt

1 tablespoon vegetable oil
1 tablespoon sugar
¼ cup milk

Starter: In quart jar combine flour, sugar, and yeast with enough water to make thin mixture. Keep at room temperature about a week. It may rise and overflow. Refrigerate after it finishes its reaction.

Night before: Add 2 cups flour to "starter" and enough water to make a thick soupy mixture. Leave at room temperature.

Pancakes: Stir mixture. Reserve 1 cup for "starter" and refrigerate for later use. To the batter add baking powder, egg, salt, oil, sugar. Add milk. Stir. Let sit 10 minutes. Cook on hot griddle or heavy skillet.

Serves 8   *Tina James*

Norwegian Pancakes "Crêpes"

Three generation favorite

1½ cups flour
1 tablespoon sugar
½ teaspoon baking powder
½ teaspoon salt
2 cups milk

2 medium eggs
½ teaspoon vanilla
2 tablespoons butter, melted
1 cup your favorite jelly, jam, or
    preserves

Combine dry ingredients. Add remaining ingredients. Mix until smooth. Heat crêpe pan or 10-inch tapered skillet. Brush lightly with butter or non-stick coating. Pour in ¼ cup batter and quickly tilt pan to spread batter evenly. Cook until lightly brown, about 1 minute. Turn and cook until brown on other side being careful not to over-cook. Place crêpe on dinner plate. Spoon preserves down center of crêpe. Roll to about 1½ inches wide. Crêpes may be made ahead and refrigerated or frozen, separating with waxed paper. When ready to serve return crêpes to room temperature before separating. Reheat in microwave.

Makes 8 crêpes   *Deb House*

German Apple Pancakes

A favorite at the lake for a late breakfast

8 large eggs
1 cup flour
2 tablespoons sugar
1 teaspoon baking powder
⅛ teaspoon salt
2 cups milk
4 tablespoons butter, melted
2 teaspoons vanilla

¼ teaspoon nutmeg
8 tablespoons butter
1⅓ cup sugar
1 teaspoon cinnamon
¼ teaspoon nutmeg
2 or 3 large Granny Smith apples,
    peeled, thinly sliced
2 10-inch iron skillets

Combine first 6 ingredients and blend until smooth. Add butter, vanilla and nutmeg. Let stand at room temperature 30 minutes or in refrigerator overnight. Divide butter and melt in 2 10-inch skillets. Brush up sides. Remove from heat. Combine sugar, cinnamon, and nutmeg. Sprinkle ⅓ cup mixture in each skillet. Divide apple slices and layer evenly. Sprinkle remaining sugar mixture over apples. Place skillet over medium heat until bubbles. Pour batter over apples and bake 15 minutes at 425 degrees. Reduce heat to 375 degrees for 10 minutes.

Serves 8   *Ingrid Brunt*

Texas Coffee Cake

Excellent for holiday brunch

2½ cups flour, sifted
2 cups light or dark brown sugar
½ teaspoon salt
⅔ cup butter or margarine
2 teaspoons baking powder
½ teaspoon soda

½ teaspoon ground cinnamon
½ teaspoon ground nutmeg
1 cup buttermilk or sour milk
2 eggs, beaten
1 cup pecans, chopped or halves

Mix first four ingredients until crumbly. Divide in half. Add next four ingredients to one half of crumb mixture. Mix well. Add eggs and milk. Mix well. Pour into greased and floured 9x12 inch pan. Top with reserved crumbs. Sprinkle with chopped pecans or lay on pecan halves. Bake at 375 degrees for 25-30 minutes. Cut into serving size pieces and serve warm.
Note: Substitute 1 tablespoon lemon juice or vinegar and sweet milk to make 1 cup sour milk. Stir and let stand 5 minutes before using.

Serves 12-15   *Katherine White*

Garpink's Biscuit Rolls

Given to us by Virginia grandmother

1 cup self-rising flour
½ teaspoon salt
 2 tablespoons shortening (1 guinea
   egg)

¼ teaspoon baking powder
¼ teaspoon baking soda
½ cup buttermilk

Combine flour, salt, and shortening. (Cut shortening into dry ingredients.) Combine baking powder and soda with buttermilk and stir until foamy. Pour milk mixture into flour mixture and form into a ball. Turn out on cloth or board and knead until smooth. Roll out thin and cut with cutter. Prick top of biscuit with fork. Bake at 325 degrees for 15-20 minutes until golden brown.

Makes 12-16 rolls   *Jeanne and Russell Smiley*

Easy Sour Cream Biscuits

1 cup margarine, melted
1 cup sour cream

2 cups self-rising flour

Combine margarine and sour cream. Add flour and mix thoroughly. Fill ungreased mini-muffin pans with heaping tablespoons of batter. Bake at 400 degrees 15 minutes. Cool biscuits for 3 minutes before removing from pan.

Makes 30 biscuits   *Peggy Dill*

Rosemary Biscuits

Good with tea or as an appetizer filled with turkey

2 cups sifted flour
1 teaspoon salt
3 teaspoons baking powder
⅓ cup sugar

6 tablespoons margarine
½ cup milk
¼ cup fresh rosemary leaves, finely
    chopped

Sift flour, salt, baking powder, and sugar together. Cut margarine into mixture. Add milk and mix to stiff dough. Add rosemary leaves. Mix well. Roll to thickness desired and cut with small biscuit cutter. Place on greased baking sheet. Bake at 425 degrees for 10 minutes or until golden.

Makes 1 dozen   *Ingrid Brunt*

"Doctored" Brown and Serve Rolls

You can't get much easier than this!!

¼ cup butter, softened
¼ cup mayonnaise

¼ cup Parmesan cheese
1 dozen brown and serve rolls

Mix butter, mayonnaise, and Parmesan cheese together in a small bowl. Frost the rolls on the top and sides with the mix. Bake on a cookie sheet at 350 degrees for 15 minutes until golden brown.

Makes 12 rolls   *Nancy Hurd*

The Phoenix, the mythical bird which rose from the ashes, is the symbol of Atlanta, here depicted in front of the Federal Reserve Bank.

Angel Biscuits

Great easy biscuit

2 cups self-rising flour

1 cup whipping cream or 1 cup half-and-half

Mix flour with cream until dough forms. Turn onto floured surface and knead briefly. Roll out on floured surface and cut with biscuit cutter. Bake at 400 degrees for 12 minutes.

Makes about 15 biscuits   *Jana Hill*

Orange Party Biscuits

2 tablespoons butter
2½ tablespoons flour
2 oranges, juiced
Grated rind of 2 oranges

Sugar to taste
Your favorite biscuit recipe using 3 cups of flour

In a double boiler, cook butter, flour, and juice of oranges until thick paste forms. Add sugar to suit taste or until it will spread well on biscuit dough. Remove from heat and cool slightly. Make biscuit dough using 3 cups of flour. Add orange rind. Roll dough to ¼ inch thickness. Spread with orange sauce. Roll jelly roll fashion. Cut with knife dipped in flour. Place on well-greased baking sheet. Bake at 450 degrees 12-15 minutes. Note: To facilitate cutting, chill rolled dough slightly.

Makes 18 biscuits   *Ingrid Brunt*

Monkey Bread

Nice to take to a new neighbor

4 cans refrigerated biscuits (10 biscuits per can)
2 cups sugar divided

2½ tablespoons cinnamon, divided
¾ cup pecans, ground fine
¾ cup butter, melted

Cut each biscuit into 4 pieces. Mix 1 cup sugar, 1 tablespoon cinnamon, and pecans. Roll each piece of biscuit in mixture. Place pieces in a large buttered tube pan. Mix remaining cup of sugar, cinnamon, and butter. Pour over biscuits in pan. Bake at 350 degrees 40-45 minutes. Let stand 5 minutes before turning onto cake plate. Do not slice, simply pull off a lump from the whole piece.

Serves 8-10   *Ginger Marks*

Easy Fresh Garlic Bread

1 1-pound loaf frozen ready dough	½ teaspoon parsley flakes
¼ cup butter, melted	¼ teaspoon oregano
2 cloves garlic, minced	½ teaspoon garlic powder
½ teaspoon dill	¼ cup Parmesan cheese

Thaw dough slightly at room temperature, about 20 minutes. Slice loaf into 12 pieces. Combine butter and remaining ingredients. Dip dough pieces in butter mixture and press back together to form loaf. Place in lightly greased loaf pan and let rise until doubled in size. Bake at 325 degrees for 30-35 minutes until golden brown. Remove from pan immediately. Serve hot.

Note: can be made night before or in the morning and then placed in refrigerator to rise slowly throughout the day.

Yields 12 slices   *Mary Williams*

The Academy of Medicine, designed by Philip Shutze and completed in 1942, was built as a home for the Medical Association of Atlanta. Now restored, it is one of Atlanta's favorite locations for weddings, parties, and chamber concerts.

Beer Bread

3 cups self-rising flour or 4 cups
   biscuit mix

3 tablespoons sugar
1 12-ounce bottle or can of beer

Combine biscuit mix and sugar. Add beer. Mix thoroughly. Spread in greased loaf pan. Bake at 375 degrees 45-60 minutes or until done. For rolls, fill muffin tins ⅔ full and bake at 400 degrees about 20 minutes.

Makes 1 loaf or 8-10 rolls
         Karen Haughey
         Anne Jordan

Persimmon Bread

2 cups persimmon purée
2½ cups flour
2 teaspoons soda
½ teaspoon salt
2 teaspoons allspice

2 teaspoons cinnamon
1½ cups butter or margarine
2 cups sugar
3 eggs
2 cups chopped pecans

Peel enough fresh ripe persimmons to yield 2 cups when puréed in blender. Sift flour, soda, salt, allspice, and cinnamon. Cream butter and sugar, add eggs and mix well. Gradually add dry ingredients to egg mixture. Add persimmon purée and pecans. Mix well. Pour into three small loaf pans which have been greased and lined with greased waxed paper. Bake at 325 degrees for 1 hour or until done. May also be baked in a tube pan or 2 large loaf pans.
Note: If persimmons are not available in your area substitute fresh peach purée for an equally delicious Peach Bread.

Makes 3 small loaves
         Sue Clark

Jenny's Own Garlic Bread

1 loaf Italian bread or 6 Italian rolls
6 tablespoons margarine or butter
4 garlic cloves, crushed

1 tablespoon olive oil
Parmesan cheese

Cut bread loaf or rolls in half. Spread margarine on bread halves. Mix garlic and oil and brush on bread. Sprinkle top with Parmesan cheese. Bake until tops are bubbly and browned lightly.

Serves 12
         Jenny Rymuza

Dilly Casserole Bread

1 cup creamed cottage cheese, heated
    to lukewarm
2 tablespoons sugar
1 tablespoon instant minced onion
1 tablespoon margarine
2 teaspoons dill seed

1 teaspoon salt
¼ teaspoon baking soda
1 egg
¼ cup warm water
1 package dry yeast
2 ¼ to 2½ cups sifted flour

Combine cottage cheese, sugar, onion, margarine, dill seed, salt, baking soda, and egg. Add water to dry yeast. Add to mixture. Gradually add flour, beating well. Dough will be very moist. Cover. Set in warm place to rise until doubled in size, about 60 minutes. Stir dough down and place in greased 1½ to 2 quart casserole dish. Let rise until doubled, about 30-40 minutes. Bake at 350 degrees for 40 minutes or until quite brown.

Serves 6-8   *Nancy Wolff*

1840's Tully Smith House

Pineapple Banana Bread

3 cups flour
1 teaspoon baking soda
1 teaspoon cinnamon
2 cups sugar
1 teaspoon salt
1½ cups oil
1 8-ounce can crushed pineapple with juice
1½ teaspoons vanilla
3 eggs
2 cups crushed bananas

Mix flour, baking soda, cinnamon, sugar, and salt by hand. Add oil, pineapple, vanilla, eggs, and bananas. Blend well. Pour into 2 greased loaf pans. Bake at 325 degrees for 1 hour and 10 minutes or until tests done.
Note: Should be mixed by hand.

Makes 2 loaves   *Marcia Steinfeldt*

"The Fabulous Fox," designed in a Neo Mideastern Eclectic style, was one of the largest movie palaces at the time of its opening in 1929. Completely restored, it is a National Historic Landmark.

Lemon-Glazed Banana Loaf

A brunch favorite

Cake:

½ cup butter

1¼ cups sugar

2 eggs, lightly beaten

1 teaspoon baking soda

4 tablespoons sour cream

1½ cups cake flour

¼ teaspoon salt, optional

1 cup mashed bananas (about 3)

1 teaspoon vanilla

½ cup chopped pecans

Icing:

Grated rind of 1 lemon

1 tablespoon lemon juice

1 tablespoon boiling water

1 cup confectioners sugar

Cake: Cream butter and sugar until fluffy. Add eggs. Dissolve baking soda in sour cream and add to mixture. Combine flour and salt and alternately add mashed bananas and dry ingredients to sugar and butter mixture. Blend thoroughly. Add vanilla and nuts. Pour into greased and floured loaf pan and bake at 350 degrees for 1 hour and 10 minutes or until tests done. Frost with lemon icing while cake is still warm to produce glaze.

Icing: Mix lemon rind, juice and water. Gradually add to sugar and whisk until smooth and thick.

Serves 15   *Karel Forrester*

Lemon Tea Bread

A sweet-tart treat

Lemony Glaze:

¼ cup lemon juice

½ cup sugar

Lemon Bread:

⅓ cup butter, melted	1 teaspoon baking powder
1 cup sugar	1 teaspoon salt
3 tablespoons lemon extract	½ cup milk
2 eggs	1½ tablespoons grated lemon peel
1½ cups flour	½ cup chopped pecans

Mix lemon juice and sugar and set aside. Cream butter, sugar, and lemon extract until fluffy. Add eggs, beating until blended. Sift flour, baking powder, and salt. Add flour and milk alternately to mixture. Stir after each addition until all is blended. Do not overmix. Fold in lemon peel and pecans. Pour batter into greased and floured loaf pan. Bake at 350 degrees one hour or until done. Remove from oven and immediately pour Lemony Glaze slowly over top. Let stand 15-20 minutes. Turn out on rack to cool.

Serves 15   *Sheryl Patwardhan*

Zucchini-Coconut-Pineapple Bread

A hearty, delicious bread/cake

3 eggs	3 cups unsifted flour
1 cup salad oil	2 teaspoons baking soda
2 cups sugar	1 teaspoon salt
2½ teaspoons vanilla	½ teaspoon baking powder
2 cups zucchini coarsely shredded	1½ teaspoons cinnamon
1 8-ounce can crushed pineapple, well drained	¾ teaspoon nutmeg
	1 cup chopped walnuts or pecans
1 cup coconut shredded	1 cup golden raisins

Beat eggs. Blend with oil, sugar, and vanilla. Beat until thick and foamy. Stir in zucchini, pineapple, and coconut. Set aside. Combine flour, baking soda, salt, baking powder, cinnamon, nutmeg, nuts, and raisins. Stir gently into mixture until just blended. Pour into 2 greased and floured loaf pans and bake at 350 degrees for 1 hour or until done. Cool in pans 10 minutes. Turn out on racks. Freezes well for several months.

Makes 2 loaves   *Jeanne Lipsitt*

Linda Bath's Cocktail Cheese Muffins

A Sewing Club favorite

¾ cup butter or margarine, melted
8 ounces sharp cheddar cheese, grated
2 tablespoons frozen chives

1 cup sour cream
2 cups self-rising flour

Mix cheese and butter in saucepan. Stir well. Cook over medium heat for 2 minutes. Add chives and sour cream. Stir well. Add flour and blend thoroughly. Fill ungreased small muffin tins two-thirds full. Bake at 375 degrees for 10-12 minutes, or until golden.

Makes 4-5 dozen

Mary Ann Marks

Druid Hills, the Dogwood Trail.

King and Prince Oatmeal Raisin Muffins

1¼ cups rolled oats
1¼ cups buttermilk
2 eggs
¾ cup brown sugar
½ cup melted butter, cooled

1 cup flour
1¼ teaspoons baking powder
½ teaspoon baking soda
½ cup raisins

Combine oats and buttermilk in bowl. Let stand one hour. Add eggs, sugar, and butter. Mix 30 seconds. Add combined dry ingredients and raisins. Mix on low speed until dry ingredients are moistened. Fill muffin tins half full and bake at 400 degrees for 15 or 20 minutes.

Makes 12 muffins

Jan Collins

Three Grain Muffins

Healthy and delicious

2 cups oatmeal (one minute type)
2 cups shredded wheat
2 cups all bran cereal
1 cup boiling water
1 cup oil
4 beaten eggs

1 quart buttermilk
1 pound box brown sugar
5 cups flour
5 teaspoons soda
1 teaspoon salt
Nuts and raisins, optional

Mix cereals in 5 quart bowl and pour in 1 cup boiling water. Add oil, eggs, buttermilk, and brown sugar. Add soda and salt to the flour and then add the flour mixture to the cereal mixture. Mix well. Store in refrigerator in plastic container. Use as needed. Add raisins and/or nuts when ready to bake, if desired. Mixture will keep 3 months in refrigerator. Fill greased muffin tins ⅔ full. Bake at 400 degrees for 12-15 minutes.

Glenda Bates

Aunt Mabel's Cornbread

1 cup margarine

2 small boxes cornbread mix (6 to 7 ounce size)

3 eggs, lightly beaten

1 16-ounce can creamed corn

8 ounces sour cream

2 teaspoons sugar, optional

Melt butter in a 9x13 inch dish. Mix remaining ingredients and pour in dish with margarine. Do not mix. Bake at 350 degrees for 25-30 minutes or until golden brown.

Serves 6-8   *Atchie Bryant*

Ansley Park with the IBM Tower and the High Museum in the background.

Armand's Mexican Cornbread

Low-fat, low-cholesterol - Great with soup!

3 tablespoons canola oil
1 egg white
1 cup skim milk
1 15-ounce can corn, drained

2 tablespoons jalapeño peppers,
   chopped
2 cups self-rising corn meal mix

Spray heavy iron skillet with low-fat corn oil cooking spray. Add canola oil to skillet and heat in oven until hot, about 5 minutes. Mix egg white, milk, drained corn, peppers, and cornmeal. Mix together. Pour in hot skillet with oil and bake until golden brown about 15 or 20 minutes at 425 degrees.
Note: You may increase peppers and also add 2 tablespoons chopped pimento.

Serves 4-6   *Armand A. DeLaPerriere, M.D.*

Grace's Cornbread Sticks

Low Cholesterol

2 tablespoons margarine
½ cup white cornmeal mix
2 tablespoons flour
1 tablespoon sugar

½ teaspoon salt
¼ teaspoon baking soda
1 egg white
½ cup buttermilk

Melt margarine in iron cornstick pan. Sift dry ingredients together. Add egg white and buttermilk. Stir with a fork until well mixed. Pour in margarine and stir. Spoon into cornstick pan. Bake at 450 degrees about 8-10 minutes or until brown on top.

Makes 7 cornsticks   *Grace Walden*

Chattahoochee Valley: DESSERTS

M. Bartholomew

The Chattahoochee Valley

Out of the hills of Habersham,
Down the Valleys of Hall,
I hurry amain to reach the plain,
Run the rapid and leap the fall.

"The Song of the Chattahoochee"
Sidney Lanier, 1877

The Chattahoochee, *an Indian word meaning "painted stone," is a river over 400 miles long originating in northeast Georgia. It tumbles down the Blue Ridge Mountains, slices through the heart of Atlanta, and meanders southwesterly across the state, forming a boundary between Georgia and Alabama and a small section of Florida.*

It is in this region that two former United States presidents, Franklin Delano Roosevelt and Jimmy Carter made their homes — one by choice and one by birth. The "Little White House" in Warm Springs is where President Roosevelt spent some of his happiest and most relaxing times. In the charming town of Plains, President Carter grew up and raised his own family.

Callaway Gardens, a nature lover's paradise, is one of the most visited spots in this area. Called perhaps the nation's finest example of ecological development, this 2,500 acre garden area boasts over 700 varieties of azaleas.

Artists:
Margaret Bartholomew — Title Page
Gloria Sampson — "The Chattahoochee Valley"

Raspberry Ribbon Brownies

A Different Kind of Brownie

Filling:

1 8 ounce softened cream cheese

⅓ cup sugar

1 egg

Bars:

4 ounces unsweetened chocolate

½ cup butter or margarine

2 cups sugar

1 teaspoon vanilla

5 large eggs

1 cup unsifted flour

½ teaspoon baking powder

½ teaspoon salt

¾ cup raspberry preserves

In a small bowl combine all filling ingredients; blend well. Set aside. In a large saucepan, melt chocolate and butter stirring constantly. Remove from heat. Cool slightly (about 15 minutes). Add sugar and vanilla. Stir well. Beat in eggs one at a time. Add flour, baking powder, and salt to chocolate mixture. Stir until blended. Pour ½ chocolate batter mixture into a greased and floured 9 x 13 inch pan. Drop filling by spoonsful and carefully spread. Spoon preserves over filling. Carefully spoon remaining chocolate batter over filling and preserves, spreading to edges of pan and smoothing top. Bake at 350 degrees until set (about 45 - 50 minutes). Test for doneness with toothpick. Cool. Cut into bars. Store in refrigerator.

3 - 4 dozen

Judy Hubrich

My Best Brownies

½ cup butter, melted

2 ounces unsweetened chocolate

1 cup sugar

½ teaspoon vanilla

2 large eggs

½ cup flour

Pinch of salt

½ cup chopped nuts

Line an 8 inch pan with foil and grease with butter. Combine butter with chocolate over low heat. Cool three minutes. Whisk in sugar and vanilla, then eggs one at a time. Add flour and salt. Stir until smooth. Stir in nuts. Bake at 350 degrees for 20-25 minutes on bottom rack of oven.

Jeanne Dille

Almond Cheesecake Brownies

Very Elegant

Cheese Mixture:
16 ounces cream cheese, softened
2 eggs

⅔ cups sugar
½ teaspoon almond extract

Chocolate Mixture:
4 1-ounce squares unsweetened
    chocolate
1 cup unsalted butter
4 eggs
2 cups sugar

1½ cups flour
1 teaspoon baking powder
1 teaspoon salt
Sliced almonds

Combine cheese mixture ingredients in a bowl. Mix until smooth. Set aside. Melt chocolate with butter in double boiler. Cool. Beat eggs and sugar. Add to chocolate mixture. Sift dry ingredients. Add to chocolate mixture blending well. Pour half of chocolate mixture into greased 9 x 13 inch pan. Spread cheese mixture on top. Cover with remaining chocolate mixture. Sprinkle with almonds. Bake at 350 degrees for 45 minutes. Cool. Refrigerate. Vanilla extract and pecans may be substituted for almond extract and almonds.

Susan Friedland

Chocolate Cream Cheese Brownies

First Layer:
½ cup butter
1 box chocolate cake mix

1 egg, beaten
1 cup chopped pecans

Second Layer:
8 ounces cream cheese, softened
1 16 ounce box powdered sugar

2 eggs

First Layer: Melt butter in a 9x13 inch pan. Sprinkle cake mix over butter. Add eggs and pecans. Stir ingredients together and pat down.

Second Layer: Cream cheese, sugar, and eggs. Spread over first layer. Bake at 350 degrees for 45 minutes. Cut while still warm.
Tester suggests drizzling melted chocolate over top in pattern.

24 to 36 bars   *Moira Brigman*

Best Brownies Ever

Icing tastes like Fudge!

Brownies:

1 cup margarine
6 tablespoons cocoa
2 cups sugar
4 eggs

2 cups flour
1 teaspoon vanilla
1 cup nuts

Icing:

½ cup margarine
3 tablespoons cocoa
1 box powdered sugar

6 tablespoons milk
1 teaspoon vanilla
1 cup nuts

Melt butter. Add cocoa and sugar. Stir well. Add eggs. Stir to blend. Add sifted flour and stir until mixed. Do not over mix. Stir in vanilla and nuts. Pour into lightly greased 9x13 inch dish and bake at 350 degrees for 25-30 minutes.

Icing: Melt butter and cocoa in saucepan. Stir in sugar and milk until icing is smooth. Add vanilla and nuts. Pour over hot brownies.

36 squares

Susie Martin

German Chocolate Brownies

50 light caramels, unwrapped
1 cup evaporated milk, divided in half
1 18.5 ounce package German chocolate cake mix (not pudding type)

¾ cup margarine
1 cup chopped nuts
1 cup chocolate chips

Combine caramels and ½ cup milk in top of double boiler. Cook over low heat until caramels melt. Combine cake mix, margarine, remaining ½ cup milk and nuts. Spread one half of cake mixture in a lightly greased 9x13 inch pan. Bake at 350 degrees for 6 minutes. Remove from oven. Sprinkle on chocolate chips. Spread caramel mixture over chips. Drop the remaining cake mixture by tiny spoonfuls over the caramel mixture. Bake 5 minutes. Remove from oven and spread to make a top layer. Return to oven and bake 13 minutes longer. Cool before cutting.

36 squares

Linda Karempelis
Bunkie Rivkin

"What's for Supper" Rocky Road Bars

½ cup margarine
1 ounce unsweetened chocolate
1 cup flour
1 cup sugar

1 teaspoon baking powder
1 teaspoon vanilla
2 eggs
½ cup chopped pecans

Filling:
8 ounces cream cheese
½ cup margarine
½ cup sugar
2 tablespoons flour
1 teaspoon vanilla

2 eggs
½ cup pecans
1 cup chocolate chips
2 cups miniature marshmallows

Icing:
¼ cup margarine
¼ cup milk
1 ounce unsweetened chocolate

3 cups powdered sugar
1 teaspoon vanilla

Melt margarine and chocolate in microwave. Combine flour, sugar, baking powder, vanilla, 2 eggs, and pecans. Add to melted chocolate mixture. Spread on bottom of greased 9x13 inch pan. Combine filling ingredients. Spread over chocolate base. Sprinkle with chocolate chips. Bake 35 minutes at 325 degrees. Sprinkle 2 cups marshmallows on this and leave in oven 5 more minutes. Mix together margarine, milk, and 1 ounce chocolate. Microwave 3 minutes. Pour over marshmallows while hot.

Makes 2 dozen squares

Kitty Beveridge

Chocolate-Peanut Butter Squares

1 pound powdered sugar
1 cup crunchy peanut butter
1 cup butter

1¼ cups graham cracker crumbs
6 ounces chocolate chips

Mix sugar, peanut butter, butter, and graham cracker crumbs. Press into 9x13-inch pan. Melt chocolate chips. Spread over top of mixture. Refrigerate.

3 dozen bars

Jan Collins

Lemon Bars

2¼ cups flour, divided
½ cup powdered sugar
1 cup margarine softened
4 eggs, beaten

1¾ cups sugar
⅓ cup lemon juice
½ teaspoon baking powder
Powdered sugar

Crust: Sift together 2 cups of flour and ½ cup powdered sugar. Cut in margarine until mixture clings together. Press into a 13x9 inch pan. Bake at 350 degrees for 25 minutes or until lightly browned.

Filling: Combine eggs, sugar, and lemon juice. Beat well. Sift together ¼ cup flour and baking powder. Stir into egg mixture. Pour over baked crust. Bake at 350 degrees for 25 to 30 minutes or until slightly brown. Sprinkle with powdered sugar. Cool. Cut into bars. Store in single layer, as they will stick together.

3 dozen bars

Myrtle Smith

Chocolate Chip Oatmeal Bars

Very Rich

1½ cups flour
1½ cups oatmeal (rolled oats)
1 cup brown sugar

½ teaspoon soda
¼ teaspoon salt
1 cup butter

Topping:
¾ cup caramel ice cream topping
3 tablespoons flour

1 cup semi-sweet chocolate chips
½ cup chopped walnuts or pecans

Combine first six ingredients to form a crumbly mixture. Press half into the bottom of a 9x13-inch pan. Bake for 10 minutes at 350 degrees. While baking, combine topping of caramel and flour. Set aside. Remove crust from oven and sprinkle with chopped nuts and chocolate chips. Pour caramel mixture over this and sprinkle with other half of crumbly mixture. Bake 15-20 minutes or until golden. Cool, cut into bars, and refrigerate.

Kim Schnell

Toffee Bars with Coconut and Almonds

Crust:
½ cup butter or margarine, softened
½ cup packed brown sugar

1 cup sifted flour

Topping:
2 eggs beaten
1 cup packed brown sugar
1 teaspoon vanilla
2 tablespoons flour
1 teaspoon baking powder

½ teaspoon salt
1 cup shredded coconut
1 cup cut up almonds or other nut of
    choice

Mix crust ingredients thoroughly. Press into bottom of ungreased 9x13 inch pan. Bake 10 minutes at 350 degrees.

Topping: Stir eggs into brown sugar and vanilla. Mix flour, baking powder, and salt and stir into egg mixture. Mix in coconut and nuts. Bake at 350 degrees 25 minutes until topping is golden brown. Cool slightly. Cut into bars.

2½ dozen bars   *Jane Taylor*

Crème de Menthe Chocolate Squares

Refreshing after-dinner treat

1¼ cups butter, divided
½ cup unsweetened cocoa
3½ cups sifted powdered sugar,
    divided
1 egg, beaten

1 teaspoon vanilla
2 cups graham cracker crumbs
⅓ cup green crème de menthe liqueur
1½ cups semi-sweet chocolate pieces

Bottom layer: Combine ½ cup butter and cocoa. Heat and stir until blended. Remove from heat and add ½ cup powdered sugar, egg, and vanilla. Stir in graham cracker crumbs. Mix well. Press into bottom of 9x13 inch pan lined with aluminum foil.

Middle layer: Melt ½ cup butter. Combine butter and crème de menthe at low speed, then beat in remaining 3 cups powdered sugar until smooth. Spread over chocolate layer. Chill 30 minutes.

Top layer: Combine remaining ¼ cup butter with chocolate pieces. Microwave until melted. Pour over middle layer. Chill 1-2 hours. Cut into 1x2 inch pieces. Store in refrigerator.

Makes 50 pieces   *Mary Marchuk*

Historic Bullard-Hart-Sampson House, Columbus, Georgia.

Spicy Raisin Squares

1 cup raisins
1 cup water
½ cup salad oil
1 cup sugar
1 egg, beaten
1¾ cups sifted flour
¼ teaspoon salt

1 teaspoon soda
1 teaspoon cinnamon
1 teaspoon nutmeg
1 teaspoon allspice
½ teaspoon ground cloves
½ cup broken nuts (optional)

Frosting:
1 cup powdered sugar

¼ cup milk

Bring to boil raisins and water. Remove from heat and stir in salad oil. Cool to lukewarm. Stir in remaining ingredients. Stir until smooth. Pour into greased 9x13 inch pan. Bake at 350 degrees for 20 minutes. Frost by drizzling blended powdered sugar and milk over warm cake. Cut in squares or bars.

36 bars

Dottie Ellis

Lemon Cream Squares

1 box lemon cake mix
½ cup butter or margarine
1 egg, room temperature
1 box powdered sugar

8 ounces cream cheese, softened
2 eggs
1 tablespoon vanilla extract or 2
   teaspoons lemon extract

Mix cake mix, margarine and egg and press into bottom of greased 9x13 inch pan. Set aside. Mix all other ingredients together for 5 minutes. Pour over cake mixture. Bake at 350 degrees for 40 minutes. Cool. Cut into small squares and sprinkle with additional powdered sugar.

24 bars

Sandra Burns
Nancy Steinichen

"Sunny" 1-2-3

Especially for those concerned with cholesterol and saturated fat

1 egg white, beaten stiff
¾ cup brown sugar, firmly packed

1 cup chopped walnuts

Gradually add brown sugar to beaten egg white. Fold in walnuts. Spray 12 inch round cookie sheet with non-stick coating. Drop cookie dough 1 inch apart, measured by a teaspoon. Bake at 250 degrees for 30 minutes. Let stand a few seconds before removing with spatula. Cool on cookie rack.

Serves 35   *Alice (Sunny) Washburn*

Chewy Molasses Cookies

These travel well and are moist, delicious, and nutritious

½ cup margarine
1⅓ cups brown sugar
2 eggs, beaten
6 tablespoons molasses
1¾ cups flour
1 teaspoon baking powder

1 teaspoon baking soda
1 teaspoon cinnamon
½ teaspoon salt
2 cups quick rolled oats
½ cup chopped walnuts or pecans
1 cup raisins

Cream together the sugar and margarine. Blend in eggs, then molasses. Combine flour, cinnamon, baking powder, baking soda, and salt; blend into molasses mixture. Add oats, raisins, and nuts and mix all together. Drop by rounded teaspoonsful onto greased cookie sheet. Bake 8 or 9 minutes at 375 degrees.

Makes 4 dozen   *Margaret Sherrill*

Pecan Puffs

1 cup margarine, softened
½ cup sugar
2 teaspoons vanilla extract

2 cups cake flour
2 cups finely chopped pecans

Cream margarine, sugar, and vanilla. Add flour and nuts. Mix well. Chill dough for 30 minutes. Shape dough into small balls a little larger than a marble. Place on greased cookie sheet. Bake at 350 degrees for 12 minutes. Remove from cookie sheet while hot and place on racks to cool.

Yield: 5 dozen   *Talitha Russell*

Fruit Cake Cookies

Even people who do not like fruit cake like these

¾ cup butter
1 cup sugar
2 eggs, beaten
1 teaspoon cinnamon
1 teaspoon nutmeg
1 teaspoon ground cloves
2 cups flour
1 pound dates, chopped

1 cup chopped red candied cherries
1 cup chopped candied pineapple
2 cups raisins
4 cups chopped pecans
½ cup boiling water
½ teaspoon soda
½ cup whiskey

Cream butter, sugar and eggs. Mix cinnamon, nutmeg, cloves, and flour. In large bowl mix dates, cherries, pineapple, raisins, and pecans. Sift flour and spices over fruit and nuts. Mix well. Add soda to boiling water and pour over mixture. Mix well. Add whiskey. Mix well. Drop by teaspoons onto greased cookie sheet. Bake at 350 degrees until lightly browned, about 15 minutes. When cool store in tin.

Yield: 8 dozen

Mary Ann Marks

The World's Best Cookie

1 cup margarine
1 cup sugar
1 cup light brown sugar
1 egg
1 cup vegetable oil
1 cup regular oats
1 cup crushed corn flakes

3½ cups flour
2 teaspoons vanilla
1 teaspoon salt
1 teaspoon baking soda
½ cup flaked coconut
½ cup sliced pecans

Cream margarine and sugars. Add egg and mix well. Add remaining ingredients one at a time as listed. Form into small balls about the size of walnuts. Flatten on ungreased cookie sheet. Bake at 325 degrees for 10-12 minutes. May be frozen.

Yield 8 dozen cookies

Connie Menendez
Janice Nicholson

Ambrosia Cookies

1 cup margarine, softened
1 cup brown sugar
1 cup sugar
2 eggs
1½ cups oatmeal
2 cups sifted flour
1 teaspoon vanilla
1 teaspoon baking powder

½ teaspoon soda
½ teaspoon salt
1 cup pecan pieces
1 cup coconut
1 cup raisins
6 ounces diced dates
Grated rind of 1 orange
Grated rind of 1 lemon

Mix all ingredients thoroughly. Roll into small balls. Drop onto greased cookie sheet. Bake at 375 degrees for 15 minutes.

Yield: 2-3 dozen cookies   *Jeanne Smiley*

Holly Cookies

The perfect Christmas Cookie

30 large marshmallows
½ cup margarine
2 teaspoons green food coloring

1 teaspoon vanilla
4½ cups cornflakes
Cinnamon candies

Melt marshmallows in margarine over low heat. Add food coloring and vanilla. Stir in cornflakes. Shape into small round wreaths and put red cinnamon candies on top for berries. Keep dry when storing.

Yield: about 2 dozen   *Jeanne Smiley*

"Haystacks"

Delicious and unusual combination

16 ounce package butterscotch
   morsels

One 6¾-ounce can salted peanuts
1 3-ounce can dry chow mein noodles

Place butterscotch morsels in top of double boiler. Heat over rapidly boiling water. When morsels begin to melt, empty peanuts into mixture. Stir well. Remove from heat. Pour in noodles. Stir well. Drop by spoonsful on waxed paper, foil, or buttered tray. Let sit overnight before serving

Virginia Logan

The $250.00 Cookie Recipe

Priceless

2 cups butter
2 cups sugar
2 cups brown sugar
4 eggs
2 teaspoons vanilla
4 cups flour
5 cups blended oatmeal (measure and
  mix in blender to a fine powder)

1 teaspoon salt
2 teaspoons baking powder
2 teaspoons baking soda
24 ounces chocolate chips
1 8-ounce Hershey bar, grated
3 cups chopped nuts

Cream butter and sugars. Add eggs and vanilla. Mix in flour, oatmeal, salt, baking powder, and baking soda. Add chips, candy, and nuts. Roll into balls and place two inches apart on a cookie sheet. Bake at 375 degrees for 6 minutes.

Yield: 9-10 dozen

Jan Collins
Joan Turcotte

Jean's Famous Oatmeal Cookies

4 cups flour
1 teaspoon cinnamon
1 teaspoon baking soda
1 teaspoon ground cloves
1½ cups margarine
1 cup sugar
2 cups brown sugar

2 teaspoons vanilla
1 cup buttermilk
1 cup molasses
4 cups oatmeal
2 cups coconut
1 15 ounce box golden raisins

Sift together flour, cinnamon, soda and cloves. Cream margarine, sugars, and vanilla. Add buttermilk and molasses to creamed mixture. Mix well. Add flour mixture. Add oatmeal, coconut and raisins. Drop by teaspoons onto greased cookie sheet. Bake at 350 degrees for 17 minutes.

Yield: 6 dozen

Kitty Beveridge

Sara's Linzer Hearts

A wonderful Valentine surprise

1½ cups sweet butter, softened
1¾ cups powdered sugar, divided
1 egg
2 cups unbleached flour, sifted

1 cup cornstarch
2 cups finely grated walnuts
½ cup raspberry preserves or other
   fruit of your choice

Cream butter and 1 cup sugar until light and fluffy. Add egg. Mix well. Sift together flour and cornstarch. Add to creamed mixture. Blend well. Mix in walnuts. Wrap dough in wax paper and chill 4 to 6 hours. Roll dough to ¼ inch thickness. Using a small heart-shaped cookie cutter cut cookies and place on an ungreased cookie sheet. Chill cookies on the sheet 45 minutes. Bake cookies at 325 degrees 10 to 15 minutes or until lightly brown. Cool cookies on rack. While they are still warm, spread half the cookies with raspberry preserves using ¼ teaspoon per cookie. Top each with one of the remaining cookies. Sift remaining sugar onto a plate. Press tops and bottoms of the cookies into the sugar to coat.

Makes 4 dozen   *Cindy Hardcastle*

*Visitors Center in the old train depot (site of Civil War
P.O.W. camp), Andersonville, Georgia.*

Killer Fudge

1⅓ cups sugar
1 7-ounce jar marshmallow cream
⅔ cup evaporated milk
¼ cup butter
¼ cup Kahlúa

¼ teaspoon salt
2 cups semi-sweet chocolate chips
1 cup milk chocolate chips
1 teaspoon vanilla

Combine first 6 ingredients in large saucepan. Bring to rapid boil and cook stirring constantly for 5 minutes. Remove from heat. Add chocolate chips. Stir until melted. Add vanilla. Stir. Pour into greased 8 inch square pan. Refrigerate until set.

About 16 large pieces   *Laurie Amerson*

Crème de Menthe Balls

Balls:
½ cup margarine, softened
1 box powdered sugar
⅓ cup crème de menthe

Few drops of peppermint extract
Toasted whole pecans

Chocolate sauce:
2 dark chocolate squares, semi-sweet
3 unsweetened chocolate squares
1 small square paraffin

1 tablespoon butter
1 teaspoon vanilla

Balls: Cream margarine and sugar. Add crème de menthe and peppermint. Refrigerate 15 minutes. Form mixture into balls. Press toasted whole pecan on each ball. Refrigerate on a cookie sheet lined with waxed paper. Dip balls into chocolate a few at a time.

Chocolate sauce: Make sauce by melting chocolates and paraffin in double boiler. Stir in butter and vanilla.
Note: Oil of peppermint may be substituted for peppermint extract.

30 to 50 balls   *Bunkie Rivkin*

Microwave Peanut Brittle

Nice gift for new neighbors

1 cup raw peanuts
1 cup sugar
½ cup white corn syrup
⅛ teaspoon salt

1 teaspoon margarine
1 teaspoon vanilla
1 teaspoon baking soda

Stir together the first 4 ingredients in a 2 quart pyrex casserole. Place in microwave. Cook on high 7 to 8 minutes, stirring after 4 minutes. Add margarine and vanilla. Stir well. Return to microwave. Cook 1 minute more. Add baking soda and gently stir until light and foamy. Pour and spread mixture quickly on buttered, flexible cookie sheet. Let cool 30 minutes. Break into small pieces.
Note: Do not change order of ingredients.

Anne Collier
Joyce Johnson

Chocolate Nut Crunch

An easy do-ahead dessert for a gift, buffet, or party

1 cup butter
1⅛ cups sugar
3 tablespoons water

1½ cups nuts, pecans or roasted
    walnuts
½ pound semisweet chocolate chips
¼ cup chopped nuts

Heat butter in a large heavy saucepan. Add sugar, then water. Cook rapidly, stirring constantly until mixture reaches hard-crack stage, 300 degrees. Add nuts. Turn candy quickly onto lightly oiled pizza pan. Spread to the sides, one nut deep. Sprinkle chocolate chips over top of the hot candy. When melted and shiny, spread chocolate evenly over top. Dust with chopped nuts. Break into pieces when cold. Stores well in tin.

Serves 10-12

Phyllis Abele

Date-Nut Log

Yum, Yum, Yum

4 cups sugar
1 cup milk
2 tablespoons butter

1 pound chopped dates
½ teaspoon vanilla
1 cup chopped pecans

Cook sugar, milk, and butter to a soft boil using candy thermometer. Add dates, cook 5 minutes longer. Remove from heat and add vanilla. Beat a few minutes. Add chopped nuts and continue to beat until thickened. Pour mixture onto a wet cloth about size of kitchen towel. Cool until able to handle. Roll into log about 3 or 4 inches in diameter. Cover again with damp cloth. Cool thoroughly. Cut into ½-inch sections. Store in air tight container.

Makes 2 logs or approximately 48 slices   *Anne Staley*

Bellevue, home of Senator Benjamin Harvey Hill, La Grange, Georgia, was built in 1853 in Greek Revival Style. Recently restored, it is on the National Register of Historic Places.

Royal Waldorf Pie

This pie is simply elegant!!! Simply, because it's easy;
elegant, as in Waldorf-Astoria, and elegant in taste.

3 egg whites
1 cup sugar
1 cup graham cracker crumbs
1 cup finely chopped pecans
½ pint whipping cream

4 tablespoons powdered sugar
1 teaspoon vanilla extract
Bittersweet chocolate (grated or
  shaved for garnish)

Beat egg whites until stiff. Gradually add sugar, then crumbs, then nuts. Pour into a 9 inch buttered pie plate. Bake at 300 degrees for 30 minutes. Refrigerate overnight. Before serving, whip cream, adding powdered sugar and vanilla gradually until stiff peaks form. Spread pie with cream. Top with chocolate shavings or shaved curls.

Serves 6-8   *Margaret Bartholomew*

"Dood's" Pumpkin Chiffon Pie

1 9 or 10 inch deep dish pie shell
1 envelope unflavored gelatin
½ teaspoon salt
½ teaspoon nutmeg
1 teaspoon cinnamon
¾ cup light brown sugar

3 eggs, separated
1½ cups pumpkin (1 15-ounce can
  pumpkin - not pumpkin pie
  mixture)
½ cup milk
¼ cup sugar

Bake pie shell according to package directions. Mix next 5 ingredients, egg yolks, pumpkin and milk in sauce pan. Mix well. Cook over medium heat, stirring constantly until gelatin is dissolved (about 10 minutes). Remove from heat and chill until mixture is slightly congealed. Beat egg whites until stiff, beating in sugar. Gently fold mixture into egg whites thoroughly. Pour into baked pie shell. Chill and serve.

Rhonda Zorn

Sweet Potato Pie

1½ cups mashed sweet potatoes
1¼ cups sugar
½ cup butter or margarine
¼ cup canned evaporated milk
3 eggs

1 teaspoon nutmeg
1 teaspoon vanilla
¾ teaspoon lemon extract
1 9 inch pie shell

Preheat oven to 350 degrees. Combine all ingredients except pie shell. After well blended, pour into unbaked pie shell. Bake for 50 to 55 minutes or until center is firm. If there is filling left over it can be baked in custard cups along with pie.

Serves 6 - 8   *Maureen Roshto*

*Plains Baptist Church, Plains, Georgia, home of former president Jimmy Carter,
who was baptized here and is an ordained deacon in the church.*

Crumb Top Apple Pie

9 inch deep dish pie crust
6-7 tart apples
⅔ cup sugar

1 teaspoon cinnamon
2 tablespoons butter

Crumb Topping:
½ cup butter, softened
½ cup brown sugar

1 cup flour

Pie: Peel apples and slice thinly. Place in 9 inch pie crust. Combine sugar and cinnamon and sprinkle over apples. Dot with butter.

Crumb Topping: Cream butter and brown sugar. Cut in flour. Mixture should be coarse. Cover apples. Press firmly. Bake at 400 degrees 50-60 minutes.
Variation: Substitute top crust for crumb topping. Prick top and bake.

Serves 12

Arlene Axelrod
Jeanie Eidex

My Mother's Chocolate Cream Pie

¾ cup evaporated milk
¾ cup water
1 cup sugar
½ cup cocoa
3 tablespoons flour
pinch of salt

3 egg yolks, beaten
1 teaspoon vanilla
1 tablespoon butter
1 frozen pie shell
3 egg whites
3 tablespoons sugar

Heat milk and water. Mix dry ingredients. Add milk and water and cook slowly, stirring, until mixture begins to thicken. Add beaten egg yolks, butter and vanilla. Pour into baked pie shell. Top with meringue.

Meringue: Beat egg whites until stiff. Add sugar and spread over filling all the way to crust. Brown top slightly, cool, then refrigerate.

Serves 6-8

Maryline Smith

Fresh Blueberry Cream Pie

Best made with Blueberries from South Georgia!

1 cup sour cream (or yogurt)
2 tablespoons flour
¾ cup sugar
1 teaspoon vanilla extract
¼ teaspoon salt
1 egg, beaten (or Egg Beater)
2½ cups fresh blueberries

1 unbaked 9 inch pastry shell
3 tablespoons flour
3 tablespoons butter or margarine,
   softened
3 tablespoons chopped pecans or
   walnuts

Combine first 6 ingredients. Beat at medium speed 5 minutes or until smooth. Fold in blueberries. Pour into pastry shell. Bake at 400 degrees for 25 minutes. Combine remaining ingredients, stirring well. Sprinkle over pie. Bake an additional 10 minutes. Chill before serving.

Serves 6

Tish Lanier

Butterscotch Pie

A Family Reunion Tradition

6 eggs, separated
1 cup brown sugar
½ cup sugar
6 tablespoons self-rising flour
1½ cups evaporated milk

1 cup milk
1½ teaspoons vanilla
⅓ cup margarine
1 graham cracker crumb crust
⅓ cup graham cracker crumbs

Beat egg yolks until light yellow. Add next five ingredients. Cook over medium high temperature until thick and firm. Remove from heat and add vanilla and margarine. Pour into crust. Then beat egg whites until stiff for meringue and place over filling. Sprinkle with graham cracker crumbs. Bake at 350 degrees 12-15 minutes until golden.

Serves 8

Willis Lanier, M.D.

Boston Cream Pie

Takes lots of pots and pans, but worth it!

Cake:
⅓ cup shortening	1¼ cups flour
1 cup sugar	1½ teaspoons baking powder
2 eggs	½ teaspoon salt
1 teaspoon vanilla	¾ cup milk

Custard Filling:
⅓ cup sugar	2 egg yolks
2 tablespoons cornstarch	1 tablespoon butter
1½ cups milk	1 teaspoon vanilla

Chocolate Glaze:
3 tablespoons water	1 cup powdered sugar
2 tablespoons butter	½ teaspoon vanilla
3 tablespoons cocoa	

Cake: Cream shortening, sugar, eggs, and vanilla until light and fluffy (3 to 4 minutes). Combine dry ingredients and add alternately with milk. Pour into greased 9 inch cake pan. Bake 30-35 minutes at 350 degrees. Cool, then slice into 2 layers. Spread Custard Filling on one layer, top with other. Ice with Chocolate Glaze.

Custard Filling: Combine sugar, cornstarch, milk and egg yolks. Cook and stir over medium heat until boiling. Cook 1 minute, then remove from heat; add butter and vanilla. Cool.

Chocolate Glaze: Combine water and butter. Bring to full boil; remove from heat and stir in cocoa, sugar, and vanilla. Beat until smooth. Pour over cake allowing it to drizzle down sides. Chill. Keep refrigerated.

Serves 8-10   *Allyce North*

Pogofenokee Chunklett Pie

¼ pound butter or margarine	2 eggs
1 square unsweetened chocolate	½ cup flour
1 cup sugar	½ cup chopped nuts, optional

Melt butter and chocolate together over low heat. Cool slightly. By hand beat in sugar and eggs. Stir in flour. Add nuts if desired. Pour into greased pie pan and bake at 325 degrees for 35 to 40 minutes. Serve warm or cold.

Sue Clark

Calypso Pie

1 16 ounce package Oreos, crushed
½ cup melted butter or margarine
½ gallon vanilla ice cream, softened
¼ cup butter
1½ squares unsweetened chocolate
⅔ cup sugar

Pinch of salt
⅔ cup evaporated milk
1 teaspoon vanilla
Whipped topping, optional
Chopped pecans, optional

Mix Oreos and ½ cup butter. Press into bottom of 9x13 inch pan. Spread ice cream over crust. Freeze. In double boiler blend ¼ cup butter and chocolate. Remove from heat. Stir in sugar, salt, and milk. Blend well. Cook and stir until thick (4-5 minutes). Add vanilla. Cool before spreading this on frozen ice cream. Freeze. May top with whipped topping and chopped pecans. A variation: Substitute a small jar of hotfudge sauce for sauce ingredients.

Serves 15

Jan Collins
Dorraine Smith
Cindy Souther

Citrus Delight

1 envelope plain gelatin
¾ cup orange juice, strained
⅓ cup lemon juice, strained
3 egg yolks, beaten lightly
4 tablespoons grated lemon rind
2 tablespoons grated orange rind
Dash salt

¾ cup sugar plus 2 tablespoons,
 divided
3 egg whites, stiffly beaten
Lemon snaps or similar cookie
1 cup mandarin orange sections
Toasted almonds
8 ounces whipping cream, whipped

Sprinkle gelatin over 2 tablespoons orange juice to soften. Combine remaining orange juice, lemon juice, egg yolks, rinds, salt, and one half of sugar. Cook over boiling water until thick and smooth. Remove from heat. Add gelatin, stirring gently until dissolved. Cool. Add remainder of sugar to stiffly beaten egg whites and fold into citrus mixture, mixing thoroughly but carefully. Line bottom and sides of glass pie plate with lemon snaps. Pour filling over cookies and chill thoroughly. Before serving, add whipped cream. Arrange sections of mandarin oranges attractively on top and sprinkle with almonds.

Serves 6-8

Sue Clark

Lemon Torte

Wonderful, wonderful

Bottom Crust:
2 tablespoons sugar
2 cups sifted flour

½ cup chopped pecans
1 cup butter or margarine

Filling:
1 tablespoon unflavored gelatin
½ cup cold water
8 eggs, separated, at room temperature
2 cups sugar, separated

½ cup lemon juice
Rind of 1 lemon
1 8-ounce carton whipped topping

Crust: Mix sugar, flour and pecans. Cut in butter. Spread in bottom of 9x13 inch pan. Bake in 350 degree oven until lightly browned, about 20 minutes. Cool.

Filling: Dissolve gelatin in water. Beat egg yolks. Add 1 cup sugar, lemon juice and rind. Cook until thickened in top of double boiler. Add dissolved gelatin. Beat egg whites until they form peaks, gradually adding 1 cup sugar. Fold in egg mixture. Pour over crust. Top with whipped topping. Refrigerate at least 3 hours before serving. Freezes well.

Serves 12-16   *Betsy Fowler*

Chocolate Fantasy

Easy and Elegant

1 box chocolate cake mix
2 3-ounce packages instant chocolate
    pudding mix

1 pint whipping cream
2 toffee-chocolate bars, crushed
2 to 4 tablespoons Kahlúa

Bake 2 9-inch round cakes according to package directions. Prepare 2 boxes of instant chocolate pudding according to package directions. Whip cream. Place one layer of cake on bottom of deep bowl or trifle dish. Pour 2 tablespoons Kahlúa on top. Allow to soak in. Spoon one-half pudding over cake. Then spread one-half whipped cream and sprinkle with one-half crushed candy. Repeat all layers. Refrigerate. Serve cold.

Serves 8   *Bunkie Rivkin*

Lemon Cheesecake Fluff

1 5-ounce can evaporated milk
1 3-ounce package lemon gelatin
1 cup boiling water
1 cup graham cracker crumbs, divided

8 ounces cream cheese, softened
1 cup sugar
1 can cherry, strawberry, or blueberry
   pie filling

Pour milk into large bowl. Chill in freezer until ice crystals form. Add water to gelatin and refrigerate until it just begins to set. Line bottom of 13x9 inch baking dish with ¾ cup graham crackers and set aside. Cream sugar with cream cheese and set aside. Whip chilled evaporated milk on high speed until it forms soft peaks (tips curl). Gradually add gelatin, beating until well mixed. Gently fold in cream cheese mixture. Turn into prepared dish. Top with remainder of crumbs and pie filling of your choice. Chill, covered, at least 8 hours.

Serves 10-12　　　　　　　　　　　　　　　　　　　　　　　　*Carole Crowder*

Pecan Praline Brownie Parfait

The ultimate

1 box Brownie mix
1 quart Pecan Praline Ice Cream
8 tablespoons praline liqueur

Whipped cream
½ cup chopped toasted pecans
8 tablespoons chocolate syrup

Make brownies according to directions. Cool completely. Crumble and layer in parfait glasses. Top with ice cream, then pecans, then ½ tablespoon liqueur. Repeat layers. Top with whipped cream. Sprinkle with pecans and 1 tablespoon chocolate syrup.

Serves 8　　　　　　　　　　　　　　　　　　　　　　　　　　*Paula Rymuza*

Fruity Ice Cream

Perfect complement to a cook-out

Juice of 3 oranges
Juice of 3 lemons
3 bananas, chopped
2 pints fresh strawberries, crushed
2 cups sugar

2 cups milk
4 eggs, beaten
½ pint whipping cream
1 pint half-and-half

Combine all ingredients. Mix well. Freeze in gallon ice cream churn.

Makes 1 gallon　　　　　　　　　　　　　　　　　　　　　*Courtenay Collins*

Scuppernong Ice Cream

4 cups scuppernong grape juice
1 quart whipping cream
2½ cups sugar (or more to taste)

Dash salt
1 tablespoon lemon juice

Combine all ingredients. Freeze in hand or electric churn.

Contributor's note: Since homemade ice cream loses some of its sweetness during churning process, it is necessary to have it slightly sweeter than tastes good before freezing. Also, ice cream will be creamier if churn is filled to a little less than recommended fill line.

Makes 1 gallon   *Sue Clark*

It Is Heaven

Or as close as you can get

1 pound package chocolate sandwich
   cookies, crushed
6 regular toffee-chocolate bars,
   crushed

1 pound can chocolate syrup
½ gallon vanilla ice cream, softened
½ gallon chocolate ice cream, softened
(Flavors are optional)

Mix cookies and candy. Place half of mixture in bottom of 10-inch springform pan. Pour half of chocolate syrup over mixture. Press vanilla ice cream on top. Sprinkle on remainder of cookie mixture. Pour remainder of syrup over this. Add chocolate ice cream and drizzle on remaining syrup. Freeze for 24 hours.

Serves 16   *Ingrid Brunt*

Custard Ice Cream

4 eggs, beaten
1 cup sugar
2 tablespoons flour
4 cups whole milk
2 teaspoons vanilla

Fresh fruit as desired
Milk
Sugar
Vanilla

Mix flour and sugar. Add milk and stir. Add beaten eggs and stir. Cook mixture over medium heat until thick. Add 2 teaspoons vanilla. Refrigerate overnight. When ready to freeze, add more milk (to "fill line" on freezer), sugar to taste, and perhaps a little more vanilla. Beat with a mixer. Add fruit if desired.

Serves 10-12   *Becky Smalley*

Tortoni

A great ending to an Italian dinner!

3 egg whites
¼ cup water
¾ cup sugar
Dash salt
¼ cup whole blanched almonds
1½ teaspoons almond extract

¼ teaspoon almond extract for cream
1½ cups heavy cream
12 maraschino cherries or candied cherries
Paper baking cups

Let egg whites warm to room temperature, about 1 hour. Mix water with sugar over low heat, stirring until dissolved. Boil, uncovered, without stirring, until the syrup spins a 2 inch thread when dropped into a glass of water (or 236 degrees on a candy thermometer). Beat whites at high speed with salt until stiff peaks form. Pour hot syrup in thin stream over whites. Beat constantly until very stiff peaks form. Refrigerate, covered, 30 minutes. Preheat oven to 350 degrees. Place blanched almonds on shallow baking pan; bake just until lightly toasted, 8-10 minutes. Chop almonds finely or grind in food processor. Turn into small bowl. Stir in 1½ teaspoons almond extract. Set aside. In medium bowl, beat cream with ¼ teaspoon almond extract and vanilla until quite stiff. Gently fold in egg white mixture until well combined. Spoon into paper-lined muffin pan. Sprinkle with almond mixture. Top with cherry. Cover with foil. Freeze until firm overnight. Can be made weeks ahead.

Serves 12-16   *JoAnn Crooms*

The Green Dessert

43 round buttery crackers
½ cup margarine, melted
2 boxes pistachio pudding (3½ ounce)
2 cups milk

6 cups vanilla ice cream, softened
1 9-ounce carton whipped topping
1 chocolate bar

Crush crackers, add margarine. Press into 9x13 inch pan. Bake 10 minutes at 350 degrees. Cool crust. Combine next 3 ingredients and pour over cooled crust. Top with whipped topping and shaved chocolate. Refrigerate.

Serves 8   *Jenny Grooms*

Chocolate Roulade

Light as a feather

6 ounces semi-sweet chocolate
3 tablespoons water
6 eggs, separated

1 cup sugar
Powdered sugar
½ pint whipping cream, whipped

Melt chocolate and water in saucepan. Cool slightly. Beat egg whites until they form peaks. Set aside. Beat yolks and sugar until creamy. Fold in chocolate, then egg whites. Oil a 12x20 inch shallow baking pan. Line with waxed paper, oil again and spray with cooking spray. Pour mixture into pan and bake at 350 degrees for 20 minutes or until toothpick comes out clean. Let cool in pan 4 to 6 hours. Refrigerate and cool 4 to 6 hours more. Spread a sheet of waxed paper big enough to hold roulade. Sprinkle heavily with powdered sugar. Turn roulade onto paper and spread with whipped cream. Roll up. The outside will crack somewhat. If this is objectionable, ice with more whipped cream. Variation: substitute 6 ounces chopped walnuts for chocolate. Spread slightly mashed bananas and strawberries before rolling up.

Serves 12-14   *Wilma Tillman*

*Trading post at early Indian crossing — oldest building
in Troup County, near LaGrange, Georgia*

Banana-Date-Nut Cake

Not too sweet - excellent for brunch or morning coffee

½ cup butter
1½ cups sugar
2 eggs
1½ cups mashed bananas
2 cups flour
1 teaspoon baking soda

1 teaspoon nutmeg
1 teaspoon cinnamon
1 teaspoon allspice
1 cup diced dates
1 cup raisins
1 cup broken pecans

Cream butter and sugar together; add eggs, one at a time while mixing. Crush bananas and beat until smooth. Add to the above mixture. Sift flour, add baking soda then add to mixture. Add spices, dates, raisins and pecans. Bake at 325 degrees in greased and floured bundt pan about 1 hour or until cake tests done. No icing needed.

Serves 20

Anne Staley

Festive Kentucky Bourbon Cake

Good with boiled custard or coffee

1 pint whiskey
1 pound red candied cherries cut in
    pieces or halves
½ pound golden raisins OR
½ pound chopped dates
1 pound shelled pecans

5 cups flour (sift before measuring)
¾ pound butter
1 cup brown sugar
1 pound sugar
6 eggs separated
2 teaspoons nutmeg

Soak cherries and raisins in whiskey, to cover, overnight. Mix nuts with small amount of flour and set aside. Cream butter and sugar until fluffy. Add beaten egg yolks and beat well. Add soaked fruit and remaining liquid and the flour to the butter mixture. Add nutmeg and baking powder. Beat egg whites and fold into mixture. Add the lightly floured pecans last. Bake in a large greased tube pan for 3 to 4 hours in a 250 degree oven. Watch baking time carefully.

To store: When thoroughly cooled place in tightly covered container. Stuff center with ½ apple to keep moist. Keep cool. Refrigerate if necessary.

Serves 15-20

Sue Ellis

Chocolate-Banana Cake

A moist 3 layer cake

2 ounces unsweetened chocolate
1 cup butter or margarine, softened
2¾ cups sugar
3 eggs
3 cups flour
2 teaspoons baking powder

¼ teaspoon baking soda
¼ teaspoon salt
1 cup mashed bananas
⅔ cup buttermilk
1 tablespoon vanilla extract
1 cup chopped pecans

Chocolate Frosting:
⅓ cup butter, softened
5 cups sifted powdered sugar
⅓ cup cocoa

¼ teaspoon salt
½ cup evaporated milk

Melt chocolate. Set aside to cool. Cream butter; gradually add sugar, beating well with an electric mixer. Add eggs, one at a time, beating well after each addition. Combine flour, baking powder, soda and salt; add to creamed mixture alternately with bananas, buttermilk, and melted chocolate, beginning and ending with flour mixture. Mix well after each addition. Stir in vanilla and pecans. Spoon batter into 3 greased and floured 9-inch round cake pans. Bake at 350 degrees for 30 minutes. Cool in pans 10 minutes; remove layers and let cool completely before frosting.

Chocolate Frosting: Combine butter, sugar, cocoa and salt in large mixing bowl. Beat at low speed of an electric mixer. Gradually add milk until frosting reaches desired consistency. Beat until smooth. Put between layers and frost cake.

Serves 25   *Annette Griffin*

Sherry Custard Cake

Delicious! So very light you don't feel guilty about having had dessert!

1 envelope plain gelatin
½ cup cold water
2 cups milk
4 egg yolks
1 cup sugar
2 tablespoons flour
Pinch salt

⅓ cup sherry wine
1 pint whipping cream, divided
4 egg whites, stiffly beaten
1 12-ounce angel food cake
Grated coconut and fresh strawberries
for garnish

Soften gelatin in cold water. Set aside. Combine milk, egg yolks, sugar, flour, and salt. Cook over low heat until thick, stirring constantly. Remove from heat. Add sherry. Dissolve softened gelatin in hot custard. Mix well. Cool thoroughly. Fold in ½ pint whipping cream and stiffly beaten egg whites. Break cake into small pieces. In 13x9 inch pan alternate layers of cake and custard. Cover and refrigerate overnight. One hour before serving whip remaining ½ pint cream. Flavor to taste with sherry and sugar and spread on top of cake. Sprinkle with coconut. Garnish with strawberries. Cut into squares and serve.

Serves 12   *Agnes Hattaway*

Carrot Cake

Rich, Rich, Rich

Cake:
2 cups flour
2 cups sugar
2 teaspoons cinnamon
2 teaspoons baking soda

1 teaspoon salt
1 cup vegetable oil
4 eggs
3 cups grated carrots

Frosting:
4 tablespoons margarine, softened
8 ounces cream cheese, softened
1 16 ounce box powdered sugar

2 tablespoons milk
1 teaspoon vanilla
1 cup chopped pecans

Cake: Mix dry ingredients. Add oil. Stir. Add eggs one at a time. Mix in carrots. Pour into greased round pans (3 8-inch or 2 9-inch) and bake at 350 degrees for 35 minutes.

Frosting: Cream margarine and cream cheese. Add sugar, milk, vanilla and mix well. Add pecans. Frost cooled cake.

Serves 15-20   *Ingrid Vega*

Company Cake

A Masterpiece

½ cup butter
½ cup sugar
4 egg yolks
4 tablespoons milk

¾ cup flour
1 teaspoon baking powder
1 teaspoon vanilla

Meringue:
4 egg whites
1 cup sugar

½ cup chopped pecans

Icing:
1 cup heavy cream, whipped,
    sweetened to taste

Cake: Cream butter and sugar. Add egg yolks, milk, flour, baking powder, and vanilla. Beat on regular speed until well blended. Divide batter evenly into 2 greased and floured 9-inch cake pans.

Meringue: Beat egg whites until stiff, gradually adding sugar. Spread over uncooked cake batter. Sprinkle with pecans. Bake at 350 degrees for 20-25 minutes, watching carefully so pecans don't burn. Turn out on cake rack, meringue side up, to cool. Wrap in plastic wrap until ready to assemble. This can be done a day ahead. To assemble, place one layer on plate, meringue side down. Spread with sweetened whipped cream. Top with other cake layer, meringue side up. Try adding fresh peaches or other fresh fruit to the whipped cream layer.

Serves 10-12   *Ann Claiborne Christian*

Lemon Nut Cake

Mildly tart and delicious

1 pound butter or ½ butter and ½
    margarine
2 cups sugar
6 eggs, whites beaten stiff
3 cups flour

1 pound white raisins
4 cups chopped pecans
1 teaspoon baking soda dissolved in 1
    tablespoon water
4 tablespoons lemon extract

Cream butter with sugar. Add beaten egg yolks. Mix flour with raisins and nuts. Add soda, floured nuts, raisins, and extract to mixture. Fold in egg whites. Pour into greased and floured angel food cake pan. Bake at 250 degrees for 2¾ hours.

Serves 15-18   *Ann Claiborne Christian*

Graham Cracker Cake

Easy, colorful, do-ahead dessert

1 pound graham crackers, crushed
1¼ cups melted margarine
2 cups sugar
5 unbeaten eggs
1 teaspoon baking powder

1 cup milk
1 cup chopped pecans
1 6 ounce can shredded coconut
2 tablespoons vanilla

Frosting:
1 16-ounce box powdered sugar
1 8-ounce can crushed pineapple with
    juice

½ cup melted margarine

Cake: Mix crushed crackers, margarine, sugar, eggs, milk, and baking powder in a large bowl. Stir until well mixed. Add pecans, coconut, and vanilla. Mix well. Bake in greased sheet cake pan at 325 degrees for 45 minutes, or until tests done.

Frosting: Mix ingredients together and spread over warm cake still in pan. You may bake cake day before serving and keep in refrigerator. Try decorating with red cherries.

Serves 24　　　　　　　　　　　　　　　　　　　　　　　*Jettie Sue Santos*

Grandma's Apple Cake

2 cups flour
1½ cups sugar
1 teaspoon baking soda
1 teaspoon salt
1 teaspoon cinnamon

3 eggs
⅔ cup vegetable oil
2 teaspoons almond extract
4 apples peeled and chopped

Mix flour, sugar, baking soda, salt, and cinnamon and set aside. Beat eggs well in separate bowl. Add oil and almond extract and blend together. Pour egg mixture into flour mixture and mix well. Add apples and stir. Pour mixture into ungreased tube pan. Bake at 350 degrees for 45 minutes or until top is brown and tests done. Cool cake in pan on rack. Remove after cake is cooled. You may sprinkle with powdered sugar. Try placing sliced almonds on top prior to baking. Also try Applejack as a substitute for almond extract.

Serves 10　　　　　　　　　　　　　　　　　　　　　　　*Beth Locandro*

Mother's Fruit Cake

½ pound butter
1 cup sugar
4 large eggs
1 cup self-rising flour
2 teaspoons vanilla flavoring
2 teaspoons cake spices

2 teaspoons almond flavoring
1 pound crystallized red cherries
½ pound crystallized white pineapple
½ pound crystallized green pineapple
3 pints pecans
¼ pound raisins

Cream butter and sugar. Add eggs one at a time and beat well. Add flour and spices. Beat well. Add fruit and nuts which have been cut up coarsely. Pour into a large greased pan and bake at 375 degrees for 15 minutes. Stir. Repeat this 2 times. After the third time, place mixture in greased and lined (brown paper bag) tube cake pan. Push cake down into pan and bake for 15 additional minutes. Let stand 15 minutes before turning out. Garnish with pecans and/or cherries.

Serves 20   *Sandra Burns*

Scrumptious Texas Chocolate Sheet Cake

Cake:

2 cups unsifted flour
2 cups sugar
1 cup margarine
5 tablespoons unsweetened cocoa
1 cup water

2 eggs, lightly beaten
1 teaspoon baking soda
½ cup buttermilk
1 teaspoon vanilla

Icing:

½ cup margarine
3 tablespoons unsweetened cocoa
6 tablespoons milk

1 pound box powdered sugar
1 cup chopped pecans

Mix together flour and sugar. Bring to boil the margarine, cocoa, and water. Pour over flour and sugar mixture, blending well. Stir soda into buttermilk. Add eggs and vanilla. Mix well. Pour buttermilk mixture over flour mixture and stir until well blended. Pour batter into greased and lightly floured 10x15 inch jelly roll pan. Bake at 400 degrees for 20-25 minutes.

Icing: While cake is cooking, heat to boiling margarine, cocoa and milk. Add sugar and pecans. Mix well. Pour hot frosting over hot cake. Cool and cut into squares.

Serves lots!   *Kris Jarrell*
                                                                                             Alice Sanders

Esther's Crumb Cake

A bridge dessert

1 cup sugar
2 eggs
½ cup bread crumbs
1 cup chopped dates

1 cup chopped pecans
1 teaspoon vanilla
Pinch of salt

Beat eggs. Add sugar and remaining ingredients. Mix well. Turn into buttered glass pie pan. Bake at 200 degrees for 40 minutes. Increase heat to 250 degrees and continue to bake until golden brown. Serve warm with dollop of whipped cream or scoop of vanilla ice cream.

Serves 6

Florence Hornsby

Day Butterfly Center, Callaway Gardens, Pine Mountain, Georgia, is the largest glass conservatory in North America and houses over 1,000 butterflies. This dream-become-reality of philanthropist Deen Day Smith is a memorial to Cecil B. Day and a gift to nature lovers everywhere.

Spice Cake

A nice cake to have on hand for any occasion

2 cups self-rising flour
2 cups sugar
1 teaspoon cinnamon
1 teaspoon nutmeg
1 teaspoon allspice

1 cup coarsely chopped pecans
1 cup vegetable oil
2 small (4.5 ounce) jars baby food
  prunes
3 slightly beaten eggs

Sift first five ingredients together in large mixing bowl. Add nuts. Combine oil, eggs, and prunes; mix well. Add to dry ingredients and mix until blended. Do not over mix. Pour into greased and floured 10-inch tube pan. Bake at 350 degrees for 55-60 minutes. Cool. Store in refrigerator.

Serves 10-12   *Margaret Bartholomew*

Dried Apple Cake

A nice alternative to Fruit Cake

Boiling water
½ pound dried apples
2 cups cane syrup
½ pound butter
1 cup sugar
3 eggs

3 cups flour
1 teaspoon ground cloves
1 teaspoon ground cinnamon
1 teaspoon ground allspice
1 pound raisins
1 pound pecans, cut up

Chop dried apples and soak for 1 hour in enough boiling water to cover. Drain off water. Add 2 cups cane syrup. Cook until tender, about 15 minutes. Cream butter and add sugar. Mix spices with flour and alternately add flour and eggs to creamed mixture. Add apples and syrup, raisins and pecans. Pour into tube pan lined with waxed paper. Bake at 250 degrees for 3 hours. Begin testing the cake with a tooth pick for doneness after 2½ hours baking time. Cool completely before removing from pan. Wrap with foil or cheese cloth. Store in cake tin. Serve with dollop of whipped cream. Best served second or third day.

Serves 16   *Barbara Tippins*

The Friendly Family Chocolate Cake

Especially good with raspberry jam spread between layers

2⅔ cups sifted flour
2 teaspoons baking powder
2 teaspoons baking soda
¼ teaspoon salt
⅔ cup margarine
2 cups sugar

2 eggs
2 teaspoons vanilla
4 squares unsweetened chocolate,
   melted
2 cups boiling water

Mix first four ingredients. In large bowl, beat next four ingredients until light and fluffy. Add dry ingredients. Mix well. Stir in chocolate. Slowly add boiling water. Mix well. Pour into 2 greased square or round cake pans. Bake at 350 degrees for 30 minutes. Cool on racks 10 minutes. Turn out. Cool well before frosting with a chocolate butter frosting.

Serves 16   *Rita Friendly Kaufman*

Double Chocolate Cake

Delicious, rich cake

1 bar German chocolate, melted or
   grated
1 box yellow cake mix
1 3½ ounce box instant vanilla
   pudding
½ cup water

4 eggs
½ cup oil
1 8-ounce carton sour cream
6 ounce package chocolate chips
1 cup chopped nuts, optional

Mix chocolate with cake mix. Add all other ingredients. Mix well. Fold in chocolate chips. Bake in bundt or tube pan at 350 degrees for 50 minutes or until it tests done.

Yield: 24 servings   *Anita Eidex*

Frozen Black Forest Cake

Frozen version of an old favorite

1 box dark chocolate cake mix
¼ cup Kirschwasser (cherry brandy)
1 pint whipping cream
½ cup powdered sugar

1 teaspoon vanilla extract
2 quarts black cherry ice cream
Shaved chocolate
Maraschino cherries

Make cake according to package directions. Cool. Slice both cake layers in half, making four layers. With a large fork make indentations on all four layers. Sprinkle with liqueur. Whip cream, adding sugar after cream begins to thicken. Add vanilla. Place one cake layer on serving dish. Spread with ice cream. Add next cake layer. Continue in this manner ending with cake layer on top. Frost sides and top with whipped cream. Garnish top with cherries. Garnish sides with shaved chocolate. Freeze. Remove from freezer 10-15 minutes before serving.

Serves 14-16 *Paula Rymuza*

Peanut Butter Pudding Cake

Delicious topped with French Vanilla ice cream

1 cup flour
1¼ cups brown sugar, packed
2 teaspoons baking powder
1½ teaspoons salt
½ cup milk

⅓ cup chunky style peanut butter
2 tablespoons cooking oil
1 teaspoon vanilla
1½ cups hot tap water

Mix flour, ¾ cup brown sugar, baking powder, and salt. Add milk, peanut butter, oil, and vanilla. Mix on medium speed 3 minutes. Spread into greased 8x8 inch baking dish. Sprinkle remaining ½ cup brown sugar over top. Carefully pour hot water over top. Bake at 350 degrees for 45 minutes. Serve warm. Can reheat in microwave.

Serves 12 *Deb House*

Chocolate Pound Cake

Good plain, with fresh fruit, or with ice cream

1 cup butter
½ cup shortening
3 cups sugar
5 eggs
3 cups cake flour

½ teaspoon baking powder
½ cup cocoa
¼ teaspoon salt
1¼ cups milk
1 tablespoon vanilla extract

Cream butter and shortening, add sugar and beat until light. Add eggs, one at a time, beating after each addition. Sift flour, baking powder, cocoa, and salt. Add dry ingredients alternately with milk. Add vanilla before last flour. Bake in a greased and floured tube pan 1 hour and 15 minutes at 325 degrees. After cooling, cake may be dusted with confectioner's sugar or a chocolate glaze. Tester suggests serving with vanilla yogurt and raspberry sauce.

Serves 20-25

Eyleen Mitchell
Lucy Skinner

Martha's Cream Cheese Pound Cake

A superb, never-fail dessert

1½ cups butter
3 cups sugar
1 8 ounce package cream cheese, softened

1 tablespoon vanilla extract
6 eggs
1 envelope dry whipped topping mix
3 cups sifted cake flour

Cream butter, sugar, and cream cheese until smooth. Add vanilla. Add eggs one at a time, beating after each. Continue beating batter at a moderate speed while gradually adding dry whipped topping mix and cake flour. Pour mixture into a greased bundt or springform cake pan. Bake at 325 degrees on center rack in oven for 1½ hours. Try serving with puréed fruit on top.

Serves 15

Martha Schwartz

Peach Pound Cake

Unusual texture

1 cup margarine, softened
3 cups sugar
6 eggs
3 cups flour
¼ teaspoon baking soda

¼ teaspoon salt
½ cup sour cream
2 cups peeled, chopped fresh peaches
1 teaspoon vanilla extract
1 teaspoon almond extract

Cream together margarine and sugar until light and fluffy. Add eggs, one at a time, beating well after each addition. Combine flour, soda, and salt in a separate bowl. Mix together sour cream and chopped peaches. Fold dry ingredients into creamed mixture alternately with sour cream and peaches, beginning and ending with dry ingredients. Stir in vanilla and almond extracts. Pour batter into greased and floured 10-inch tube pan and bake at 325 degrees 75-80 minutes or until cake tests done.

Serves 20   *Barbara Meehan*

Rainbow's Cream Cheese Pound Cake

A special cake for a special occasion

8 ounces cream cheese, softened
1½ cups margarine or butter, softened
3 cups sugar
½ teaspoon salt
2 teaspoons vanilla-butternut flavor
   (if margarine used) OR

1 teaspoon vanilla extract (if butter
   used)
6 eggs
3 cups flour
2½ cups chopped pecans, divided

Cream butter and cream cheese. Add sugar, salt, and flavoring. Add eggs alternating with the flour. Grease bundt pan. Sprinkle bottom of pan with chopped pecans. Add 2 cups chopped pecans to batter. Bake at 325 degrees for about 1½ hours. Remove from pan immediately.

Serves 16   *Susan Daus*

A True Pound Cake

A bride's dream come true - an easy, never fail homemade pound cake

1 pound butter
1 pound box powdered sugar
1 pound eggs (6 extra large)

2 tablespoons vanilla extract
1 tablespoon almond extract
1 pound flour

Have everything room temperature. Cream butter and sugar (save box). Add eggs, one at a time. Add vanilla and almond extracts. Fill empty sugar box with unsifted flour. Gradually add to creamed mixture. Mix well. Pour into well buttered and floured 10-inch tube cake pan. Bake at 325 degrees for 1 hour and 15 minutes.

Serves 20   *Pat Tanner*

Fresh Coconut Pound Cake

1 cup butter, softened
3 cups sugar
6 eggs
3 cups flour
¼ teaspoon baking soda

8 ounces sour cream
1 cup fresh (or frozen, thawed)
   coconut
1 teaspoon vanilla extract
1 teaspoon coconut extract

Icing:
½ cup vegetable shortening
1 pound box powdered sugar
¼ cup milk
⅛ teaspoon salt

1 teaspoon vanilla
½ cup grated coconut for top of cake,
   if desired

Cream together butter and sugar until light and fluffy. Add eggs, one at a time, beating well after each addition. Sift flour, soda, and salt together to mix well. Add to creamed mixture alternately with sour cream, beginning and ending with flour mixture. Fold in coconut and flavorings. Pour batter into a greased and lightly floured 10 inch tube pan. Bake at 350 degrees for 1 hour and 20 minutes or until a wooden pick inserted in the center comes out clean. Cool in pan for 10 or 15 minutes; remove from pan and cool completely before icing or cutting.

Icing: Combine all ingredients in a large bowl and mix at high speed until fluffy. Frost top and sides of cake, sprinkling a little coconut on top of cake, or place cake on serving plate and sift powdered sugar over cake.

Serves 16   *Jeanette Steed*

Chocolate Chip Cheesecake

Moist and creamy and not for dieters!

1½ cups finely crushed chocolate
    sandwich cookies (18 cookies)
¼ cup butter, softened
24 ounces cream cheese
1 14-ounce can sweetened condensed
    milk

3 eggs
2 teaspoons vanilla
1 cup mini chocolate chips, divided
1 teaspoon flour

Combine crumbs and butter. Pat firmly on bottom of 9 inch springform pan. In large bowl, beat cream cheese until fluffy. Add condensed milk. Beat until smooth. Add eggs and vanilla. Mix well. Combine ½ cup chips with flour to coat. Stir into cheese mixture. Pour onto crust. Sprinkle remaining chips evenly over top. Bake at 300 degrees for 1 hour or until cake springs back when lightly touched. Cool to room temperature. Chill. Remove sides of pan. Garnish as desired. Refrigerate leftovers.

16 slices   *Jane Schwartz*

Supreme Cheesecake

2 cups graham cracker crumbs
1 teaspoon cinnamon
¼ cup sugar
½ cup butter, melted
36 ounces cream cheese, softened
1 tablespoon lemon juice

1¼ cups sugar
4 eggs
2 cups sour cream
4 tablespoons sugar
1 teaspoon vanilla

Grease 10 inch springform pan. Mix graham crumbs, cinnamon, ¼ cup sugar, and melted butter. Press firmly into pan. Blend cream cheese with lemon juice. Add 1¼ cups sugar and eggs, 1 at a time. Beat well 1 to 2 minutes. Pour into pan on top of crust and bake at 375 degrees for 25 minutes. Remove cake and turn oven to 450 degrees. Blend sour cream, sugar and vanilla. Pour on top of cake. Return to 450 degree oven and bake 12-15 minutes. Remove. Cool. Refrigerate 12 hours. Garnish with chocolate shavings or fresh fruit.

Serves 10-12   *Pam Woodward*

Strawberry Kiwi Cheesecake

14 tablespoons butter, softened and divided
1⅓ cups crushed coconut bar cookies
⅓ cup flaked coconut, finely chopped
1 16-ounce container ricotta cheese
2 8-ounce packages cream cheese, softened
1 cup sugar
4 eggs

6 tablespoons flour
1 tablespoon lemon juice
1 teaspoon vanilla
2 cups sour cream
½ cup apple jelly
3 kiwi fruit, sliced into ¼ inch slices
1 pint strawberries, sliced into ¼ inch slices

Crust: In a small saucepan, melt 6 tablespoons butter. Stir in cookies and coconut until well mixed. Press into sides and base of 9 inch springform pan. Bake 10 minutes. Cool on wire rack.

Filling: In a large bowl with a mixer at medium speed, beat ricotta, cream cheese and remaining butter until well blended. Beat in sugar until light and fluffy. Beat in eggs, one at a time, beating well after each addition. Blend in flour, lemon juice, and vanilla. Stir in sour cream. Pour over crust. Bake at 350 degrees for 1 hour or until slightly set in center. Turn off oven. Cool in oven with door open for one hour. Cool completely on wire rack. Refrigerate several hours or overnight. One or two hours before serving, slice fruit. Arrange kiwi slices around perimeter of cake with slices overlapping. Arrange strawberry slices in a similar manner inside kiwi circle. Melt apple jelly. Drizzle over fruit on top of cheesecake. Refrigerate at least an hour.

Serves 12

Delphine DeMauro

Pistachio Nut Cheesecake

Delicious and visually appealing

Crust:
2 cups flour
3 teaspoons sugar

3 teaspoons white vinegar
½ pound unsalted butter

Filling:
1 pound cream cheese, softened
1¾ cups sugar
6 eggs
1½ cups ground pistachio nuts

1 teaspoon vanilla
1 teaspoon almond extract
1 teaspoon lemon juice

Topping:
1 cup sour cream
¼ cup sugar

chopped pistachio nuts for garnish

Crust: Mix crust ingredients and press into a well buttered springform pan.

Filling: Cream cheese, sugar, eggs, and nuts. Add vanilla, almond extract, and lemon juice. Pour into crust. Bake at 350 degrees for 1 hour.

Topping. Mix sour cream and sugar and spread over hot cheesecake. Sprinkle with chopped pistachios. Refrigerate at least 4 hours.
Note: Pistachios can be chopped in a food processor.

Serves 16   *Kim Schnell*

Westville Handicrafts Village, Lumpkin, Georgia —
a living history village where its always 1850.

Chocolate Cheesecake with Kahlúa

Yummy spectacular make-ahead dessert

1½ cups chocolate wafer crumbs
¼ cup butter, softened
1 tablespoon sugar
1½ cups semisweet chocolate chips
¼ cup Kahlúa
2 tablespoons butter

16 ounces cream cheese, softened
2 large eggs
⅓ cup sugar
¼ teaspoon salt
1 cup sour cream

Combine chocolate crumbs, butter, and sugar. Press firmly in the bottom of a 10-inch springform pan. Set aside. Melt chocolate with Kahlúa and butter in microwave. Stir until smooth. Set aside. In large bowl cream cheese. Add eggs, sugar, salt, and sour cream. Beat until smooth. Gradually blend in chocolate mixture. Turn into crust. Bake at 350 degrees 40-45 minutes until barely set in center. Remove from oven and let stand at room temperature for 1 hour. Refrigerate several hours. Garnish with whipped cream flavored with Kahlúa and fresh raspberries or strawberries.

Serves 10-12   *Allyce North*

German Chocolate Cheesecake

Sinfully delicious

1 8½ ounce package chocolate wafers crushed

6 tablespoons butter or margarine, melted

3 8-ounce packages cream cheese, softened

1¼ cups sugar

3 tablespoons cake flour

¼ teaspoon salt

4 eggs

1 4 ounce package melted sweet baking chocolate

¼ cup evaporated milk

1 teaspoon vanilla extract

Topping:

2 teaspoons cornstarch

¼ cup sugar

⅔ cup evaporated milk

¼ cup melted butter or margarine

¾ cup chopped pecans

¾ cup flaked coconut

1 teaspoon vanilla extract

Combine wafer crumbs and butter, mixing well. Press into bottom and 1¾ inches up sides of a 9-inch springform pan. Set aside. Beat cream cheese until light and fluffy. Gradually add sugar, flour, and salt, mixing well. Add eggs, one at a time, beating well after each addition. Add chocolate, milk, and vanilla; mix well. Spoon into prepared crust. Bake at 325 degrees for 1 hour. Remove from oven; cool 15 minutes. Loosen sides of cheesecake from pan with spatula. Cool 30 minutes. Remove sides of pan.

Topping: Combine cornstarch and sugar in a saucepan. Gradually add milk and butter. Cook over medium heat, stirring constantly, until mixture thickens and comes to a boil. Boil 1 minute, stirring constantly. Remove from heat; stir in pecans, coconut, and vanilla. Cool. Spread topping on cheesecake leaving about an inch of cheesecake showing around outside edge. Cover and chill 8 hours. Garnish with toasted coconut and pecan halves around edge.

Serves 10-12   *Jan Rhodes*

Crema Caramella

Excellent light dessert

2 cups sugar, divided
½ cup water
1 quart milk

8 large eggs
1 teaspoon vanilla
Pinch of salt

In a heavy saucepan over moderate heat, stir together 1 cup sugar and water until sugar dissolves. Continue cooking over moderate heat, without stirring until golden brown. Pour the syrup into warm round 10x2 inch cake pan. Tilt to coat bottom and sides. Cool pan for 30 minutes. Heat milk until lukewarm. In large bowl beat until blended the eggs, remaining 1 cup sugar, vanilla, salt, and one cup lukewarm milk. Add remaining milk and beat until blended. Strain into prepared pan. Place pan in another larger pan with enough water to come up as high as the custard mixture. (Water bath). Bake in a 350 degree oven until knife inserted near the center comes out clean, about 50 minutes. Cool. Cover and chill. Place a large shallow serving plate upside down over the flan and invert. When the pan is removed there will be a generous amount of syrup. Serve chilled.

Serves 12

Julie Davies
Noula Kokenes

Interior of Plains Baptist Church, Plains, Georgia

Mocha Brûlée

This is divine!

Caramel:
⅔ cup sugar

3 tablespoons water

Custard:
2 cups half-and-half
¼ cup sugar
2½ teaspoons instant coffee granules
4 ounces imported milk chocolate

3 large egg yolks
1 large egg
1 teaspoon almond extract

Ganache:
1½ teaspoons instant coffee granules
4 ounces imported milk chocolate

2 tablespoons cream

Caramel: Place 6 ½-cup ramekins in baking pan and warm slightly. Place sugar and water in heavy saucepan over low heat until sugar dissolves. Increase heat to medium high and boil, without stirring until mixture turns golden brown, about 9 minutes. Immediately divide caramel between the ramekins, tilting to coat bottoms.

Custard: Place half-and-half, sugar, coffee granules, and milk chocolate in a pan on low heat. Stir until chocolate is melted. Mix eggs and almond extract in small bowl. Remove chocolate mixture from heat and whisk in egg mixture. Pour custard mixture into ramekins. Cover each with foil and place in baking pan. Bake in water bath at 325 degrees 35-40 minutes. Remove from bath, uncover and cool completely. Refrigerate about 4 hours or over night.

Ganache: Melt chocolate, cream and coffee granules over low heat. Spread ganache on top of custards. Refrigerate at least 30 minutes or over night. To serve loosen edges of custard with sharp knife. Invert onto dessert plates. Garnish with whole sweet strawberries.

Serves 6   *Kate Zoercer*

Flan

Very popular in Cuba

1 cup sugar
8 ounces cream cheese, softened
4 eggs and 2 yolks
1 14-ounce can condensed milk
1 5-ounce can evaporated milk

3 cups milk
3 tablespoons sugar
1 teaspoon vanilla
¼ teaspoon cinnamon

Melt sugar in heavy skillet over low heat, stirring constantly until sugar turns light brown . Immediately pour into 2 quart round pan which has been kept warm in the oven. Set aside. Blend cream cheese with eggs and yolks. Add milks and remaining ingredients. Stir. Pour mixture into prepared dish. Bake in water bath at 350 degrees for 1 hour. Cool and keep in refrigerator for at least 8 hours. Invert onto serving dish. Garnish with half peaches and cherries.

Serves 12   *Lidia Delgado*

Cuban Bread Pudding

½ cup sugar for caramel
2 cups milk
2 cups bread cubes
2 eggs
¾ cup sugar

Pinch of salt
¼ teaspoon cinnamon
Raisins (optional)
¼ cup brandy or sherry

Stir ½ cup sugar constantly in heavy pot on medium heat until brown. Pour into heated mold. Soak bread in milk. Add remaining ingredients and mix. Pour into mold. Place mold in pan of hot water. Bake at 375 degrees until done, about 35-45 minutes. Knife inserted in center will come out clean. Refrigerate. Unmold when cold.

Serves 8   *Renee Hernandez*

Gee-Gee's Bread Pudding

Best served warm and freshly cooked

1 cup light brown sugar
5 slices raisin bread, well buttered and
    cubed with crust removed

2 cups milk
2 eggs, beaten
1 teaspoon vanilla

In double boiler, layer sugar, then bread cubes. Do not stir. Combine milk, eggs, and vanilla. Blend well. Pour over bread cubes. Do not stir. Cook over simmering water 2 hours To serve ladle sauce from bottom of pan over each serving

Serves 6-8   *Nancy Story*

Bread Pudding with Whiskey Sauce

3 eggs
1½ cups sugar
3 cups milk
1 teaspoon vanilla extract
1 teaspoon cinnamon

4 cups stale bread, cubed
½ can stewed apples with syrup (slice apples into smaller pieces)
¾ cup raisins
3 teaspoons butter

Whiskey Sauce:
1 stick butter
1 cup powdered sugar

1 egg, well beaten
Whiskey or rum to taste

Pudding: Beat eggs, sugar, milk, vanilla, and cinnamon until well blended. Place bread in a casserole and cover with the mixture. Soak several minutes. Fold in the apples and raisins. Do not fill to top of bowl. Top with butter. Bake at 350 degrees covered until boiling. Uncover and cook for additional 25 minutes. Serve topped with whiskey sauce.

Whiskey Sauce: Mix butter and sugar. Heat until well blended. Gradually add egg, stirring rapidly. Add liquor to taste.

Serves 6-8   *Maureen Roshto*

Brown Rice Pudding

High fiber, low cholesterol

2 cups uncooked brown rice
2 egg whites
¼ teaspoon cream of tartar
4 cups skimmed milk

½ cup honey
2 teaspoons vanilla
¼ teaspoon nutmeg
¼ teaspoon cinnamon

Cook brown rice according to directions with no salt. Beat egg whites and cream of tartar until fluffy. Mix all ingredients together. Bake in dish which has been sprayed with oil at 350 degrees for 1 hour.

Serves 10   *Toni Shiver*

Red Candied Apples

A children's favorite

10-12 wood skewers (popsicle sticks)	⅔ cup water
10-12 medium sized apples	1 teaspoon lemon juice
3 cups sugar	15 whole cloves
½ teaspoon cream of tartar	1-2 teaspoons red food coloring

Stick skewers into stem end of apples securely. Combine sugar, cream of tartar, water, lemon juice, and cloves in heavy sauce pan. Stir over heat until sugar dissolves. Add coloring. Boil, without stirring, to 300 degrees or "hard-crack" stage. Remove from heat. Skim out cloves. Twist apples in syrup quickly. Set on buttered cookie sheet. Serve same day.

Yield: 10-12   *Becky Smalley*

*President Franklin D. Roosevelt at the Little White House, Warm Springs, Georgia.
He first came here in 1924 encouraged that the Warm Springs would be beneficial
to his hoped-for recovery from infantile paralysis. FDR built a modest home here,
called "The Little White House" and visited frequently until his death here in 1945.*

Apple Strudel

5 or 6 tart apples
Cinnamon and nutmeg
1 cup sugar, divided
1 egg

1 cup flour
6 tablespoons butter
Juice of one lemon and enough water
to make ½ cup

Peel and slice apples. Place in buttered 8x11 inch dish. Sprinkle with cinnamon, nutmeg, and ¼ cup sugar. Beat egg, add sugar and flour and spread over apples. Sprinkle with cinnamon and nutmeg. Melt butter and pour over top. Add lemon juice and water in one corner. Bake at 350 degrees for 30 minutes or until lightly browned. May serve warm with ice cream.

Serves 6-8   *Betty Jones*

Easy Fruit Cobbler

Peach, blueberry, or blackberry

½ cup butter
¾ cup flour
1 cup sugar
1 cup buttermilk
2 teaspoons baking powder

⅛ teaspoon salt
1½ pints of fruit of your choice pre-
sweetened and cooked for 10
minutes

Melt butter in oven in 9x13 inch pan. Mix remaining ingredients at medium speed. Pour batter over butter. Add fruit. Bake at 425 degrees for 20-25 minutes or until golden brown.

Serves 12-14   *Sally Woods*

Chef Mario Massari's Strawberries Romanoff

This recipe appeared in Jean Thwait's column in the Atlanta Constitution, *October 20, 1966. The Junior Women's Committee of the Atlanta Symphony Orchestra hosted a black tie pre-concert dinner at the Chateau Fleur de Lis. Chef Mario shared this recipe.*

1 cup heavy cream
1 pint vanilla ice cream, softened
juice of ½ lemon
2 ounces Cointreau

1 ounce rum
2 quarts strawberries, hulled
powdered sugar

Whip cream. Combine with ice cream. Add lemon juice, Cointreau, and rum. Pour over whole chilled, sugared strawberries.

Serves 8   *Barbara Tippins*

Marge's Strawberry Dessert

Definitely delicious

Crust:

1 cup self-rising flour

½ cup margarine, melted

¼ cup sugar

½ cup chopped nuts

Filling:

8 ounces cream cheese, softened

2 cups confectioners sugar

8 ounces whipped topping

1 tablespoon vanilla

Glaze:

1 cup sugar

3 tablespoons cornstarch

1 cup water

1 quart strawberries, sliced

Crust: Mix flour, margarine, sugar, and nuts. Bake at 375 degrees for 15 minutes. Cool.

Filling: Mix cream cheese, sugar, whipped topping, and vanilla and pour over cooled crust.

Glaze: Cook sugar, cornstarch, and water, stirring until thickened. Cool. Add strawberries. Pour over filling. Refrigerate.

Serves 8   *Marge House*

Providence Canyon State Park, Stewart County, known as Georgia's "Little Grand Canyon." This area has the highest concentration of natural wildflowers in Georgia.

Scenic Lowlands:
POTPOURRI

Scenic Lowlands

Called "Land of the Trembling Earth" by the Seminole Indians, the **Okefenokee Swamp** is truly one of nature's most unique creations. Two rivers, the Suwannee and the St. Marys, flow through the shallow 950 square mile basin.

Despite repeated efforts by generations of entrepreneurs to harness and utilize its resources, the Okeefenokee remains an unconquered wilderness. In 1937, President Roosevelt designated this area a National Wildlife Refuge, preserving forever the primeval beauty of the swamp and safeguarding its wild life resources.

Along with the bears, deer, wildcats, otters, raccoons, and alligators, the most well-known animal of the Okefenokee is the fictional opossum Pogo. First created in 1943 by artist Walt Kelly for his popular cartoon strip, Pogo makes a guest appearance in **Georgia Land** courtesy of Mrs. Selby Kelly.

Artists:
Margaret Bartholomew — Title Page
Tina Highsmith Rowell — "Scenic Lowlands"

Lemon Cheese Icing

A tart treat

3 whole lemons
3 cups sugar

4 egg yolks, beaten lightly
1/8 teaspoon salt

Grate all three whole lemons, seeding when necessary. Combine all ingredients and cook in double boiler stirring constantly until thickened and mixture changes color and is slightly darker. Spread between 4 thin layers of your favorite white or yellow cake. Save enough for top and sides.

Ingrid Brunt

Fresh Cranberry-Banana Sauce

Tangy addition to holiday feasts

2 12-ounce packages fresh
   cranberries, washed
1 1/4 cups water

1 1/4 cups sugar
3 very ripe mashed bananas

Place berries in large pot. Add water. Cook on medium heat until most berries pop open. Add sugar to mixture. Stir well. Place large sieve over deep mixing bowl. Press cranberry mixture through sieve until pulp remaining is dry. Discard pulp. Scrape underside of sieve often to remove sauce. Add bananas and mix well. Chill.

Amy Swindle

New England Hot Chocolate Sauce

2 squares unsweetened chocolate
2 cups cold water
2 cups sugar

2 teaspoons vanilla
2 tablespoons butter

Cut chocolate into 5 or 6 pieces. Add cold water and cook over direct heat until smooth and thick. Add sugar and stir until dissolved. Boil three minutes. Add vanilla and butter. Serve hot. Delicious over ice cream or strawberries.

Makes 1 pint

Pellie Manning

Talitha's Horseradish Mold

Especially good with roast beef

1 tablespoon plain gelatin
½ cup cold water
¾ cup mayonnaise, not cold

½ cup horseradish
¼ teaspoon salt
1 cup heavy cream, whipped

Soften gelatin in water. Dissolve over low heat, or microwave for 30 seconds. Mix mayonnaise and gelatin. Add horseradish and salt, and fold in whipped cream. Pour into quart mold. Let congeal. Unmold and serve.

Talitha Russell

Lemon Curry

Use on gingerbread, pound cake, English muffins, or cheesecake

5 tablespoons butter, softened
1½ cups sugar
2 eggs

⅛ teaspoon salt
2 lemons, juiced

Cream butter. Gradually add sugar. Beat well. Add eggs and mix. Slowly add salt and juice. Cook in top of double boiler until thick.

Serves 8

Ingrid Brunt

People Puppy Chow

A great munchie

6 ounces milk chocolate chips
6 ounces semi-sweet chocolate chips
1 cup peanut butter

½ cup butter
12.3-ounce box crispy square cereal
2 cups powdered sugar

Over low heat melt chocolate chips, peanut butter, and butter. Pour over cereal. Stir. Cool. Place mixture in brown paper bag. Add sifted powdered sugar. Shake. Variation: Add nuts, raisins, and any other diced, dried fruit.

Makes 1 gallon   *Jacqueline Clark*

Barbara Kanto's Natural Cereal

Great nibble food

7¾ cups (1 box) regular oatmeal
1 cup flaked coconut
¾ cup packed brown sugar
1 cup wheat germ
⅓ cup salted sunflower seeds
1 2-ounce jar sesame seeds
1½ cups Grapenut cereal
½ teaspoon salt

⅓-½ cup pancake syrup
¾ cup vegetable oil
⅓ cup water
1½ teaspoons vanilla
Vegetable spray
½-1 cup raisins, to taste
½ cup chopped dates, to taste

In a 6 quart bowl combine the first 8 ingredients. Mix. Drizzle syrup over. Stir. Combine oil, water, and vanilla and pour over cereal. Mix well. Spray 2 15x10 inch jelly roll pans with vegetable spray. Pour one half of mixture into each pan. Cook 45 minutes, stirring every 15 minutes. Cool. Add raisins and dates. Store in quart jars.

Makes 4 quarts   *Barbara Kanto*

Orange Ginger Dip

Marvelous as dip or dressing for fruit

1 cup mayonnaise
¼ cup orange juice
2 tablespoons honey

½ teaspoon grated orange peel
¼ teaspoon ground ginger

Combine all ingredients and stir until blended. Cover and thoroughly chill. Serve with fresh fruit.

Joan Turcotte

Tina Highsmith Rowell, '92

Jeanne's Swedish Nuts

Wonderful little holiday packages

2 egg whites
1 cup sugar
½ cup butter or margarine

1 pound pecan halves
Dash of salt

Beat egg whites until stiff not dry, folding in sugar gradually. Add salt. Melt butter in 15x12inch pan. Add pecan halves. Spoon egg white mixture over nuts and butter. Bake at 325 degrees for 30 minutes or until butter is absorbed and nuts begin to brown. Stir every 10 minutes. Cool on wire rack and break up with wooden spoon.

Makes 1 pound   *Jeanne Smiley*

"Brandied" Pecans

Nice to have or give for holidays

½ cup sugar
½ cup brown sugar
¼ teaspoon cream of tartar
¼ cup orange juice

¼ teaspoon cinnamon
1 teaspoon vanilla
2-3 "squirts" of spirits of choice
2 cups pecan halves

Combine and bring to boil the first seven ingredients. Reduce heat to medium. Cook 10 minutes. When a drop tests firm in cup of cold water add the pecan halves. Stir carefully until pecans begin to crystallize. Turn out onto oiled cookie sheet. Cool. Separate with fork. Store in tight glass covered jar.
Note: Try using bourbon, Grand Marnier or brandy.

Makes 2 cups   *Dea Porter*

Pecans Foo Weung

Hot and spicy

1 pound pecan halves
3 tablespoons butter, melted
2 teaspoons salt
3 tablespoons Worcestershire

¼ teaspoon cayenne
½ teaspoon cinnamon
Dash hot pepper sauce

Mix all ingredients except pecans. Pour mixture over pecans on baking sheet. Mix well. Roast in oven uncovered for 45 minutes at 275 degrees, stirring frequently. Turn oven off and leave pecans in oven for 30 minutes.

Carol Ann Hardcastle

My Favorite Dove or Quail

A favorite in South Georgia

8-10 shallots finely chopped
½ cup butter, divided
1 4-ounce can sliced mushrooms
1 teaspoon salt
½ teaspoon pepper
1 teaspoon Worcestershire
Dash hot pepper sauce
½ teaspoon thyme
¼ cup olive oil

12 doves or quails
Flour
1 clove garlic, finely chopped
⅓ cup cognac
½ cup flour
1 10½-ounce can chicken broth
1 tablespoon currant jelly
1 cup burgundy wine

Sauté shallots in ¼ cup butter in small skillet. Add mushrooms, salt, pepper, Worcestershire, hot pepper sauce, and thyme. In Dutch oven or roasting pan heat olive oil and ¼ cup butter. Dredge birds in flour. Add birds and garlic to oil mixture. Turn birds until browned on all sides. Heat cognac in small pan. Pour over birds and flame. When flame dies remove birds from pan and keep warm. Add ½ cup flour to pan working into paste. Pour in chicken broth. Add jelly and wine. Stir until well blended and slightly thickened. Stir in shallot mixture. Cook 5 minutes, stirring constantly. Return birds to Dutch oven. Cook, covered over low heat 1½ hours or until tender.

Serves 6   *Bette Turner*

*"Obediah's Okefenok," Waycross, restored swamp homestead
of Obediah Barber, legendary "King of the Swamp."*

Wild Turkey

Hunters' favorite

1 wild turkey (whatever size you are
    fortunate enough to kill)
1 turkey size roasting bag
1 tablespoon flour
2 onions, quartered and chopped

2 or 3 stalks celery, chopped in large
    pieces
Vegetable oil
Salt and pepper to taste

Day before serving wash wild turkey thoroughly. Pat dry. Sprinkle bird cavity with salt and pepper. Stuff with onion and celery. Rub outside of turkey with oil, salt, and pepper. Place flour in roasting bag. Shake to coat. Place turkey in bag, closing end with tie. Place turkey in refrigerator and let sit overnight. When ready to cook cut 2 or 3 slits in bag to let air escape. Follow instructions on bag container for cooking time. Let turkey sit 30 minutes before carving.

Eyleen Mitchell

Grilled Venison

Excellent hot or cold

1 large venison roast, tenderloin, or
    other portion (3-4 pounds)
1 clove garlic, cut in half

Salt
Lemon pepper

Marinade:
1½ cups soy sauce
2 cups red wine
1 clove garlic, crushed

2 tablespoons butter or margarine,
    melted
Juice of 1 lemon

Trim and prepare venison for cooking. Pat dry. Rub cut garlic over venison. Sprinkle generously with salt and lemon pepper. Place in large container. Mix soy sauce, red wine, and garlic. Pour over venison. Marinate for several hours or overnight, turning periodically. When ready to cook, remove venison from marinade. Mix butter and lemon juice. Brush on venison. Place venison on grill over hot coals. Turn fire to low. Cook to desired doneness, about 15-20 minutes per pound. While cooking baste frequently with marinade and lemon juice. Slice thin. Serve hot with béarnaise sauce or cold for sandwiches with herb mayonnaise.

Miles Marks

Paella

1 to 1½ cups olive oil
2 onions, chopped
2 to 4 garlic cloves, minced
2 large green peppers, chopped
2 bay leaves
1 to 1½ pound chicken, cut into
   serving pieces
2 crabs, cleaned and cut up, or 1 4-
   ounce can crab meat
2 lobster tails, cut up
½ pound ham, diced
½ pound pork loin, diced
½ pound fish (red snapper), cut up

1½ pounds shrimp, cleaned and
   peeled
1 pound clams or 1 can smoked
   oysters
1 8-ounce can tomato sauce
1 4-ounce jar pimientos
2½ tablespoons salt
2 teaspoons paprika
¾ teaspoon pepper
4 cups brandy or dry white wine
1 teaspoon vinegar
4 cups chicken broth
2 pounds rice (Valencia or yellow
   saffron)

In large Dutch oven sauté onions, garlic, and pepper in olive oil until tender. Remove from pan. Add to oil in pan chicken pieces, seafood, ham, pork, and fish. Cook, turning constantly until golden brown. Return onions, garlic, and peppers to pot. Add tomato sauce, undrained pimientos, salt, paprika, bay leaves, vinegar, and wine. Bring to boil and add broth. Cook until chicken is tender. Add rice and clams or oysters. Cover and simmer or place in 300 degree oven for 30 minutes or until rice is done. Remove bay leaves and serve in paella pan. Garnish with petit pois and chopped pimiento. Note: Do not overcook.

Serves 12-15   *Cecilia Baute*

Vegetable Chili

1 medium eggplant, unpeeled, cut into ½ inch cubes
1 tablespoon coarse salt
½ to ¾ cup olive oil
2 medium onions, diced
4 cloves garlic, finely chopped
2 large green peppers, cored, seeded, and diced
1 35-ounce can Italian plum tomatoes
1½ pounds fresh ripe Italian tomatoes, cubed
2 tablespoons chili powder
1 tablespoon ground cumin
1 tablespoon dried oregano
1 tablespoon dried basil
2 teaspoons freshly ground black pepper
1 teaspoon salt
1 teaspoon fennel seeds
½ cup chopped fresh Italian parsley
1 15½-ounce can red kidney beans, drained and rinsed
1 15-ounce can garbanzo beans, drained
½ cup chopped fresh dill
2 tablespoons fresh lemon juice
Shredded cheddar cheese, optional

Place eggplant in colander. Sprinkle with salt. Let stand 1 hour. Pat dry and set aside. Heat ½ cup oil in large skillet. Add eggplant and sauté until almost tender, adding oil as necessary. Remove eggplant to dutch oven. Heat remaining oil in same skillet over low heat. Add onion, garlic, and green peppers. Sauté just until softened, about 10 minutes. Add to eggplant. Add undrained canned tomatoes, fresh tomatoes, and next 8 ingredients. Cook over low heat, uncovered, stirring frequently, for 30 minutes. Stir in beans, dill, and lemon juice. Cook additional 15 minutes. Stir well. Adjust seasonings. Serve over rice. Garnish with shredded cheddar cheese, if desired.

Note: For variety, sauté 2 diced zucchini with onion, garlic, and peppers. Also may add 1½ cups fresh corn kernels with beans. For spicier chili add hot sauce as desired. If thinner chili is desired add 1 cup vegetable broth.

Serves 8-10

Sara Beecham
Martha Schwartz

Vegetarian Chili

8 ounces dried red beans, picked and rinsed, or 3 cups rinsed and drained canned red beans

1 tablespoon olive oil

3 medium onions, chopped

5 large celery ribs, chopped coarsely

¼ cup minced garlic

2 cups chopped carrots

2 cups chopped cabbage

2 cups finely chopped mushrooms

1 cup finely chopped red peppers

1 cup finely chopped green peppers

½ cup chili powder

1 tablespoon unsweetened cocoa powder

1 tablespoon brown sugar

½ tablespoon cumin seeds

1 tablespoon oregano

1 teaspoon fennel seeds

1 teaspoon thyme

½ teaspoon ground cinnamon

1 tablespoon salt

1 teaspoon freshly ground black pepper

1 28-ounce can chopped Italian plum tomatoes and liquid

4 cups water

2 tablespoons soy sauce

2 tablespoons dry sherry, optional

1 teaspoon hot pepper sauce

Topping:

1 cup sour cream

2 cups sliced green onions, white and green tops

½ pound sharp cheddar cheese, grated

Cook dried beans according to package driections. Drain. In dutch oven heat oil over moderate heat and sauté onions and celery until translucent, 6-8 minutes. Add garlic and cook 1 minute longer. Add remaining chopped vegetables and cook until tender, stirring occasionally, about 10-15 minutes. Stir in next nine seasonings and ½ teaspoon black pepper. Stir in tomatoes. Add beans, tomato liquid, and water. Simmer over low heat 2 hours. Remove from heat and cool. Cover and refrigerate overnight. To serve, reheat chili over low heat, add remaining black pepper. Remove from heat. Stir in soy sauce, sherry, and hot sauce. Ladle into bowls. Top with sour cream, onions, and cheese.

Serves 8   *Jeanne Smiley*

Pogo, Georgia's Official State Possum, says "Bon Appetit, ya'll!"

Index

W

Z

Auxiliary to the Medical Association of Georgia
938 Peachtree Street, N.E.
Atlanta, Georgia 30309

Please send me _____ copies of **Georgia Land**   @ $16.95 per copy _____
                          Add postage and handling   @ $ 2.00 per copy _____
                          Georgia residents add sales tax @ $ 1.02 per copy _____
                                                          Total _____

Please make check payable to A-MAG COOKBOOK FUND.

Ship to:

Name _____

Address _____

City _____ State _____ Zip _____

- -

Auxiliary to the Medical Association of Georgia
938 Peachtree Street, N.E.
Atlanta, Georgia 30309

Please send me _____ copies of **Georgia Land**   @ $16.95 per copy _____
                          Add postage and handling   @ $ 2.00 per copy _____
                          Georgia residents add sales tax @ $ 1.02 per copy _____
                                                          Total _____

Please make check payable to A-MAG COOKBOOK FUND.

Ship to:

Name _____

Address _____

City _____ State _____ Zip _____

- -

Auxiliary to the Medical Association of Georgia
938 Peachtree Street, N.E.
Atlanta, Georgia 30309

Please send me _____ copies of **Georgia Land**   @ $16.95 per copy _____
                          Add postage and handling   @ $ 2.00 per copy _____
                          Georgia residents add sales tax @ $ 1.02 per copy _____
                                                          Total _____

Please make check payable to A-MAG COOKBOOK FUND.

Ship to:

Name _____

Address _____

City _____ State _____ Zip _____